Practising
Existential Therapy

SAGE was founded in 1965 by Sara Miller McCune to support the dissemination of usable knowledge by publishing innovative and high-quality research and teaching content. Today, we publish more than 750 journals, including those of more than 300 learned societies, more than 800 new books per year, and a growing range of library products including archives, data, case studies, reports, conference highlights, and video. SAGE remains majority-owned by our founder, and on her passing will become owned by a charitable trust that secures our continued independence.

Los Angeles | London | Washington DC | New Delhi | Singapore

Practising Existential Therapy

The Relational World | Second Edition

Ernesto Spinelli

Los Angeles | London | New Delhi
Singapore | Washington DC

Los Angeles | London | New Delhi
Singapore | Washington DC

SAGE Publications Ltd
1 Oliver's Yard
55 City Road
London EC1Y 1SP

SAGE Publications Inc.
2455 Teller Road
Thousand Oaks, California 91320

SAGE Publications India Pvt Ltd
B 1/I 1 Mohan Cooperative Industrial Area
Mathura Road
New Delhi 110 044

SAGE Publications Asia-Pacific Pte Ltd
3 Church Street
#10-04 Samsung Hub
Singapore 049483

Editor: Susannah Trefgarne
Assistant editor: Laura Walmsley
Production editor: Victoria Nicholas
Copyeditor: Christine Bitten
Proofreader: Louise Harnby
Indexer: Silvia Benvenuto
Marketing manager: Camille Richmond
Cover design: Shaun Mercier
Cover image: *Veil 20*. Oil on linen, 2007
© Paul Winstanley
Typeset by: C&M Digitals (P) Ltd, Chennai, India
Printed by: Henry Ling Limited at the Dorset
Press, Dorchester, DT1 1HD

Library of Congress Control Number: 2014940294

British Library Cataloguing in Publication data

A catalogue record for this book is available from the British Library

ISBN 978-1-4462-7234-3
ISBN 978-1-4462-7235-0 (pbk)

At SAGE we take sustainability seriously. Most of our products are printed in the UK using FSC papers and boards. When we print overseas we ensure sustainable papers are used as measured by the Egmont grading system. We undertake an annual audit to monitor our sustainability.

This book is dedicated to my dear friends and colleagues
Bo Jacobsen, Rimas Kociunas, Arthur Jonathan and Ismail Asmall.

Thank you for your unlimited optimism and encouragement … and your wisdom.

And to the memory of
Hans Cohn,
who, I suspect, would have both appreciated and disapproved of this book,
and
Freddie Strasser,
the most wonderfully optimistic pessimist (or pessimistic optimist?) I have ever had the
pleasure to know,
and
Al Mahrer
who asked all the right questions and dedicated his life to searching out their answers.

Contents

About the Author

Professor Ernesto Spinelli has gained an international reputation as one of the leading contemporary trainers and theorists of existential analysis as applied to psychology and psychotherapy and, more recently, the related arenas of coaching and conflict mediation. He is a UKCP registered existential psychotherapist, a Fellow of the British Psychological Society (BPS), and the British Association for Counselling and Psychotherapy (BACP), as well as an accredited executive coach and coaching supervisor. In 1999, Ernesto was awarded a Personal Chair as Professor of psychotherapy, counselling and counselling psychology and in 2000 was awarded the BPS Division of Counselling Psychology Award for Outstanding Contributions to the Advancement of the Profession. Ernesto is Director of ES Associates, an organisation dedicated to the advancement of psychotherapy, coaching and supervision through specialist seminars and training programmes.

Acknowledgements
(Second Edition)

I am grateful to SAGE Publications and, in particular, Susannah Trefgarne and Laura Walmsley, for having encouraged me to prepare a new edition of this book. It is a great gift for an author to be given the opportunity to clarify and extend a number of his more obscure ideas and arguments, as well as add some new ones.

If this new incarnation of my book strikes its readers as being somewhat more accessible, it is largely so because of the input and suggestions of a number of people whom I am honoured to call my friends. Thank you, Stuart, Bill, Yaqui, Mick, Greg and Todd. I can't express in words how touched I am by your generosity.

My professional life has changed substantially since the publication of the first edition. Following a great deal of 'soul-searching', I decided to leave my academic 'home' of 20 years. While my leave-taking was not without sadness and more than a touch of anger, over and above anything else, I remain very much in debt to the School of Psychotherapy and Counselling for the opportunities it provided for me to develop my thinking and to find my voice as lecturer and writer. More than that, my affection towards, and respect for, the many colleagues, trainees and students whose lives touched mine during those years far outweigh whatever institutional toxicity we all endured. I have no doubt that if anything of interest, much less wisdom, exists in this book, it is largely due to the dialogues and encounters we engaged in with one another. Thank you.

Finally, as ever, a heartfelt, if all too inadequate, thank you to my wife, Maggi Cook, for her tireless support, her patient reminders to 'just get on with it' and, more than anything, her being.

Ernesto Spinelli
London, 2014

Acknowledgements
(First Edition)

The origins of this book can be traced back to a series of seminars that I facilitated on the Advanced Diploma in Existential Psychotherapy programme offered at the School of Psychotherapy and Counselling, Regent's College, London. I am grateful to all of the trainees who participated in these seminars for the wealth of critical insight that they brought to our discussions. I am grateful, as well, to my colleague and Director of the programme, Ms Lucia Moja-Strasser, for having permitted me to present my views and ideas even though she was well aware of some of the confusion and controversy that they might provoke for the trainees.

I would also like to acknowledge the very generous and equally patient staff at SAGE Publications and, in particular, Alison Poyner, Senior Commissioning Editor. Alison's faith in this book at times surpassed my own. I hope that she will find her efforts to have been worthwhile.

I am very grateful to have been given the opportunity to travel to many parts of the world in order to meet with all manner of colleagues and trainees who share this odd passion for, and fascination with, existential psychotherapy. The informal discussions we have had have influenced and shaped this book in a multitude of ways. Thank you all and in particular to my friends from The Society for Existential Analysis, UK; the I-Coach Academy, UK and South Africa; The Forum for Existential Psychotherapy, 'The London Group', 'The Copenhagen Group' and The New School of Psychology in Denmark; the Portuguese Society for Existential Psychotherapy; the East European Association for Existential Therapy in Lithuania; the Australian Existential Society and Psychotherapy in Australia; the International Society for Existential Psychology and Psychotherapy in Canada; the Psychology Department at Duquesne University, Pittsburgh, Pennsylvania, USA; the International Human Science Research Group; and, of course, my comrades – past and present, staff and students – at the School of Psychotherapy and Counselling, Regent's College.

I am also remarkably lucky to have known the late Hans W. Cohn. While he was alive, Hans and I held regular 'irregular' lunch-time discussions in Regent's College's Faculty Dining Room. These were occasions that we both used to discuss our shared and divergent views regarding existential psychotherapy, engage in peer supervision and, just occasionally, catch up on the latest gossip from the existential world. I have no way of pinpointing just how or in what ways something of these discussions has seeped its way into this book. But I am certain it has.

Finally, let me simply state that this has been by far the most difficult book I have yet written. In my naivety, before I began it I was happily telling one and all how easy it would be. Unfortunately, the gods must have heard me. Fortunately for me, however, I have been blessed with friends whose good humour, encouragement and just plain insistence that I get on with it and stop moaning kept me at it. So ... Thank you to Peter and Stuart and Barbara and Charles and Laurence and Susanna and James and Helen and Abbey. And, as always, to my 'best friend', Maggi.

Ernesto Spinelli
London, 2006

Publisher's Acknowledgements

'Seeker of truth' is reprinted from *Complete Poems 1904-1962*, by e.e. cummings, edited by George J. Firmage, by kind permission of W.W. Norton & Company. Copyright © 1991 by Trustees for the e.e. cummings Trust and George James Firmage.

Extracts from Fromm, E *Man for Himself: An Inquiry into the Psychology of Ethics* © Erich Fromm and from Foucault, M *The Order of Things: Archaeology of the Human Sciences* © Michel Foucault are reproduced by kind permission of Taylor and Francis.

Lyrics from 'Hallelujah' by Leonard Cohen and 'Caroline Says II' by Lou Reed are included by kind permission of Sony/ATV EMI Music Publishing.

Notes on the Text

All names, distinguishing characteristics and identifying details of the clients discussed in this book have been altered in order to ensure their anonymity.

A recurring attempt to distinguish between *being* and being – as in 'every being is an expression of *being*' exists within existential literature. It is usually addressed by use of the terms as 'being' and 'Being'. My personal preference is to clarify this distinction via italics and bold highlighting when referring to *being* in its more general sense as the originating basis to all expressions and experiences of being.

Readers are likely to notice that terms such as 'my self', 'your self', 'her self' and 'our selves' appear in this divided form throughout the text. The dividedness is intentional in that it seeks to emphasise the existential phenomenological view of 'self' as a reflectively derived construct rather than the foundational starting point to all humanly lived experience.

Introduction to the Second Edition

This – is now my way – where is yours? Thus did I answer those who asked me 'the way'. For the way – it doth not exist. Friedrich Nietzsche

A few years ago, I chanced upon an intriguing journal article by the American existential therapist and phenomenological researcher, Paul Colaizzi. Entitled 'Psychotherapy and existential therapy', Colaizzi's paper sought to make a case for the uniqueness of existential therapy. I will address some of his points below and in the first chapter of this text. For now, I simply want to alert the interested reader of my ongoing difficult relationship with this particular paper. Yes, it is difficult because a great deal of what it has to say is challenging. But also, though I hate to admit it, it is difficult because it confronts me with my intellectual limitations: I remain uncertain as to whether I have accurately understood some of its more pivotal arguments. Mostly, however, the difficulty lies in the risible fact that I keep losing and then finding and then losing the article yet again. In preparing to write this second dition, I came across it, told my self that I wanted to refer to it and so should place it somewhere accessible ... and then promptly lost it again. As things stand today, I know that it is safely tucked away in some as yet unknown somewhere. Only through the kind – and much appreciated – efforts of my colleagues, Les Todres, Scott Churchill, Fred Wertz and Mo Mandic, have I been able to locate and access an electronic version of it. Why this keeps happening (and only with this one paper!) and what its meaning might be, I leave to my analytically minded compatriots to decipher. Why I am writing about this 'here it is/now it's gone' relationship I am in with Colaizzi's paper is that, in many ways, it expresses in microcosm what I have come to conclude about my relationship with existential therapy in general. Namely, every time I think I have my grasp on it, it eventually succeeds in eluding me, vanishing to some unknown mysterious 'elsewhere' from which it can continue to tantalise me without giving away its secrets.

Even so, acknowledging the influence Colaizzi's article has had upon me, and, as well, in keeping with a stance I have upheld for quite some time (Spinelli, 1994), I have replaced the term 'psychotherapy', which appeared in the title of the first edition, with that of 'therapy' so that this new edition's title reads as *Practising Existential Therapy: The Relational World*. This shift to the broader term intends to make it more obvious that the views and practices being presented herein are as applicable to the related professional areas designated as counselling and counselling psychology as they are to that of psychotherapy. Indeed, although it is beyond the remit of this text, the great majority of what is being presented, I believe, is also applicable to the areas of coaching, mediation and leadership training (Spinelli, 2014b; Spinelli et al., 2000; Spinelli & Horner, 2007; Strasser & Randolph, 2004). There is, however, a further, more significant, reason, arising directly out of Colaizzi's (2002) paper, that has led me to make this change in the title. Colaizzi argues that the 'psycho-' in psycho-therapy severely limits the radical challenge that existential therapy can provide and, as well, obscures its distinctiveness from every other form of contemporary therapy. I think that this is an important point and the change in title reflects my overall agree-ment with it (even if I continue to disagree with some of Colaizzi's other conclu-sions). Hopefully, readers will be able to discern its influence throughout the whole of this text.

I have been practising, lecturing and writing about, as well as training profes-sionals to practise, existential therapy for around 30 years now. I have the cre-dentials, the affiliations, the titles, and the recognition that permit me to claim an expertise in the area. But just what is this expertise? And what is it that allows this claimed expertise to label itself as 'existential'? These are the questions that have pushed me towards writing – and now re-writing – this text.

In common with all other contemporary systems of therapy, existential therapy is concerned with issues of unease and disturbance or what might be called, more broadly, 'dilemmas in living'. However, unlike the majority of contemporary sys-tems, whose primary indebtedness is allied to medicine and natural science, the pivotal focus for existential therapy rests upon a number of seminal ideas and conclusions drawn from a philosophical system which has become most gen-erally known as existential phenomenology (Barnett & Madison, 2012; Cohn, 1997; Cooper, 2003; Jacobsen, 2007; Langdridge, 2013; Spinelli, 2005; Strasser & Strasser, 1997; Valle & King, 1978; van Deurzen & Arnold-Baker, 2005; Yalom, 1980). Because of this allegiance, existential therapy, at least as I understand it, steps back from providing various change-oriented directive interventions and, instead, emphasises the attempt to remain 'still' with the issues under focus so that they may be opened to description, clarification, and the explication of the embodied values, meanings, 'moods' and behaviours which accompany them. Why it does so, and what there is about existential phenomenology that pretty much neces-sitates its doing so, is not open to simple and brief explanations. In a culture that demands 'fast everything', existential therapy does not 'go with the flow' terribly well. Indeed, one of the great mysteries surrounding existential therapy might well be this: how is it that it still exists and continues to be practised? Perhaps, as will be discussed in Part One, it is because it offers a distinctively different perspective on matters of living. But what is so different about this perspective?

Existential phenomenology is made up of several closely affiliated, but also at times significantly competing, philosophical investigations centred upon questions of existence such as 'What is it to be?' and 'What is it to be human?' Such questions provoke multiple responses that focus upon several 'grand themes' of existence, such as life/death, meaning/meaninglessness, relation/isolation and choice/determinism.

Among therapists who have been influenced by existential phenomenology, the dominant tendency has been to identify these thematic existence concerns as the pivotal features of the approach. Although they may disagree with one another on any number of specific issues, the wide range of writers who have sought to describe and delineate the theoretical underpinnings of existential therapy tend to share this thematic emphasis (Barnett & Madison, 2012; Boss, 1963, 1979; Cohn, 1997, 2002; Cooper, 2003; Jacobsen, 2007; Langdridge, 2013; May, 1969, 1983; van Deurzen-Smith, 1997; Yalom, 1980). As well, more recently, it has been through this thematic focus that attempts have been made to address the more practical, or skills-based, aspects of existential therapy (Adams, 2013; Langdridge, 2013; van Deurzen-Smith, 1997; van Deurzen & Adams, 2011; van Deurzen & Arnold-Baker, 2005).

As I will seek to show in Part One, in highlighting these thematic existence concerns as the foundational features of existential therapy, the arguments for its distinctiveness are often blunted of their more radical implications. All too frequently, as a result, the practice of existential therapy ends up falling well within the structural assumptions and applied framework of other existing approaches, most obviously psychoanalytic and humanistic approaches. Such integrative attempts, while valuable and deserving of closer consideration, also unwittingly lead to conclusions regarding the practice of existential therapy that do not fit well with, and at times contradict, its key philosophical underpinnings. In focusing upon thematic existence concerns, existential therapy presents itself as being no different to all the other models and approaches that address the very same broad spectrum of life issues. It cannot justifiably be identified through these thematic concerns nor can it claim proprietary rights to them simply because they are concerned with questions of existence. While it would be nonsensical to claim that the various existence themes and ultimate concerns that are explored by existential authors and practitioners are unimportant, it is the emphasis given to them as the baseline or starting point to an understanding of existential therapy that, I believe, is mistaken. Instead, as will be argued in Part One, it is not these themes in themselves but existential therapy's way of addressing them that is the basis for its distinctiveness. As will be discussed in Chapter 1, this way is guided by the foundational Principles of existential phenomenology. I have highlighted three of these Principles in particular – relatedness, uncertainty and existential anxiety – as being pivotal to the clarification of what is unique about existential therapy and how its aims and practices can be contrasted with those of other models and approaches.

In addition, this text argues that the tendency to emphasise broad-based existence themes rather than existential phenomenological Principles raises several other confusions and concerns that could otherwise be avoided. Among these, a commonly recurring one centres on the oft-repeated misunderstanding that existential therapy's singularity lies in the fact that, unlike other therapeutic systems which are primarily, if not exclusively, psychologically derived, it is uniquely philosophically grounded. This is, of course, utter nonsense. All therapeutic theories are underpinned by philosophical assumptions and postulates, even if, in many cases, these remain implicit and covert for the majority of their adherents and practitioners. It could be reasonably argued that existential therapy initially stands out from other approaches precisely because it acknowledges explicitly and utilises overtly its foundational philosophical assumptions. But this should not lead anyone to conclude that its openly admitted philosophical grounding in itself is its distinguishing feature. Valid arguments along very similar lines have been made by, and for, any number of other therapeutic models (Lundin & Bohart, 1996; Thorne & Henley, 2004). As a broader concern, the tendency by some authors to locate existential therapy predominantly – if not exclusively – within philosophy leads to the incorrect implication that it is an approach open only to those deeply steeped and trained in philosophy. Of course, it would be absurd to claim an allegiance to existential therapy without a continuing immersion in, and willingness to grapple with, *at least* the main literature dealing with its philosophical foundations. But, it would be equally absurd to argue that the understanding necessary to the practising of existential therapy can be gained solely through the reading of that literature.

Here is the crux of the matter: in spite of their many disagreements and divergences, the great majority of contemporary models of Western therapy typically share the very same, or highly similar, foundational philosophical Principles. Their differences, while no means minimal and often rancorous, stem from opposing interpretations of thematic issues that arise out of these Principles. In contrast, the foundational Principles of existential therapy are of a different kind. In being so, they approach the thematic existence concerns which shape the issues brought to therapy from an alternative, often radically dissimilar, perspective. In sum, it is not that existential therapy is philosophically grounded, but rather what its specific philosophical grounding argues that remains the critical issue.

As a brief example of this point, let us consider the theme of 'the self'. At a surface level, both existential and other therapeutic approaches place great emphasis on the issue of 'the self'. However, the moment one goes beyond this surface agreement, critical divergences begin to emerge. The guiding Principles upon which existential therapy rests contradict a persistent assumption regarding 'the self' held not only by the majority of therapeutic approaches but by Western culture in general – namely, that 'the self' is best viewed and understood from an isolationist perspective as an individual, separate and distinct entity. As such, the dominant ethos of therapy assumes the foundational primacy of the discrete individual subject. In doing so, it becomes commonplace to suggest that it is only once 'the self' has been 'found', 'accepted', 'authenticated' or 'self-actualised' that it is then capable of focusing upon and addressing the possibilities of relationship with others and the world in general. In contrast to this view, the Principles underpinning existential phenomenology lead it to argue that no self can be 'found', nor 'emerge', other than via an a priori grounding in relatedness. From this perspective, any form of self-awareness is an outcome of, rather than the starting point leading toward, relational issues. This conclusion has many implications for therapeutic practice, as will be discussed throughout this book.

There is yet another general issue to confront. While I can readily attest that it is no easy task to describe and discuss the practice of existential therapy, nonetheless, a somewhat unusual reticence to attempt to do so permeates the approach. In part, this reserve highlights the concern shared by many existential practitioners that any such attempts might only succeed in 'technologising' or 'operationalising' practice, thereby limiting it to a rigid set of techniques which, in turn, severely contradict its aim of an immediate and open encounter between therapist and client. In brief, the argument runs that to discuss the practising of existential therapy encases it in such a way that it contradicts and misrepresents precisely that which is being attempted – a classic case of 'whatever is said about what it is, it isn't' (Korzybski, 1995). This reluctance, however, also harbours another less appealing and rarely acknowledged contributing factor. This is, as I see it, the tendency on the part of existential therapists to somewhat over-mystify the numinous practice-based qualities and skills which they claim to bring to any given encounter. This latter stance has a whiff of dubious superiority that evokes a self-aggrandising sense of arcane 'specialness'. Far too many times, when questioning colleagues as to their unwillingness to attempt some delineation of practice, I have received replies that are all too reminiscent of Wittgenstein's celebrated injunction: 'Whereof we cannot speak, thereof we must pass over in silence' (Wittgenstein, 2001: 90). Personally, I have found my self over the years becoming increasingly irritated by my colleagues' near-adoration of this quote. Were it the case that practising existential therapy was something which, of necessity, must remain unspoken, then so be it. Personally, I remain unconvinced.

Part Two of this text sets out my counter-argument. I have provided a structural model for the practice of existential therapy that remains alert to the grounding Principles from which its practical applications arise. Further, my aim throughout this text is fourfold:

1. That it provides a coherent and consistent structure for therapeutic practice that remains grounded in the existential phenomenological Principles being espoused.
2. That the ideas discussed will inform and clarify for readers what it is that may be said to be distinctive about practising existential therapy.
3. That the views and arguments being presented may serve to provoke readers, regardless of the model or approach they adopt, to reconsider critically and re-appraise their own understanding and application of therapeutic practice.
4. That via the challenges contained in the above points, readers will be able to express more clearly, and to own with deeper understanding and commitment, that which is their way of therapeutic practice.

As an aid to this overall aim, I have included various practical exercises throughout the Chapter discussions which will, hopefully, serve to connect the reader in a more experiential way to the challenges raised by the issues and practices under consideration. I hope that readers find them to be stimulating and enjoyable as well as useful.

Finally, acknowledging my own concerns surrounding the potentially undesirable consequences of such an enterprise, and in an attempt to reduce the likelihood of the fulfilment of both my colleagues', and my own, worst fears as far as possible, let me state two critical points as plainly as I can. First, let us all be clear that just as there exists no single means by which to practise psychoanalysis, or CBT or person-centred therapy, or any other of the principal contemporary therapies, so too is it that there is no exclusive or singular form of existential therapy. Acknowledging this in no way makes it impossible to set out an explicable and coherent structural framework for practice that can be critically considered, compared to and contrasted with other frameworks, whether they be within existential therapy or, perhaps as importantly, with competing models and systems of therapy.

Secondly, this text seeks to reflect my own attempts to understand, describe and apply the practice of existential therapy as derived from existential phenomenology. While I would not be writing this book if I presumed that such an idiosyncratic account would be of little, if any, value to anyone else, at the same time it is not my purpose to convince readers that what is discussed herein should be treated as a 'tool-kit' for, much less anything approaching 'the final word' on, practising existential therapy.

Taken together, these two points emphasise that this text considers one particular interpretation that I am hoping readers will find to be accessible and thought-provoking. I am aware that some, perhaps many, existential therapists will find this version to be a considerable challenge to their own understanding as to how to define and practise existential therapy. It has not been my intent to dismiss nor denigrate alternate perspectives and approaches but rather to stir up possibilities and encourage open-minded – and open-hearted – dialogue. In summary, what is being presented is *a* way rather than *the* way of practising existential therapy.

PART ONE
Theory

Chapter 1

*Existential Phenomenology's
Three Foundational Principles*

Relatedness
Uncertainty
Existential Anxiety

Chapter 2

*Thematic Existence Concerns as
Viewed by Existential Phenomenology*

Existence Precedes Essence
Meaning/Meaninglessness
Choice, Freedom and Responsibility
Authenticity and Inauthenticity
Isolation and Relation
Death Anxiety
Temporality
Spatiality

Chapter 3

Worlding and the Worldview

Embodied Existential Insecurities in
Continuity/Dispositional Stances/Identity
Primary Structures in the Worldview
The Self-Construct
The Other-Construct
The World-Construct
Worldview Sedimentations and Dissociations

Chapter 4

*Existential Phenomenological Critiques of Key
Foundational Beliefs in Therapy*

Change
Causality
Conflict
Symptoms
Sexuality and Spirituality
Consciousness

↓

Chapter 5

Existential Therapy – an Overview

Historical Background
Existential Therapy Viewed from the Perspective of the
Three Foundational Principles
Existential Therapy as an Investigative Enterprise
Existential Therapy and the Therapeutic Relationship
The Existential Therapist as the Present Other
The Existential Therapist's Acceptance
The Existential Therapist's Experiential Immediacy
The Existential Therapist's Dialogical Attitude
Un-knowing

FIGURE 1.1

1

Existential Therapy: Three Key Principles

The Im/possibility of Existential Therapy

Existential Therapy is no kind of therapy. Paul F. Colaizzi

In an approach that is already overflowing with paradoxes, here is yet another – currently, the living therapist and author most often associated with contemporary existential therapy and recognised by professionals and public alike as *the* leading voice in the field is the American psychiatrist, Irvin Yalom. For example, in a recent survey, over 1,300 existential therapists were asked to name the practitioner who had most influenced them. Yalom ranked second on that list (following Viktor Frankl (1905–1997), the founder of Logotherapy) and was at the top of their list of living practitioners (Correia, Cooper & Berdondini (2014); Iacovou, 2013). Nevertheless, Yalom has stated that there is no such thing as existential therapy *per se* (Yalom, 2007). Instead, he has argued that therapies can be distinguished by the degree to which they are willing and able to address various existence themes, or ultimate concerns, such as death, freedom, meaning and isolation, within the therapeutic encounter (Cooper, 2003; Yalom, 1980, 1989). From this Yalomian perspective, any approach to therapy that is informed by these *thematic existence concerns* and addresses them directly in its practice would be an existential therapy.

As an existential therapist, I continue to admire Yalom's contributions and to learn from his writings and seminars. It has been my honour to have engaged in a joint seminar with him during which we each presented some of our ideas and perspectives (Yalom & Spinelli, 2007). Nonetheless, as the title of this text makes plain, unlike Yalom I see existential therapy as a distinct approach that has its own specific 'take' on the issues that remain central to therapy as a whole. Further, as I understand it, existential therapy's stance toward such issues provides the means for a series of significant challenges that are critical of contemporary therapy and its aims as they are predominantly understood and practised (Spinelli, 2005, 2007, 2008).

Viewing both perspectives, holding them in relation to one another, an interesting and helpful clarification emerges – an important distinction can be made between therapies that address thematic existence concerns and a particular approach to therapy that is labelled as existential therapy.

Like me, the great majority of writers, researchers and practitioners who identify themselves as existential therapists would disagree with Yalom's contention that there cannot be a distinctive existential model or approach to therapy. Nonetheless, as I see it, they would also tend to be in complete agreement with him in that they, too, place a central focus on the various thematic existence concerns such as death and death anxiety, meaning and meaninglessness, freedom and choice as the primary means to identify existential therapy and distinguish it from other models. As was argued in the Introduction, in my view they are making a fundamental error in this because, as Yalom correctly argues, these various thematic existence concerns also can be identified with numerous – perhaps all – therapeutic approaches. For example, a wide variety of models other than existential therapy address issues centred upon the role and significance of meaning, as well as the impact of its loss, its lack and its revisions (Siegelman, 1993; Wong, 2012). Similarly, the notion of death anxiety is as much a thematic undercurrent of psychoanalytic models as it is of existential therapy (Gay, 1988).

A further problem also presents itself – if *only* thematic existence concerns are highlighted as defining elements of existential therapy then it becomes possible to argue (however absurdly) that any philosopher, psychologist, scientist or spiritual leader who has ever made statements regarding some aspect of human existence can be justifiably designated as 'an existential author/thinker/practitioner'. In similar 'nothing but' fashion, from this same thematic perspective, any number of therapeutic models can make claims to being 'existential', just as existential therapy can argue that, at heart, all models of therapy are, ultimately, existential. While there may well be some dubious value in pursuing such arguments, nonetheless they impede all attempts to draw out just what may be distinctive about existential therapy.

In my view, it is necessary to step beyond – or beneath – thematic existence concerns themselves and instead highlight the existential 'grounding' or *foundational Principles* from which they are being addressed. In doing so, a great deal of the difficulty in clarifying both what existential therapy is, and what makes it discrete as an approach, is alleviated.

I believe that very few existential therapists have confronted the significance of these two differing perspectives. As suggested in the Introduction to this text, one therapist who has done so is Paul Colaizzi. In his paper entitled 'Psychotherapy and existential therapy' (Colaizzi, 2002), Colaizzi highlights what he saw as the fundamental difference between existential therapy and all other psychotherapies, that is, whereas psychotherapy models confront, deal with and seek to rectify the problems of living, existential therapy concerns itself with the issues of existence that underpin the problems of living. In order to clarify this distinction, Colaizzi employs the example of a bridge. He argues that if we were to identify all of the material elements that go into the creation of the bridge, none of them can rightly be claimed to *be* the bridge. The material elements are necessary for the bridge to exist, but no material permitting the construction of the bridge is itself 'bridge-like'. For the bridge to exist requires a 'boundary spanning' from the material elements to the existential possibility that permits 'the bridgeness of the bridge'. In similar fashion,

> Life is the unbridgelike, unstretching material of the bridge of existence. And acts of living as the segments of life are the pieces of material which fit into the spanning of existence. But these life contents are not themselves existence; they do not stretch or span across the whole of individual, finite temporality.

> It is existence which infuses life contents with any meaning they have, just as spannedness infuses bridge material with the meaning of bridge material. Just as no parts of the bridge span across boundaries but rather fit into spannedness, no life contents span across space and time. (Colaizzi, 2002: 75–76)

For Colaizzi, psychotherapy concerns, and limits, itself with life issues which he sees as being the equivalent of the material elements that are necessary for bridges to exist. Existential therapy, on the other hand, should be more concerned with the 'boundary spanning' or 'stretching' of life issues so that it is 'the lifeness of life issues' (just as 'the bridgeness of the bridge') that becomes its primary focus.

Colaizzi's argument is often poetically elusive. However, I believe the issues he addresses are central to the understanding of existential therapy. Although I am not always in agreement with some specific aspects of his discussion, I think that Colaizzi is correct in pointing out that existential therapists have tended to over-emphasise the thematic concerns that make up the 'materials' of existence. If, instead, we were to take up his challenge and focus more on what may be 'the existentialness of existential therapy', what might we discover?

What are Key Defining Principles?

We face each other in the betweenness between us. Watsuji Tetsurō

Most models of therapy are able to embrace competing interpretations dealing with any and every aspect of theory and practice. Regardless of how different these may be, they remain 'housed' within a shared model. What allows this to be so? All models and approaches contain shared *foundational Principles*, what existential phenomenologists might refer to as 'universal structures' that underpin all the variant perspectives within a model, thereby identifying it and distinguishing it from any other. Both psychoanalysis and cognitive behavioural therapy (CBT), for example, are each made identifiable and distinctive through such foundational Principles. For instance, the assumption of a separate and discrete mental processing system – the *unconscious* – in contrast to that of conscious processing – is a foundational Principle to be found in all variants of psychoanalytic thought. In the same way, the foundational Principles of transference and counter-transference run through all modes of psychoanalytic practice (Ellenberger, 1970; Smith, 1991). Similarly, within CBT, which consists of a huge diversity of views and, at times, quite starkly contrasting emphases, there also exists at least one key underlying Principle that runs across, and to this extent unifies, its various strands – their shared allegiance to, and reliance upon, formal experimental design as the critical means to both verify and amend clinical hypotheses (Salkovskis, 2002).

As important as they are in providing the means by which both to identify a model and to reveal its uniqueness, it is surprising to discover that these foundational Principles are rarely made explicit by the majority of practising therapists. This seems somewhat odd since it is through such Principles that the uniqueness of any specific model is revealed. Whatever this might say about the state of contemporary therapy, what is important to the present discussion is the acknowledgement that if an agreed-upon set of foundational Principles for existential therapy can be discerned, then it becomes more possible to clarify what unites its various and diverse interpretations.

When considering existential therapy, it is difficult not to conclude that there are as many unique expressions of existential therapy as there are unique beings who engage in and practise it. Thus, it is something of a challenge to claim, much less provide evidence for, the existence of shared underlying Principles in the practice of existential therapy – unless one were to argue that the one governing Principle was that of *rejecting* any foundational Principles. Avoiding that conclusion, this book argues that existential therapy rests upon three key foundational Principles. I will discuss these below and in Part Two I will provide a structural model for practising existential therapy that I believe remains true to these Principles.

Implicit in this enterprise lies a desire to challenge existential therapists to consider critically whether their ways of 'doing' existential therapy might be taking on board attitudes, assumptions and behavioural stances that originate from other models but which might not 'fit' all that well, if at all, with the aims and aspirations of existential therapy. For example, when considering issues such as therapist disclosures and anonymity might existential therapists be unnecessarily adopting stances that are indistinguishable from those assumed by other approaches? Perhaps, with reflection, the decision to do so might well turn out to be both sensible and appropriate. But it may also be possible that, much like Medard Boss' *daseinsanalysis*, which maintains the basic structural stance of psychoanalysis but 'situates' this within a distinctly different, even contradictory, theoretical system (Boss, 1963, 1979), existential therapists have *assumed* attitudes, stances and structures borrowed from other traditions and considered them as required for the practice of therapy without sufficient questioning of these assumptions. Again, in Part Two, I have provided a structural model for practising existential therapy that acknowledges and utilises various contributions from other models while at the same time avoiding being unnecessarily burdened by the structural stances, assumptions and practices derived from them that are inconsistent with its foundational Principles.

Obviously, no enterprise that attempts to respond to these challenges should either dismiss or deny current standards and ethics of practice as delineated by Governing Bodies for the profession of therapy. If it wishes to be acknowledged and approved by these Bodies, any model of existential therapy must remain situated within the facticity of their professional rules and regulations. As such, there is nothing considered or discussed in this text that does not adhere to currently existing standards of practice as presented by the major UK and international Professional Bodies. Nonetheless, at its broadest level, the model under discussion seeks to bring back to contemporary notions of therapy a stance that re-emphasises a crucial aspect that is contained within the original meaning of *therapeia* – namely, the enterprise of 'attending to' another via the attempt to stand beside, or with, that other as he or she is being and acts in or upon the world (Evans, 1981). Although I believe this notion to be a broadly shared enterprise of all existential therapists, why they should take this stance is best clarified when linked to the foundational Principles of the approach.

Which leads to the obvious question: Just what are existential therapy's foundational Principles?

Existential Therapy's Three Foundational Principles

What is spoken is never, and in no language, what is said. Martin Heidegger

Existential phenomenology, as a unique system of philosophically attuned investigation, arose in the early years of the twentieth century. Although it is composed of many interpretative strands and emphases, at its heart is the attempt to grapple with the dilemma of dualism. Dualism has multiple manifestations: the distinctiveness of mind and matter – or lack of it – has been the source of centuries-spanning ongoing debates between idealists and materialists. Such debates, in turn, have confronted issues centred upon everything from the nature of reality in general, to the (assumed) dichotomy between consciousness and the brain, self and other, intellect and emotion, good and evil, male and female and so forth. From the standpoint of structured investigation, which is the hallmark of Western science, dualistic debates have focused on the interplay between the 'subject' (the observer/ investigator) and the 'object' (the observed/the focus of investigation) and whether claims made regarding truly objective data entirely detached from the investigator's influence are valid and reliable.

Yet another, somewhat different, aspect of dualism can be seen in contemporary theories of physics wherein two mutually exclusive mechanisms are *equally* required for the most adequate understanding of a particular principle. Theories addressing the wave–particle duality of matter would be an example of this (Selleri, 2013). It is important to recognise that this second expression of dualism differs significantly from the others in that it does not adopt the more prevalent 'either/or' stance that separates the contradictory categories under focus. Instead, the contradictory categories are viewed from a 'both/and' stance of necessary complementary co-existence.

This 'both/and' perspective is uncommon in Western thought. We prefer our dualities to be mutually exclusive and separate rather than complementary and often paradoxical. Our language is so significantly geared toward this preference that, when seeking to express a 'both/and' stance, it exacerbates the dilemma by imposing the terminology of contradiction/separatism upon that of complementarity/paradox. For example, other than via mathematics, it seems to be impossible to express the complementary/paradoxical view of 'wave–particle theory' without resorting to contradictory/separatist language.

I raise this last point because it highlights a critical dilemma. Existential phenomenology has often been presented as an approach that has sought to remove the dominance of dualism from our thought and practice. While not incorrect, this conclusion often leads to the assumption that existential phenomenology is linked entirely to monist perspectives which deny any apparent dualism through the reductive emphasis upon a single unifying mechanism or substance. For example, dominant monist stances on body–mind dualism insist that either no truly distinct and separate 'mind' exists and all seemingly mental phenomena are solely materially (i.e. brain-) derived or that mental phenomena can be identified but only as outcomes of (admittedly complex) brain activity. Following this monist stance, neuroscientists are broadly in agreement that consciousness *is* the electrical activity of cortex neurons that have been assembled in a series of inter-connecting networks (Smythies, 2014).

While many would argue that an existential phenomenological perspective rejects dualism and in some way must espouse some sort of monist position, I don't think that such a hard-line stance is necessary to adopt without diminishing the impact of its challenges. Instead, I would like to suggest that existential phenomenology's foundational perspective, being neither exclusively idealist nor exclusively materialist, is much more akin to that of the complementary/paradoxical stance adopted by theoretical physics. In promoting this 'both/and' perspective, it addresses dualist concerns without favouring one aspect of the perceived duality over the other but, rather, by arguing that the dual opposites co-exist equally and inseparably as mutually influencing continuum *polarities*. For instance, from this existential phenomenological perspective, mind–body dualism shifts away from 'either/or' debates which prioritise one component over the other, and attempts to give equal value to seemingly separately existing components (i.e. mind *and* body) by arguing for a paradoxically 'indivisible dualism' (i.e. 'mindbody' or 'bodymind') that is expressed via polarities.

Nonetheless, this proposed shift retains the same problems of language as were noted in the attempts by contemporary physics to address various theories such as those that consider matter from wave–particle perspectives. The English language, for example, seems to be structured in ways that are inimical to the articulation of existential phenomenological perspectives. As a consequence, all attempts to do so must resort to statements that are inevitably imbued with an inherent separatist, 'either/or' dualism which, in turn, confounds the meaning of the statement and confuses its intent. For instance, in order to assert the key principle of indivisible relatedness (as will be discussed below), existential therapists often employ the term *being-in-the-world* (Cooper, 2003). Even so, and in spite of the attempt to express a polarity-derived unified duality via the hyphenation between the words, the term still suggests a conjunction of two separate and distinct entities, namely 'the being' and 'the world'. On further consideration, even the introduction of novel terms, such as *dasein* (Heidegger, 1962), that attempt to convey that this polarity cannot be defined without recourse to an explanatory language imbued with contradictory separatism. As such, not only does the 'alien language' of existential phenomenology fail to fulfil its intent, it adds substantially to the (in my opinion, erroneous) view held by many that the ideas and concepts being propounded are too difficult, too abstract and too limited to have any useful therapeutic applications.

Is there *any* way out of this linguistic dilemma? Probably not. Still, problematic as novel terms can be, at least they serve to expose the separatist dualism that is so embedded in our thought and language. That challenge in itself, even without the provision of a fully developed alternative, can have significant impact. Perhaps, as well, *indirect* challenges that point us toward the alternative perspective through metaphor and allusion, can also provoke an experiential understanding that shifts us beyond the limitations of the language being employed so that we grasp more adequately what it is intending to express. What is evident nonetheless is that, in spite of such difficulties, existential phenomenology's arguments and concerns continue to tantalise many of those who come upon them, be they philosophers, psychologists or therapists. I suspect that it is these very same difficulties which are the key to its continuing allure. Most significantly, in attempting to investigate fundamental issues of existence from a complementary and paradoxical ('both/and') perspective, the foundational Principles of existential phenomenology become much more readily identifiable. Three of these Principles in particular – *relatedness, uncertainty and existential anxiety* – are, in my view, not only critical to existential phenomenology as a whole; they also provide the basic rationale to any attempt at practising existential therapy.

The First Principle: Existential Relatedness

The world and I are within one another. Maurice Merleau-Ponty

The principle of *relatedness* is so pivotal to the whole rationale of existential phenomenology that its presence and influence resonates through its every point and argument. Because it is so foundational, and at the same time so often counterintuitive to Western thought, it requires extended consideration.

Relatedness can be understood at both a surface and deeper level. The former is more initially accessible, but, I think, ultimately too limiting of what is intended. The latter, for the linguistic reasons discussed above, cannot be expressed directly but can be approached through analogies which can be helpful but, in common with any analogy, remain unable to express or contain all that the Principle proposes.

At its simplest, surface level, relatedness argues that everything that exists is always in an inseparable relation to everything else. From this understanding of relatedness, every thought, feeling and action experienced or undertaken by me is said to arise not only from the interaction of systems and components *within* me as a boundaried organism, but also from the interaction *between* boundaried organisms (which is to say, between self and others and between self and world). Even at this surface level, the Principle of relatedness can be seen to have enormous implications, not least because it no longer permits an exclusively isolationist subjectivity capable of generating its own internally generated reflections upon its experience of being. At the same time, numerous other approaches, perhaps most obviously systemic approaches, would argue something pretty much identical to this viewpoint (Hills, 2012). What makes the existential phenomenological perspective on relatedness significantly different only becomes clearer when its deeper implications are considered.

A Cup of *Being* Tea: An Analogy of Relatedness

> Nevertheless, suppose that Descartes had written ...: We think, therefore *we* are. Suppose that the solipsist constraint is dropped, and that intersubjectivity is taken as a primitive postulate .... John Ziman

Imagine a cup of tea. Now, imagine that the tea is '*being* tea' in that it is the tea through which all beings emerge. Each spoonful 'bit' of *being* tea expresses and gives rise to a unique, special, unrepeatable, individual being. And, as well, each spoonful 'bit' of *being* tea that is extracted and held up to investigation and then returned to the cup of *being* tea is never exactly the same as any previous or future spoonful. No individual spoonful 'bit' of *being* tea is somehow *more being* tea than any other. Nor is it *less* than any other. Every 'bit' of *being* tea is unique and every 'bit' of *being* tea *is* the *being* tea.

Now imagine each individual spoonful 'bit' of *being* tea declaring that not only is it unique and unrepeatable, it is also its own originator. It exists out of its own making and can be understood and defined within its own boundaries, separate and distinct from any and all other 'bits' of *being* tea each of whom, as well, can be understood and defined in and of itself without any relational recourse to any or every other 'bit' of *being* tea. Such declarations allow each 'bit' of *being* tea to exist *as if* its existence had nothing whatever to do with the shared cup of *being* tea from which all individual *being* tea 'bits' emerged. Indeed, such declarations allow each 'bit' of *being* tea to forget or deny its source-point.

What this, admittedly silly, analogy highlights is the central challenge that existential phenomenology poses to all those viewpoints and systems that assume an exclusively individually derived, separatist subjectivity as the starting-point to our experience of being. Most obviously, this challenge addresses all those views that in various ways begin with the primacy of an isolated self that is entirely comprehensible within its set of subjectively derived meanings, felt experiences and behaviours. The Principle of relatedness presents us with an alternative to this perspective. It argues that it is only via its prior grounding in relatedness that the self's distinctive and unique sense of being becomes possible. As should now be clearer, an existential phenomenological notion of relatedness argues much more than that each of us, as a separate being, is always in relation to and with all other separate beings. Far more significantly, what it is proposing is that *seemingly separate beings exist only because of a foundational precondition of relatedness*. Each being stands out in a wholly unique and unrepeatable way of being *and* is able to be and do so through a foundational relatedness that is not only shared by all beings but which is also the necessary condition through which individual beings emerge.

As I see it, existential phenomenology argues that Western views of existence, especially since Descartes, have promoted a specifically divisive dualistic mode of interpretative reflecting. In its broadest sense, this way of reflecting has allowed us to construe **being** only as 'boundaried' or 'bounded' (Gergen, 2009) as well as individualistically/subjectively dominated rather than relationally attuned. In short, such forms of reflection have served to reduce relatedness to mere relationship – that is, the interaction of, by and between separate beings whose existence is claimed to be understandable and explicable from an originating, individualistically boundaried perspective. Viewed from an existential phenomenological perspective, however, whatever the stance taken towards relationships – whether seen as desirable or problematic, to be embraced or avoided, sufficient or lacking – it always remains an expression of relatedness. One can avoid, reject or even deny that they are 'in' any sort of relationship; at the same time, those very claims of avoidance, denial or rejection reveal the foundational relatedness from which they emerge. Relatedness is not something that becomes established only under certain circumstances or as a result of particular conditions or which we work towards. Rather, 'relatedness is'. Always.

The significance of, and implications arising from, this first foundational Principle become most apparent when considering the related notions of *subjectivity* and *the individual*.

Relatedness and Subjectivity

Why should the healthy hand attend to the wounded foot? The Buddha

One of the most interesting and important recent attempts to challenge the dominance of subjectivity within Western thought can be found in Kenneth Gergen's book, *Relational Being: Beyond Self and Community* (Gergen, 2009). Gergen states that the view of the individual as separate and singular is a conception that in the

West took root only four centuries ago. However sensible or obvious this view might seem to us to be today, it remains an unusual idea within a wider cultural context. Gergen's enterprise is to explore the ways in which the idea of bounded being can be replaced by that of relational being. As with the existential phenomenological Principle of relatedness, this enterprise is an attempt

> to generate an account of human action that can replace the presumption of bounded selves ... I do not mean relationships between otherwise separate selves, but rather, a process of coordination that precedes the very concept of the self .... There is no isolated self or fully private experience. Rather we exist in a world of co-constitution. (Gergen, 2009: xv)

Gergen makes his aims clear: he wants to develop a view steeped in relatedness in which there is no prioritising condition of an independent subjectivity. In attempting this, he highlights the action-based consequences of this shift. For example, he challenges the reader to consider the possibility of our language containing no nouns whatsoever. Immediately the stability of a 'thing-based' noun-world is replaced by flow-like, action-based process. In this new language, it would be difficult 'to contain the flow of action into discrete, noun-like entities; like waves of the ocean it is not clear where one movement ends and another begins .... [T]he world might not appear to us as separate entities ... not discrete "forms" but continuous "forming"' (Gergen, 2009: 30).

Relational Being's arguments and concerns are too rich and numerous for me to provide anything approaching an appropriate summary. I strongly urge readers to discover and engage with this text for themselves. Nonetheless, Gergen's position on relatedness resonates strongly with that being presented here, as are, alas, the linguistic difficulties incurred.

Similar conclusions are presented in one of the last papers written by John Ziman prior to his death in 2005. Coming from a background of theoretical physics, Ziman presented a view of relatedness that challenges 'the axiom of subjectivity' (Ziman, 2006: 18) which runs through scientific enquiry. Specifically, Ziman argues: 'I have not come across any evidence that the subjective mode of consciousness is prior − in the species or in the phenotypical modern individual − to its intersubjective copartner' (ibid.: 23). Acknowledging his agreement with this view and extending its focus, the anthropologist Alan Macfarlane responded to Ziman's conclusion by arguing:

> With the growth of comparative anthropology it became clear that our individualistic, capitalistic, self-consciousness, rather than being the normal state of things, is indeed a western peculiarity, something produced by the strange form of individualistic, monotheistic religion and western law and economy. When anthropologists reported back on what they had found in South American or South East Asian jungles, or in New Guinea or among Australian aborigines, they described relational, inter-subjective, world views not wholly different from that which Ziman is suggesting. (Macfarlane, 2006: 46)

Macfarlane argues that it would be wrong to believe that 'these societies could be ignored as to a certain extent peripheral vestiges of a disappearing world' (ibid.: 47). On the contrary, he states that

> as anthropologists and historians turned their attention increasingly to large, literate, market-based, peasant civilizations outside western Europe they found that they also were based on the premise of inter-subjectivity .... One example was Chinese civilization .... A second was India .... A third comes from the attempts to understand Japanese civilization .... (ibid.: 47)

All these arguments resonate with existential phenomenology's assertion that subjectivity is just one variant of a prior foundational state of relatedness and should be understood as an expression of that relatedness. Viewed in this way, subjectivity does not arise or exist in contrast to, nor is it distinct from, relatedness, nor can it be placed alongside relatedness as a separate and alternative mode of *being* and experiencing. Rather, subjectivity is seen as a particular, perhaps culturally specific, emergent consequence of relatedness.

Relatedness and the Individual

> It is not that there is experience because there is an individual, but that there is an individual because there is experience. Kitaro Nishida

Addressing the issues surrounding notions of the individual, Gergen has argued that the '"I" does not index an origin of action, but a relational achievement' (Gergen, 2009: 133). In line with this view, the philosopher David Midgley (commenting upon the work of John Ziman as discussed above) agrees with Ziman's contention that the 'bias towards atomic individualism not only bedevils the human and social sciences: it distorts the whole philosophy of nature' (Ziman, 2006: 21). Midgley then extends this view by arguing that 'individual consciousness is actually a part or subsystem of a larger [interrelational] consciousness' (Midgley, 2006: 100).

Perhaps the most radical reconsideration of currently dominant views surrounding the individual can be found in the writings of Martin Buber, a philosopher whose ideas have had a major impact upon existential phenomenology. Buber's now famous contrast between 'I–It' and 'I–Thou' states that relations between self and other can be viewed in two ways: 'The other' can be experienced as a separate *object* whose meaning in relation to the scrutinising 'I' is shaped by that 'I's' imposition of its preferred meaning stance. Alternatively, 'I' can approach 'the other' as an inter-related co-subject through which mutually revealing, unpredictable and impermanent meaning possibilities unfold themselves (Buber, 1970, 2002).

The former is an 'I–It' attitude that is grounded in an object-focused stance of separateness and control. The latter is an 'I–Thou' attitude that expresses the instability of ever-emergent, co-created engagement *between* persons. If the former demands that the 'I' must 'fix' him or her self in an attitude of authority, the latter's impact opens the 'I' to the reconstituting and redefining of its own meaning base via the equalising attitude taken toward the other. If 'I–It' objectifies both the 'I' and the other ('It'); 'I–Thou' reveals that both 'I' and the other ('Thou') co-exist as an inseparable inter-relation whose truthful meanings are not handed down, directed toward, imposed or predetermined via a process of objectification (Buber, 1970). It is important to clarify that Buber saw both stances as expressions of relatedness. His was not yet another 'either/or' position. Rather, he argued that although relatedness lay at the foundation of each, 'I–It' engagements seek to express relatedness through its denial, while 'I–thou' relations move ever towards its embrace.

Buber further clarified these differing responses to relatedness via his distinction between 'individuals' and 'persons'. He was deeply critical of Western culture's (and much of therapy's) elevation of the isolated, self-sustaining individual. He railed against the sort of 'fascism of self-autonomy' that runs rampant through Western thought and is so alien in its views from those of so many other philosophies and systems in the world (Kirschenbaum & Henderson, 1990). In contrast, his view of the person served as an expression of what it is to be human – a being who inhabits an inseparable relation with the world, and is an expression of that relation. For Buber, being a person means far more than simply individuating. Being a person requires *inclusion,* engaging 'in real reciprocity with the world' (Kirschenbaum & Henderson, 1990: 63).

In taking this view, I suggest, Buber was uncommonly prescient. Today, the constant blathering of marketeers and politicians about the sanctity and protection of 'the individual', and the wants or pursuits associated with it, has permitted an unprecedented and highly manipulable allegiance to blandness, mediocrity and predictability in people's goals, aspirations and experience of their existence. In minimising, if not removing, the foundational constituent of relatedness from our understanding of individuality, our relations – be they with self or others – have become all too commonly enmeshed in the objectifying strictures of 'I–It' encounters.

Relatedness: A Summary

I am who I am because of everyone. Orange Telecom 2008 Ad Campaign

Much of the difficulty in existential phenomenology's attempts to convey the Principle of relatedness stems from the limitations of language. As I have argued above, the English language, for example, immediately imposes a 'split' upon all discourse that seeks to express relatedness in a direct way. If I were to state, for instance, that you and I are both co-defined and co-active expressions of **being**, I would be attempting to communicate a key inter-relational axiom via the 'split' language of 'I' and 'you'. Such an attempt blunts and diminishes what is intended; in effect, it expresses relatedness via a language that, at best, obscures the inseparability that encompasses terms such as 'I' and 'you', 'us' and 'them'. Equally, attempts to create a novel way of expressing the relatedness underpinning these terms reveal that a major part of the problem is that what is being attempted is a description and communication of some*thing* – be it 'I' or 'you'. Instead, what relatedness posits is more akin to a *process*. Or, to put it another way, what is being pointed to is more *verb-like* than it is *noun-like*. In considering relatedness from a noun-like perspective, tensions and problems come into being that complicate an already confusing enterprise.

Once again, this confusion can be seen to have its parallel in the attempts to communicate various concepts and ideas from contemporary physics. Here, too, when the conclusions drawn from mathematical equations are communicated in terms of more everyday language, what emerges is a confusion of apparently distinct and contradictory statements which, nonetheless, are all held to be 'true'. If we consider the many conceptual conundrums to do with time, space, locality and materiality thrown up by quantum physics it is both evident and somewhat startling to note how closely such conundrums resonate with those presented by the Principle of relatedness (Bohm & Hiley, 1995).

The terms we employ to grasp and express relatedness encase and restrain. They impose a passivity and/or closure upon a notion that yearns to communicate movement, openness and a perpetual 'becoming'. In like fashion, the terms that existential phenomenologists have tended to apply, such as 'being-in-the-world' or 'dasein' or 'figure/ground', remove all sense of movement and indeterminacy, are too noun-like and remain too static for that which they seek to embrace. At the same time, terms like relatedness are also subject to being perceived from a separatist, noun-like standpoint. Relatedness is not either action or stasis, or either verb-like or noun-like; it is always 'both/and'. Nonetheless, important distinctions arise when relatedness is viewed from each focus point. As will be discussed in Chapter 3, I have elected to employ the terms *worlding* and *worldview* as a means of more adequately expressing the human experience of existence both in general and as contrasting expressions of relatedness. For now, in spite of the limitations of language, I hope that something sufficient has been expressed regarding the existential phenomenological Principle of relatedness.

As a way of summarising the key concerns expressed by the Principle of relatedness, I want to put forward the South African notion of *ubuntu*. Ubuntu is a term open to multiple cultural interpretations (Gade, 2012). Nonetheless, a recurring theme embedded within the term challenges all views which address the person in isolation rather than from an inter-connected standpoint. Indeed, ubuntu suggests that we can only become human, and experience our humanity, when we no longer perceive of our selves as isolated individuals, separate and distinct from all others. According to Michael Onyebuchi Eze, ubuntu proposes that

> humanity is not embedded in my person solely as an individual; my humanity is co-substantively bestowed upon the other and me. Humanity is a quality we owe to each other. We create each other and need to sustain this otherness creation. And if we belong to each other, we participate in our creations: we are because you are, and since you are, definitely I am. The 'I am' is not a rigid subject, but a dynamic self-constitution dependent on this otherness creation of relation and distance. (Eze, 2010: 190–191)

Through terms like ubuntu, we can better grasp the intended meaning of existential phenomenology's Principle of relatedness. Its implications reach out to challenge the dominance of an isolated and separatist subjectivity and remind us of a grounding through which the experience of existence includes all subjectivities.

An Exercise Exploring Existential Relatedness

1. Write five statements that convey something about who you are, or how you feel about your self or some other selected person or event, or what you did earlier today or intend to do later on.
2. Examine the statements and note how noun-based they are.
3. Following Kenneth Gergen's challenge, try to re-write your five statements so that all nouns are eliminated and, instead, what they attempt to convey is expressed only in a verb-like or action-focused language. Alternatively, try to communicate your five statements only via action – such as movement or dance. For example, try to convey a statement such as 'I will holiday in Italy this May' from an action-focused stance conveying 'I-ing' 'holidaying', 'Italy-ing' and 'May-ing'.
4. Consider and explore your experience of shifting from noun-dominated statements to action-focused language. For instance, how, if at all, does it affect your sense of self? How, if at all, does it affect your connection to, or relationship with, the statements you have made and the persons or events or feelings and behaviours contained within them?

The Second Principle: Uncertainty

> Explanations exist; they have existed for all time; there is always a well-known solution to every human problem — neat, plausible, and wrong. H. L. Mencken

The second foundational Principle of existential phenomenology, *uncertainty*, arises as an immediate consequence of relatedness. Uncertainty expresses the inevitable and inescapable openness of possibility in any and all of our reflections upon our existence.

As was concluded with regard to the Principle of relatedness, our reflections upon existence, be they in general or having to do with 'my own' existence, can no longer be held *solely* by me or exist in some way exclusively 'within' me. Instead, relatedness exposes the many uncertainties that impinge upon every attempt at reflection. The Principle of uncertainty asserts that I can never fully determine with complete and final certainty or control not only *what* will present itself as stimulus to my experience, but also *how* I will experience and respond to stimuli. An immediate consequence of this stance is that even how I will experience my self under differing stimulus conditions cannot be predetermined.

Does this imply that existential phenomenology recognises no certainties whatsoever? Not at all. There exist any number of preconditions – including environmental and bio-chemical variables – that are required for the establishment and maintenance of life. Without them, no life is possible nor can be sustained. These are the certainties upon which life is able to come into, and continue, being. This second Principle concerns itself with those uncertainties that arise *within* the context of these preconditions. It argues that the person's lived experience within the certain preconditions of existence is constantly open to multiple possibilities – and hence remains uncertain. As Simone de Beauvoir reminds us, '[f]rom the very beginning, existentialism defined itself as a philosophy of ambiguity' (de Beauvoir, 1986: 9). The Principle of uncertainty exemplifies this conclusion. At any moment, for example, all prior knowledge, values, assumptions and beliefs regarding self, others and the world in general may be open to challenge, reconsideration or dissolution in multiple ways that might surprise or disturb. Common statements such as 'I never thought I would act like that', or 'She seemed to turn into someone I didn't know', or 'World events have convinced me that I just can't make sense of things any longer' point us to positions that at least temporarily acknowledge the uncertainties of being. Social psychological studies on obedience to authority and social conformity provide powerful evidence of how easily we can think, feel and act in ways that we would never have predicted (Milgram, 1974; Zimbardo, 1969).

As a 'way in' to the further clarification of the Principle of uncertainty, let me first consider it from the standpoints of contemporary physics and from Isaiah Berlin's argument for value pluralism. Although approaching the question from a different perspective to that of existential phenomenology, I hope to demonstrate that their conclusions regarding uncertainty are not only compatible; they also serve to make the Principle more accessible.

Uncertainty in Contemporary Physics

We are all agreed that your theory is insane. The question that divides us is whether it is insane enough to have a chance of being correct. Neils Bohr to Wolfgang Pauli

I have long been fascinated by the temporal resonance between the development of existential phenomenology and the revolutionary changes taking place in Western physics. I have often wondered whether one body of thought impacted on the other in any way. Although I know of no historical research that has been carried out along such lines, I find it difficult to imagine that philosophers such as Edmund Husserl, who came from a background in mathematics, would have remained unaware of the radical theories being propounded by his scientific colleagues.

At the beginning of the twentieth century, theories of physics with regard to light assumed that light was best understood if viewed as a wave. Albert Einstein's equations argued instead that light was a stream or 'packet' of energy particles, which he named quanta. Unlike waves, quanta have mass. This view was initially seen as being fantastical because light could not possibly have weight. Nonetheless, Einstein's hypothesis could not be disproven. However, although Einstein was correct in arguing that light was made up of quanta, older experiments which showed that light was also wave-like also continued to be verified. Depending upon the investigator's focus of observation, light could be simultaneously both a packet of energy (quanta) and a wave. Uncertainty in physics was established (Al-Khalili, 2009, 2012).

With the publication of Einstein's *Theory of Special Relativity* in 1905 (Einstein, 2001), the certainties of a mechanical and predictable universe began to be dismantled. Relativity theories argued that the one fixed constant – the speed of light – did not ever alter regardless of the conditions under which it was placed. However, the same could not be said of space and time. These now could be seen to be *relative*. For example, distance could no longer be understood as a relation between two points. Distance also involved the observer, whose relation to these two points directly affected the outcome of their measurement. Equally, intervals of time were seen to have no absolute value since the flow of time was demonstrated to be dependent on the relation between object and observer (Einstein et al., 2000).

Now, two competing and contradictory truths could co-exist. Uncertainty was introduced as a basic given of our relationship to the universe. The relativity of time and space was extended to become a relativity of knowledge. Whereas nineteenth-century physics had assumed that the more we understand, the more we can know with absolute certainty, twentieth-century physics began to reveal that the more we understand, what we can know becomes less predictably certain (Al-Khalili, 2009).

Contemporary dynamical systems theories of physics, such as Chaos Theory, are often misunderstood as arguing that the behaviour of complex systems is unpredictable. Instead, as was summarised by the theoretical physicist Jim Al-Khalili, what is actually being proposed is that: 'All the complexity of the universe emerges from mindless simple rules, rules repeated over and over again. But as powerful as this process is, it is also inherently unpredictable' (Al-Khalili, 2009). In other words, at the heart of all our certainties lies uncertainty. Whereas classical physics had assumed that unpredictable events were caused by some *external* interference upon a system that was otherwise coherent and predictable, dynamical systems theories have shown that this unpredictability is built into the system itself. And more, that it is this very same systemic unpredictability that generates what we experience as pattern and structure. Contemporary theories of physics view Order and Chaos, waves and matter, structure and process as interweaving paradoxical polarities (Al-Khalili, 2012).

Not being able to be certain should not, paradoxically, lead us to assume the certainty of uncertainty. From an either/or stance, I can claim that something is either certain or uncertain. If I declare it certain, then I am adopting a position of certainty. Equally, however, my opposite declaration of uncertainty is also rooted in certainty in that I am now arguing that I am certain that something is uncertain. Both these claims can be seen to rely upon a foundational stance of certainty. In effect they are saying: ultimately all statements about either certainty or uncertainty are statements of certainty.

The existential phenomenological Principle of uncertainty, like dynamical systems theories in physics, proposes an alternative stance – that of *the uncertainty of uncertainty*. This stance treats both our claimed certainties as well as our claimed uncertainties as uncertain. In doing so, it seeks to emphasise the inseparable interweaving between certainty and uncertainty. Because of this inter-connectedness, no certainty (including the certainty of uncertainty) can ever be wholly certain; there can only be uncertain certainties and uncertain uncertainties.

Uncertainty: Isaiah Berlin's Value Pluralism

Uncertainty is a quality to be cherished, therefore – if not for it, who would dare to undertake anything? Villiers de L'Isle-Adam

Although it would be seriously misleading to suggest that he was an existential phenomenological philosopher, and he would almost certainly have been displeased to be so labelled, it is my view that, in his theory of *value pluralism*, Isaiah Berlin provides the most insightful analysis of several key implications arising from the Principle of uncertainty. Berlin's central argument criticised the general Western assumption that any theories or conclusions concerned with human values such as liberty, kindness, and equality could only be deemed to be true or correct if they revealed a coherence and consistency between all the various human values. If any conflicts or contradictions between values were identified, then the theory had to be wrong in some way. In his review of Berlin's posthumous book, *Political Ideas in the Romantic Age: Their Rise and Influence on Modern Thought* (Berlin, 2006), John Gray summarises this persistent assumption that

all genuine human values must be combinable in a harmonious whole. Conflicts of values are to be seen as symptoms of error that in principle can always be resolved: if human values seem to come into conflict that is only because our understanding of them is imperfect, or some of the contending values are spurious; and where such conflicts appear there is a single right answer that – if only they can find it – all reasonable people are bound to accept. (Gray, 2006: 20)

Berlin emphatically rejected all of these claims. Instead, his counter-argument to this view, which he rightly saw as having dominated Western intellectual tradition, asserted that, on the contrary, 'conflicts of values are real and inescapable, with some of them having no satisfactory solution .... [C]onflicts of value go with being human' (Gray, 2006: 20). From a political standpoint, Berlin contended, this

Enlightenment idea of an ideal and monistic harmony and perfection in human values generated the cataclysms of tyranny which had overshadowed his lifetime. For, at the heart of this idea lay 'the intellectual roots of some of the major political disasters of the twentieth century' (Gray, 2006: 20). When considering the excesses of political intolerance and curtailment of freedom of expression associated with both extreme right-wing and left-wing twentieth-century regimes, for example, Berlin's view was that these were not explicable as errors in the application of a particular ideology, but, rather, were 'the result of a resolute attempt to realize an Enlightenment utopia – a condition of society in which no serious conflict any longer exists' (ibid.: 21).

The point being made by Berlin addresses the key concerns and assumptions to be found in the second Principle of existential phenomenology. Together, they ask us to embrace existence's lack of completeness, and the inevitable failure of any attempt to complete it by realising all our possibilities (Cohn, 2002). Some critically minded therapists have arrived at very similar conclusions: In their text, *Pluralistic Counselling and Psychotherapy,* Mick Cooper and John McLeod argue that both an existential therapy steeped in certainty as well as an existential therapy that is certain about its uncertainty is a contradiction in terms; existential uncertainty always holds open plural possibilities (Cooper & McLeod, 2011). In summarising Berlin's value pluralism, John Cherniss provides a particularly revealing and relevant passage. He writes:

> Man is incapable of self-completion, and therefore never wholly predictable; fallible, a complex combination of opposites, some reconcilable, others incapable of being resolved or harmonised; unable to cease from his search for truth, happiness, novelty, freedom, but with no guarantee . . . of being able to attain them. (Cherniss, 2006, quoted in Gray, 2006: 21)

This quote, it seems to me, provides us with a powerful summary of the Principle of existential uncertainty.

Existential Uncertainty: Implications

It is not certain that everything is uncertain. Blaise Pascal

All of us are likely to have had the experience of changing our view with regard to someone or some event. A close friend acts in a way that betrays my trust and brings the friendship to an end. I discover a new-found ability that alters the direction of my professional life. I watch a film that I initially thought to be a work of genius but which now seems superficial and pedestrian. If such obvious possibilities of uncertainty were all that this second Principle sought to highlight, then it would hardly be deserving of much attention. Surprising and unexpected events come upon us all at some time or other during our lives. However, rather than just being an occasional and temporary consequence of unusual circumstances, existential phenomenology proposes that uncertainty remains a constant of existence. Shattering in its implications, this Principle remains initially counter-intuitive. Uncertainty expresses its presence not only in the surprising events in our lives, but just as equally and forcefully in the expected and (seemingly) fixed meanings and circumstances of everyday life. The existential phenomenological Principle of uncertainty urges us to treat each instance of 'the expected' as novel, full of previously unforeseen qualities and possibilities.

This 'both/and' way of considering the implications of the Principle of uncertainty is not always sufficiently addressed by existential therapists. Yet it offers potentially valuable insights. For example, this view of uncertainty suggests that a couple's experience of sexual boredom within their relationship is not directly due to the rigidity of habitual behaviour, but rather to the degree to which they have detached themselves from experiencing the uncertainty that exists within the rigid conditions being maintained. Television 'lifestyle' experts or newspaper agony aunts, for instance, forever suggest novel positions or activities as ways of 'spicing up' a couple's moribund sexual life. In taking this stance, they fail to consider how it is that any number of other couples may be happily satisfied with, and require no 'spicing up' of, their sexual relations, even though what they do and how and when they do it might be characterised as being habitual and predictable. Equally, such pundits avoid alerting their audience to the likelihood that even the suggested novel position or activity may all too rapidly come to be experienced as tedious and bland. What such examples make plain is that the experience of pleasurable excitement in one's sexual relations, or the lack of it, has little to do with matters of novelty or habit, but rather reveals the consequences of an openness toward, or an avoidance of, the uncertainty that exists at all times and is expressed in all actions. In sum, uncertainty reminds us that every reflectively structured pattern of certainty nonetheless is grounded in uncertainty.

In general, Western culture perhaps overvalues the comfort of certainty and underestimates the benefits of uncertainty. We assume a 'naturalness' to the former and impose a sense of the unusual or the unwanted in the latter. We tell our selves that it is better to act as though we were certain of our selves or some viewpoint rather than reveal our selves to be uncertain. Certainty is strength; uncertainty weakens us. In contrast to this, consider the following existential alternatives:

Most days, when either I or my wife leave our home on our own, we embrace one another at the doorway and say something like, 'See you, later.' Our statements are full of certainty. There will certainly be a 'later' during which we will see one another. However, were we to acknowledge the impact of existential uncertainty, what we would have to say to one another, at best, would be, 'Hopefully, we'll see one another again'. At first, this latter statement strikes us as being decidedly odd, perhaps even ghoulish. But consider it this way: If we truly accepted its implications, and placed uncertainty upon our desire and hope to meet again, then might it not be likely that our embrace, our potentially temporary but also potentially permanent 'goodbye' to one another would be imbued with a value, a quality, a fervour that would be far less likely to exist in that 'goodbye' which assumes there will be many other future 'goodbye's and 'hello's to come? The 'goodbye' that assumes a future 'hello' permits me to put off until another time that which I might want to express or will punish my self for not expressing if, unexpectedly, no further opportunities become possible.

A client of mine, Sharon, came to see me because she was so upset by her mother's worsening of dementia and the effect it was having upon their relationship. Sharon's mother had been in a Home for some eight months and Sharon had arranged her life in such a way that she could visit her three times a week. However, as the impact of the dementia increased, Sharon was finding it more and more difficult to force her self to visit her mother. She explained to me that their encounters had become increasingly painful because her mother now rarely recognised Sharon and when told by her that they were mother and daughter, rejected such statements as nonsense. Sharon's insistence as to their relationship only succeeded in generating ever increasing levels of disturbance for her mother such that she became verbally abusive towards Sharon and demanded that she leave. Sharon felt deeply guilty about her increasing lack of desire to visit her mother as well as her growing anger towards her. During therapy, we addressed these feelings and, as well, Sharon's expectations and feelings of loss. Though still alive, her mother had begun to feel relationally dead to Sharon and several times, breaking down in fits of anger and shame, she expressed the wish that her mother would now die physically as well as relationally. The breakthrough came for Sharon when, on one of her visits, having given up all hope, she approached her mother as a stranger. No longer able to be mother and daughter, they were now two people meeting for the first time and attempting to engage with one another. Much to Sharon's amazement, their discussion soon turned to the topic of their children and Sharon heard her mother talk lovingly and with great accuracy about her daughter, who, quite by coincidence, was also named Sharon. Having given up her insistence that she be seen as her mother's daughter, Sharon had found a way to experience that mutually significant and deeply felt mother–daughter relationship for which she had longed.

As readers can ascertain, the first example challenges us to embrace the uncertain in that which we have made certain. The second example alerts us as to how we can limit the possibilities of uncertain circumstances when we insist upon imposing a preferred, but unavailable, certainty upon them.

An Exercise Exploring Uncertainty

Ask your self the following questions:

1. What is one thing, (a), about me that I feel truly certain about?
2. What is one thing, (b), about me that I feel truly uncertain about?
3. What is my felt experience of each? What is the same about (a) and (b)? What is different about them?

(Continued)

(*Continued*)

4. What would happen if I became uncertain about (a)?
5. What would happen if I became certain of (b)?
6. What is my felt experience of (a) having become uncertain? What is my felt experience of (b) having become certain? What is the same about these new experiences of (a) and (b)? What is different about them?

The Third Principle: Existential Anxiety

Freedom's possibility announces itself in anxiety. Søren Kierkegaard

The Principle of existential anxiety follows as a direct consequence of the first two Principles in that it expresses *the lived experience of relational uncertainty*. It is necessary to note from the outset, however, that existential anxiety is not only an expression of disabling and unwanted levels of unease, nervousness, worry and stress. The Principle of existential anxiety certainly *includes* these disturbances and disorders, but it seeks to convey a much more generally felt experience of incompleteness and perpetual potentiality which is expressive of an inherent openness to the unknown possibilities of life experience. In its wider scope, existential anxiety can be both exhilarating and debilitating, a spur to risk-taking action as well as stimulus to fear-fuelled paralysis. Because of this wider meaning, and as well in their attempt to avoid confusion with more restricted, clinically derived definitions of anxiety, some existential phenomenologists prefer to employ the term *angst* (Langridge, 2013). Acknowledging the possible debates and confusions in definition that can be provoked, nonetheless my own preference is to retain the more widely accessible term.

What is pivotal about the notion of existential anxiety is that it is to be seen as an inevitable 'given' of our lived experience of being human. The notion of homeostasis serves as a useful analogue of existential anxiety. Homeostasis refers to the body's attempt to maintain a state or condition of equilibrium or balanced stability. This attempt remains just that – an attempt rather than an achievement. Stimuli from within and external to the organism prevent homeostasis from being a permanent accomplishment. As a condition of life, the body is in a perpetual state of dis-equilibrium endeavouring to achieve permanent balance. Although the body is continually frustrated in its attempts to achieve the perpetual stability of homeostasis, it is nonetheless this very same failure that stimulates the organism to act and to experience. As with the Principle of existential anxiety, it would be misleading to view homeostatic dis-equilibrium solely as a disorder. Instead, both existential anxiety and homeostatic dis-equilibrium serve as stimuli towards strategies whose intent is that of balance.

The dilemma of existential anxiety is not so much *that* it is, but rather *how* each of us 'lives with' it. Existential anxiety encompasses *all* responses to the relational uncertainties of existence. Anxiety may, and often does, arouse feelings of despair, confusion and bewilderment. But the experience of anxiety can also be stimulating, can re-awaken or enhance our connectedness to being alive, and elicits creativity. In not only responding to the challenges of life, but, as well, in provoking challenge through such felt experiences as curiosity, desire, hope, and care we welcome the anxiety that accompanies all these experiences because of its ability to 'awaken' and stimulate us.

The Principle of existential anxiety also alerts us to the disturbing realisation that whatever the stance we adopt towards anxiety, it cannot be removed from our experience of existence. If I embrace anxiety, anxiety remains. Equally, my attempts to resist, reject or deny anxiety typically generate anxiety as expressed, for example, through rigid and restrictive patterns of thought and behaviour or, conversely, as persistent demands and quests for the unknown and novel. What both these stances reveal is a shared rigidity and inflexibility of attitude and stance. Commonly expressed in terms such as obsessive or compulsive behaviours, phobias and addictive disorders these instances of unease reveal themselves as *anxieties about anxiety*. As will be discussed in Part Two, existential therapy can confront us with our attempts to evade and escape anxiety and the anxiety-riddled consequences that can result from this. In important ways, rather than propose or provide the means to reduce or eradicate anxiety from our lives, as is often offered by other models of therapy, existential therapy challenges us to reconsider our anxiety-evasive strategies, weigh up more accurately what their 'price' is and what consequences they generate, and to assess what alternate 'price' there might be in attempting stances that are more open to meeting or engaging with existential anxiety. At the same time, we should not delude our selves into supposing that by facing up to our attempts to avoid or deny existential anxiety we somehow manage to surmount it or disengage our being from it. Whichever stance we take, it will be imbued with existential anxiety. There is 'no way out'.

An Exercise Exploring Existential Anxiety

1. Identify one recurring anxiety that you experience.
2. What is it about this anxiety that is problematic for you?
3. What would change in or about your life if you no longer felt this anxiety?
4. What would change in your life if the anxiety intensified?
5. How does your anxiety affect or impact upon your relations with others? Or a particular other?
6. When you consider your anxiety as an example of the attempt to evade existential anxiety what, if anything, is further clarified about your anxiety?

The Three Principles: A Summary

Our own life is the instrument with which we experiment with the truth.
Thich Nhat Hanh

Existential phenomenology argues that Western thought and reflections upon our existence, especially since Descartes, have seen human existence in a dualistic mode. Self/other, subject/object, inner/outer, thought/emotion are examples of our particularly separatist Western way of dualistic reflection. This way of reflecting has allowed us to construe *being* as 'boundaried' or 'bounded' and individualistically/ subjectively dominated rather than relationally attuned. In contrast, I have argued that, through its foundational Principles of relatedness, uncertainty and existential anxiety, existential phenomenology can present a view of existence which rests upon the attempt to 'hold the tension' between apparently contrasting, separate and contradictory concerns so that they can be reflectively experienced as co-existent and inter-dependent unifying polarities.

Existential therapists have often claimed that this approach, or their particular interpretation of it, is radical (Langdridge, 2013; van Deurzen & Adams, 2011; van Deurzen-Smith, 1988). In my view, such claims are weakened because of the centrality of focus given to various thematic existence concerns without first placing these within the specific context of existential phenomenology's underlying Principles. In not doing so, I believe that existential therapy's specific 'take' or perspective on these broad themes, which in various ways all models of therapy address, often remains unclear and difficult to separate from the perspectives of other models. Further, in emphasising the thematic concerns without contextualising them within existential phenomenology's Principles, the novel possibilities regarding the *practice* of existential therapy remain obscure such that it is often difficult to discern what there is about practising existential therapy that is different, distinctive or, indeed, radical.

I think that such claims can be made valid by reconfiguring existential therapy so that what it says and does is far more clearly aligned with its foundational Principles. As a starting point to this argument, the present chapter has sought to summarise three key foundational Principles of existential phenomenology – relatedness, uncertainty and existential anxiety. It is my view that these three Principles are *necessary* to any adequate explication of existential phenomenological theory. That they may be *sufficient* as well as necessary remains debatable. My own view is that these three conditions are sufficient in so far as they provide the most basic 'sketch' or 'ground-plan' of the existential phenomenological terrain as delineated by its foundational philosophical contributors – Edmund Husserl (1965, 1977, 2012), Martin Heidegger (1962, 1976, 2001) and Jean-Paul Sartre (1973, 1985, 1991). This is not to suggest that the contributions of these three philosophers, much less those of pivotal thinkers such as Martin Buber (1970, 2002), George Gadamer (2004), Karl Jaspers (1963), Immanuel Levinas (1987, 1999) and Maurice Merleau-Ponty (1962, 1964a, 1964b), among numerous others, can simply be *reduced* to these three

Principles. Nor is it being suggested that anyone claiming to espouse existential phenomenology is no longer required to grapple intellectually with many, if not all, of these philosophers (and any number of others left unmentioned).

What *is* being proposed is that in considering these three Principles as pivotal constituents, a great deal of the confusion and dividedness regarding what existential phenomenology proposes, what its implications for therapy might be and how an existential therapy that exists in contrast and comparison to other approaches to therapy would be substantially reduced. For one thing, it would become clearer that it is not so much *that* it is philosophically based, but rather *what* philosophical Principles it upholds that makes it distinctive. Second, the diversity between existential approaches which arises through the differing emphases and interpretations given to thematic existence concerns can be considered within the context of these foundational Principles. Third, a genuine distinction could be made between those philosophers and theorists who address existence themes from a wide range of perspectives (often in highly pertinent and significant ways) and those whose exploratory perspective on such themes is derived from existential phenomenological Principles. For example, as was discussed with regard to the Principle of uncertainty, Isaiah Berlin's writing on value pluralism has much to say that illuminates various thematic existence concerns such as meaning and authenticity. At the same time, claims that Berlin's arguments reveal him to be an existential phenomenological thinker would be absurd and degrading of his achievements. Personally, acknowledging its potentially divisive danger, I would argue that the writings of Friedrich Nietzsche provoke a similar conclusion. A great many of the thematic existence concerns that inform Nietzsche's writings are of vast significance to existential phenomenological thought and practice and help to elucidate its specific stance regarding such themes. But to argue that Nietzsche's contributions to psychoanalytic thought are not at least as significant would be, I think, misguided.

But let me be clear – I am making no claim that a single, all-encompassing approach to existential therapy must exist, or more, that the interpretation being presented in this text *is* that approach. In keeping with the focus of this chapter, I want to emphasise the openness and uncertainty that are characteristic of existential therapy. At the same time, it would be pointless to claim that anything can be existential therapy without also claiming that whatever that 'anything' might be was in some way contained and contextualised within certain conditions. In my view, these conditions are best understood as foundational Principles, which I have attempted to identify and clarify. That these may stimulate further clarification or other contrasting ways of thinking is about the best any author can hope for.

Having provided an introductory overview centred upon these Principles, it is now possible to consider those thematic existence concerns most closely associated with existential phenomenology – concerns surrounding meaning and meaninglessness, choice, freedom and responsibility, authenticity and inauthenticity, isolation and relation, death anxiety, temporality and spatiality – so that an existential phenomenological perspective on them can be argued.

2
Existence Themes and Concerns

Introduction

Consciousness is inherently paradoxical. Benny Shanon

As was discussed in the previous chapter, I have proposed that existential phenomenology is founded upon several foundational Principles through which the recurring *themes and concerns of existence* are considered. Although open to multiple means of investigation, these themes are so closely identified with existential phenomenology that their relevance to existential therapy is unquestionable. This chapter provides an overview of the most relevant of the themes. In doing so, it is hoped that it will provide sufficient stimulus and challenge for readers to pursue more detailed analyses through their own reading, thought and analyses.

Existence Precedes Essence

The world is undifferentiated being. We differentiate it. Maurice Merleau-Ponty

Sartre's (in)famous summary of existential thought, 'existence precedes essence' (Sartre, 1991: 28), has been derived from a sentence in Heidegger's *Being and Time:* 'the "essence" of dasein lies in its existence' (Heidegger, 1962: 67). At first, the statement suggests a reversal of the more common Western philosophical view that in order to exist, whatever exists must first be 'some thing' (i.e. essence precedes existence). If we stay with this reversal, we become aware that our assumptions regarding such 'things' as human nature and inherent identity are *outcomes* rather than foundational conditions of existence. A key to understanding Sartre's argument can be found in the title of his most famous work, *Being and Nothingness* (Sartre, 1991). The 'nothingness' to which Sartre refers is not intended to suggest the equivalent of a lack, or emptiness. Rather, Sartre is pointing out the primal 'no-thing-ness' of existence. Every 'thing' is an outcome expression of no-thing (or pre-thing-ified) existence. Hence, existence precedes essence.

But what 'things' are we talking about here? Nothing less than the most basic 'things': the structures or constructs that we label 'I' or self, others and the world. No-thing, or pre-thing-becoming existence precedes all its essentialist expressions. Once again, language complicates and confuses. We have to be attentive to how we express what is intended otherwise we end up with statements in favour of essence preceding existence. For example, in their recent text, *Skills in Existential Counselling & Psychotherapy,* Emmy van Deurzen and Martin Adams rightly assert that 'existence precedes essence' encapsulates all of the thematic concerns of existential phenomenology (van Deurzen & Adams, 2011). Unfortunately, they then go on to write: 'What [existence precedes essence] … means is that the fact *that* we are is more basic than *what* we are. We *are* first and define ourselves later. Moreover we are always in the process of becoming something else' (van Deurzen & Adams, 2011: 9; emphases in the original).

This attempt at clarification only succeeds in misdirecting the argument back to a primary focus on 'things' – namely the structures labelled as 'we' and 'our selves' – thereby, however inadvertently, declaring the precedence of essence. The problem lies in the emphasis placed on the subject, be it 'I' or 'we' or 'self', as that which both *is* existentially and *becomes* as essence. This primacy fails to clarify that, from an existential phenomenological standpoint, the subject who ponders its existence and essence *is itself an essence.* That is to say, the 'I' is already a reflective construct attempting to clarify its own construction. In brief, to argue '*that* we are is more basic than *what* we are' (ibid.) is, at best, a limiting dilution of the existential phenomenological argument. Why? Because the issue is not concerned with any false foundational primacy of the 'we' but with **being** *per se.*

As I see it (and to be fair, what I think van Deurzen and Adams tried to express), the argument that existence precedes essence is more accurately an attempt to clarify that pre-substantive **being** precedes any particular form or structure – such as 'I' – that **being** might adopt. Acknowledging the limitations of language, which impose a noun-like bias of fixedness upon a verb-like process, the argument can be expressed as: *That existence is, precedes whatever structure existence adopts.*

But what is it that makes the argument for existence preceding essence so significant? Is it not just some abstract debate of little worth to everyday life? I think not. The radical shift being proposed by the argument challenges the dominance of viewing existence as a fixed, mainly permanent and immutable structure. In doing so, it invites an awareness that any subjective statement asserting or captured by its own essence is inadequate and incomplete. Some initial lived sense of this awareness becomes possible when the essence-loaded statement '*I am*' is re-stated as '*I am being*'. Though still essence-loaded, the latter statement opens up the experience of existence to at least an acknowledgement that this 'I' is far less fixed in its particular expression of essence than might have been assumed. Perhaps even more accurately, though admittedly relying upon a highly unusual language, we can further re-phrase the statement in this way: **Being** *is being expressed as that being who is being* …. Still inadequate in its structural, noun-like emphasis, and far too clumsy to stand a chance of ever being adopted into everyday discourse, nonetheless, it expresses a challenge to the naive essentialism of our culture.

'Existence precedes essence' has multiple implications for therapeutic thought and practice. Perhaps most significantly, it challenges the overriding emphasis given to the injunction to 'be true to your self'. Instead, in taking a view that fore-grounds existence over essence, existential phenomenology rejects this injunction on the grounds that focusing upon a reflective structure – the self – as the source for truth maintains an essentialist primacy. In contrast, 'being true to **being**' would be a more accurate, if relationally uncertain, existence-focused aspiration.

An Exercise Exploring the Theme of Existence Precedes Essence

1. Fill in the remainder of the following five statements:

    o I am [your name]
    o I am [your age]
    o I am [your gender]
    o I am [your relation to a family member] (e.g. a daughter/a brother/a cousin/a father)
    o I am [a currently felt experience] (e.g. hungry/in love/lonely/amused)

2. Say each statement aloud. Note what felt experience you have as you make each statement as well as the overall feeling you have once you have made all the statements.

3. Now, fill in the remainder of the following five statements:

    o I am being [your name]
    o I am being [your age]
    o I am being [your gender]
    o I am being [your relation to a family member] (e.g. a daughter/a brother/a cousin/a father)
    o I am being someone who feels [a currently felt experience] (e.g. hungry/ in love/etc.)

4. Say each statement aloud. Note what felt experience you have as you make each statement as well as the overall feeling you have once you have made all the statements.

5. What differences, if any, did you find in your felt experience of expressing statements of being from an 'I am' to an 'I am being' focus?

(Continued)

(Continued)

6. Now, fill in the remainder of the following five statements:

    o **Being** is being expressed as that being who is being [your name]
    o **Being** is being expressed as that being who is being [your age]
    o **Being** is being expressed as that being who is being [your gender]
    o **Being** is being expressed as that being who is being [your relation to a family member]
    o **Being** is being expressed as that being who is being someone who feels [a currently felt experience]

7. What differences, if any, with the previous two statements on **being** did you find in your felt experience of expressing statements of **being** from a '**being** is expressing itself' focus?
8. How, if at all, has this exercise assisted your understanding of the existential phenomenological contention that 'existence precedes essence'?

Meaning/Meaninglessness

> The way of life means continuing. Continuing means going far. Going far means returning. Tao Te Ching

It has become commonplace for contemporary theories of mind to argue that our unique form of evolutionarily derived consciousness has as its primary function the reflectively grounded construction of a meaningful reality, or, as I have suggested as the title to an earlier book, an *interpreted world* (Spinelli, 2005). Existential phenomenology agrees that we are meaning-making beings. From existence to essence, no-thing becomes some-thing or any-thing. Viewed in this way, however, it has to be asked: what 'meaning' exists in a pre-essence existence? Does not meaning only emerge through 'thing-ification'? To say: 'This is what it means', or 'I no longer hold those meanings' requires us to have gone through some essentialising process. Even if our existence is always meaning-*oriented*, at a pre-essentialist level no meaning yet exists. Instead we are faced with the *meaninglessness* or the as-yet meaning-openness of existence.

Many existential authors, particularly those most influenced by the ideas of Viktor Frankl (Frankl, 1988), have rightly emphasised the critical importance of meaning and the dilemmas encountered when meanings become too rigidified, or are inadequate, or appear to have been lost and cannot be found. What is far less often discussed is the equal importance of meaninglessness. On initial consideration, we appear to be deeply intolerant of meaninglessness. Our confrontations with instances or examples whose meaning is unknown or ambiguous or novel stimulate us to figure out their meaning. And if meanings cannot be discerned, it is a common stance either to impose inadequate, barely sustainable meaning upon them or, just as often, to reject, denigrate or deny the value or, indeed, the very existence of the agitative event or entity (Cohn, 2002; Spinelli, 2005; Strasser & Strasser, 1997). The recurring dismissive cultural response to 'the shock of the new' (Hughes, 1991) provoked by movements in Fine Art, architecture and music is but one obvious example of the unease which accompanies that which challenges our demand for meaning. Usually, once meaning has been constructed, the event or entity no longer disturbs us. Its meaning makes it acceptable. Indeed, again as with diverse examples from the Arts, from Impressionism to The Beatles, stances can shift dramatically so that what was once the focus of disgust and dismissal becomes venerated as being among the most exquisite expressions of meaningfulness.

In my view, one of the great strengths of existential phenomenology is that it can avoid imposing a divide between meaning and meaninglessness. Instead, it can consider both as extremes within the context of an inseparable, co-existent polarity wherein each extreme is of equal standing and import. The human tendency to search for meaning is counter-balanced by our ability to remain open to the meaninglessness within those meanings we claim to have found. Through the questioning and challenging of existing meanings emerge the possibilities of creativity, discovery, playfulness and imagination. Paradoxically, the willingness to tolerate, perhaps even embrace, a temporary engagement with meaninglessness serves to strengthen the lived value and validity of those meanings that emerge from a person's confrontations with the unknown, the unexpected and the uncertain. Equally, in avoiding instances of meaninglessness, established meanings rigidify, stagnate and become the inflexible truths or dogmas that nurture cultural, political, religious, sexual and intellectual fundamentalism.

All instances of meaning reveal themselves to be 'captured', essentialised moments of meaninglessness. Conversely, because, inevitably, all meanings retain novel interpretative, re-constitutive possibilities, they are always open to the challenge of meaninglessness. This ever-present tension expresses itself experientially via the Principle of existential anxiety.

The anxious experiencing of the constant relational interplay between meaning/ meaninglessness helps to clarify the wide range of meaning dilemmas that arise for persons. Meanings that are maintained so rigidly that no doubt or alternative is possible can be experienced as being negative, debilitating and destructive. But they might also be interpreted as liberating, transformational and life-enhancing. In the same way, experiences of loss of meaning or prolonged moments of meaninglessness may be terrifying and disorienting but may also be yearned for and attempted through intoxicants or techniques designed to 'free up' experience. Such contradictory experiences reveal a complexity to the assumptions we might hold regarding meaning and meaninglessness. The ability to maintain meanings may be generally associated with well-being just as the loss or search for meaning may be stressful. But such generalities miss the significant point that I have understood existential phenomenology to be making: *Meanings that can permit no meaninglessness may be the source to both well-being and disturbance, just as the loss or search for meaning and the associated experience of meaninglessness may both reduce and intensify unease and distress.* What seems to me to be worthy of consideration is whether the direction taken toward well-being or disorder is determined by the degree to which the interplay between meaning and meaninglessness is permitted or denied. It may well be that the importance given by many existential therapists to the search for meaning requires some further clarification in that it may not be the search in itself, but *how* the search is carried out with regard to its tolerance for the perpetual challenge of meaninglessness that makes all the difference.

The issues raised by meaning and meaninglessness tie into the closely related attempt to discover 'the truth' that reveals the reason and purpose to our existence. Heidegger made explicit the ever-elusive finality of any quest for 'the truth'. The resolution of such quests, he argued, depends upon both the possibility and actuality of 'capturing' meaning in such a way that it is no longer open to novel and alternative possibilities. If I have discerned *the* truth to my existence, or to any aspect of it, then its meaning is bound, its interpretation is final and fixed forever, and cannot be subject to alternative interpretative meanings that are shaped through the interplay with meaninglessness. Instead, for Heidegger, the origin of our idea of truth reaches back to the notion of *aletheia* – the ever-disclosing, ever-revealing, openness to being. From this standpoint, my meaning may be 'truthful' in that it both reveals that which is there for me and, at the same time, *opens* that meaning which is there for me to further possibilities of meaning-extending (or meaninglessness-disclosing) truthfulness. Truth, in this sense, is never complete or completed. The implications of this view, not least for therapeutic practice, are extensive and significant. Elegantly expressed by the relational psychotherapist Leslie Farber, they propose that 'speaking truthfully is a more fitting ambition than speaking the truth' (Farber, 2000:10).

All therapies will inevitably challenge a client's relationship to the meanings in his or her life. Even the most skilful and responsible of such challenges will provoke the temporary experience of meaninglessness for the client, which, in turn, may be felt as either destructive and debilitating or liberating and creative. As well, all therapies confront the therapist with challenges to his or her own stance toward the polarity of meaning/meaninglessness, and how this stance may be impacting upon his or her interventions and interactions with clients. Indeed, as will be discussed in Part Two, the existential therapist's ability to embrace and work with both the client's and his or her own experience of the interplay between meaning/meaninglessness within the therapeutic encounter will enhance, rather than limit, the quality of that encounter both at process and outcome levels.

An Exercise Exploring the Theme of Meaning/ Meaninglessness

1. Complete the following statement: 'One thing that is truly meaningful for me is —'
2. Examine and explore your felt experience when you hear your self make the above statement.

(Continued)

(Continued)

3. Explore and consider the following challenge: What would it mean to you if that which you have identified above as being meaningful were to suddenly become meaningless? How would your life be affected? How would the life of significant others be affected?
4. Examine and explore your felt experience of the above challenge. What is there, if anything at all, in your reaction that you would identify as disabling or destructive? What is there, if anything at all, in your reaction that you would identify as liberating or creative?
5. Consider how your responses might clarify or raise new questions for the discussion on the existential theme of meaning/meaningless.

Choice, Freedom and Responsibility

You are not the Do-er. The Buddha

Choice has all too often been understood to suggest an open-ended or unlimited ability to choose how and what 'to be' or 'to do'. Similarly, views of *freedom* tend to emphasise its individualistic, subjectively focused possibilities. Likewise, *responsibility* is usually assumed from a bounded or divided self/other perspective such that responsibility can be distinguished between boundaries demarcating 'my' responsibilities from 'your' (or 'others") responsibilities. As I will show below, each one of these conclusions is contradicted by existential phenomenology's Principles of relatedness, uncertainty and existential anxiety.

Existential phenomenology's interpretations of choice, freedom and responsibility rely upon an *a priori* assumption of relatedness. Placed in this context, the approach avoids examining these thematic existence concerns from a standpoint that assumes distinct and separate entities such as 'I' and 'other', each of whom is individually choosing, free and responsible for itself alone. Instead of individualistic notions of choice, freedom and responsibility, which, to employ Ken Gergen's term, are contained within a 'boundaried self', existential phenomenology challenges us to re-consider these themes from the standpoint of 'relational selves' (Gergen, 2009). This distinction has vast implications. From a boundaried perspective each of us can choose to act in ways that will 'free up my own possibilities', even if another or others experience these as oppressive or painful or undesirable. Equally, from this isolationist standpoint, each individual 'I' can respond to the other's experience as being 'the other's choice' and can abdicate any sort of responsibility for it. I suggest that, in contrast to this all-too-familiar perspective, valued and so often repeated by politicians, self-help gurus and marketeers of every persuasion, existential phenomenology, in keeping with its foundational Principles, argues that 'no choice can be mine or yours alone, no experienced impact of choice can be separated in terms of "my responsibility" versus "your responsibility", no sense of personal freedom can truly avoid its interpersonal dimensions' (Spinelli, 2001: 15–16).

Choice

Life is the sum of all your choices. Pythagoras

The issues and questions surrounding choice tend to be understood from a non-relational, 'boundaried' bias that interprets existential choice from an overly solipsistic viewpoint which, in addition, is almost always incorrectly perceived as being 'multi-optional.' This view is summarised as: 'I make my choices in life and you make your choices in life. And, as well, we can each always choose alternatives to current conditions'. I think that this view makes no sense at all within the context of existential phenomenology. Instead, a much more challenging – and less optimistic – perspective is being presented.

Sartre makes it plain: choice is more accurately a condemnation than it is a matter of celebration. Every choice made has its pay-off and its price and which is which in many of our choices is not readily predictable or foreseeable (Sartre, 1991). Even the best, most desirable and fulfilling choice will provoke some degree of regret since every choice confronts us with the 'what might have been' which has been lost as a result of having made that choice.

From the standpoint of existential phenomenology, the question of choice is distinct from that of *origination*. No claim is made with regard to our capacity or ability to cause, control or determine the plethora of event stimuli that occur at any and every moment of our lives. Viewed in this way, choice is not about choosing the stimuli themselves. Rather, our choices lie in how we *respond to* these stimuli. For example: I walk out the door and slip on a banana peel, twisting my ankle so that I cannot walk for a period of time. I did not 'choose' the presence of the banana peel. Nor did I cause it into being, or being where it was. My choice lies in how I interact with the stimulus event. Do I choose to experience it as a catastrophe because now I must cancel that long-standing lecturing engagement or do I choose to experience it as a relief because I didn't really want to embark upon a lecturing tour at this point in my life? Or do I choose to experience the event as something that is both disappointing as well as a relief? All such choices suggest nothing of origination. Rather, *choice emerges out of the response given to the presenting conditions of life.*

But now, it must be asked: what, if anything, determines the *actual* chosen response given to any stimulus event? Here, too, existential phenomenology accepts that the choices we make are always situated, or contextualised, within various conditions, such as our time and place of birth, our biological make-up, our socio-cultural backdrop, our nationality. These situational conditions are usually referred to as our *facticity*. Our facticity is an ever-present variable in all our responses to experiential stimuli. The choices that appear to us as *possible* choices are shaped through facticity. For example, as a result of my slipping on a banana peel I could, in theory, choose to make the event an opportunity for me to become pregnant or to offer my services to Bletchley Park so that the 'Enigma Code' might be broken. The facticity of my being male and living in 2014 make it unlikely that such choices will emerge as genuine options for me to enact.

Our facticity is not a separate set of conditions existing in opposition to choice, nor is it an obstacle to choice. Our choices rest upon and *include* facticity. If a tension exists, it is not between choice and facticity *per se,* but rather between a stance toward choice that includes facticity or one that seeks to exclude it. Again, as an example, my slipping on a banana peel presents me with choices that either include my facticity or reject its presence and influence. In rejecting my facticity, I convince my self that as a result of this incident I really should take the opportunity to become pregnant. In choosing outside of the conditions of my facticity, I am making *false choices* – that is to say, choices that could only be mine were the circumstances of my facticity different to what they are. False choices can often be tempting, and it is often painful to put aside those choices that 'could have been mine had my facticity been other than what it is'. Indeed, many of the dilemmas brought to therapy arise through the client's determination to pursue false choices.

In acknowledging the role of facticity within any choice, it can be argued that the actual choices available in response to any experiential stimuli may not often be at a *multi-optional* level. The conditions of facticity may well impose a *single-option choice.* As Heidegger puts it, my choice '*is* only the choice of *one* possibility – that is, in tolerating one's not having chosen the others and one's not being able to choose them' (Heidegger, 1962: 331, as quoted in Cohn, 2002: 97; emphases in the original). Choice, from this existential phenomenological perspective, and the possibilities that emerge through it, rests on the choosing or embracing of that choice that is there, already present, rather than adopting a false-choice stance that assumes or insists that *something other* than that one choice can be, and in some sense is already, present. In many instances, choice rests upon the choice of 'A or A'. But how can this be claimed to be any sort of choice at all? Consider the following example:

Jessica finds the idea of abortion to be morally repugnant. Unfortunately, she finds her self pregnant as a result of a brief fling with a man whom she has subsequently decided would not make either a good father or partner. While *from another set of facticity conditions* Jessica might be able to choose between continuing with her pregnancy or terminating it, from the actual current facticity-derived standpoint adopted by Jessica, there is only the single-option choice of continuing with the pregnancy that is available to her. Jessica could choose this single option. But, she could also claim to have the availability of a false choice, or what the existential philosopher Paul Tillich termed as a 'what if' option (Tillich, 1980). In Jessica's case, this 'what if' choice might be one that placed the power of choice in someone else's control, or that placed the power of choice in the hands of a separate and 'possessed' Jessica, or that imbued the pregnancy with a 'special' significance, or that simply denied the pregnancy. All of these possibilities permit the appearance of a seemingly genuine alternative to Jessica's one-option choice. But, equally, they are all 'false' choices. *In order to make these alternative choices, Jessica would have to be someone other than who she is being; she would have to be someone whose conditions of facticity allowed for different choice possibilities.* Jessica can imagine all manner of alternative choices, but these choices are only available to other possible versions of Jessica. They are always theoretically possible, but they present a different choice dilemma: is Jessica prepared to become another Jessica, one who can choose what to do about her pregnancy in a different way, or under different conditions of facticity, to that of the current Jessica?

In order to continue being the Jessica that she currently identifies her self as being, Jessica is faced with a single-option choice: Does Jessica choose that which is there for her to choose under existing conditions? Or does she choose a non-existent alternative that could be chosen were she a different Jessica? Of course, Jessica can always play 'what if' games giving rise to false choices by supposing that a theoretical alternative possibility was actually available to her. But these alternatives only become genuine choices if Jessica is prepared to give up being the Jessica she *is* being and who no longer holds views and values surrounding abortion that she *does* hold.

Of course, like Jessica, we are 'always at liberty to make a change or abandon whatever lifestyle we have adopted' (van Deurzen & Arnold-Baker, 2005: 7). But in order to make changes or abandon lifestyles requires the 'I' who makes that choice to also choose to risk its own existence and to bring into being a novel, unknown and unpredictable newly choosing 'I'. The possibility of being or doing as an 'other' is always there, but its price – which is to become and act *as an unknown other* – is not often an option that we find easy or are willing to make, as will be discussed more fully in the next chapter. For now, we are confronted with a discomforting view of choice – not *all* choices are available at *all* times. Rather, genuine choice can only be that which is there as 'part of the basis of our total present situation' (Cohn, 2002: 96). At times, perhaps more often than we suppose or would like to think, the choice that is there is a single-option choice. How can a single-option choice be seen to be a choice at all? It remains a choice because it can always be denied as the one choice that is available, which is to say: 'I choose not to choose it but rather to experience its impact and consequences as that which was imposed upon me or which was chosen by someone or something other than me.' Equally, it remains a choice because, ultimately, it directs attention to the 'I' who chooses and reveals that 'I' as itself being a choice.

This last point acts as a reminder – when the claim is made that 'I' choose X, what is being suggested is the implicit notion of a discrete 'I', whose existence is separate from that of all other 'I's', and whose choices reside or are experienced somewhere *within* the confines of its 'I-ness'. When considered from an existential phenomenological perspective, however, this choosing 'I' is not an isolated, exclusively self-defining 'I' but rather an 'I' whose uniqueness and individuality is a consequential expression of the Principle of relatedness. In this way, 'my' choice is not mine alone to make. Nor are its impact and consequence directed solely to, or for, me.

This complex view of choice makes plain how choice is not solely, or even primarily, a pleasant or desirable enterprise. Indeed, the attempt to abdicate from, or deny, choice may provide a desired reduction of tension as well as an escape from the regret arising from the often difficult and uncertain demands which accompany choice. Further, this view of choice shows how many of the disruptions and tribulations that provoke such pain and unease arise when we insist upon claiming the ability to choose that which is not open to our choosing.

An Exercise Exploring the Theme of Existential Choice

1. Complete the following statement: 'One choice that I believe I have made in my life is —'
2. Examine and explore your felt experience when you hear your self make the above statement.
3. Complete the following statement: 'Something that has happened in my life that I did not choose is —'
4. Examine and explore your felt experience when you hear your self make the above statement.
5. Compare and contrast your felt experiences to the two statements. What, if any, experiences were similar? Different? Surprising?
6. Go back to the two statements that you made and reverse them so that your example of something you chose becomes your example of something unchosen, and vice-versa.
7. Compare and contrast your felt experiences to the two statements. What, if any, experiences were similar? Different? Surprising?

Freedom

> In willing freedom we discover it depends entirely on the freedom of others and that the freedom of others depends on ours .... I can take my freedom as a goal only if I take the freedom of others as a goal as well. Jean-Paul Sartre

We speak of 'the freedom to choose' or we enjoin someone to 'choose freely': thus freedom and choice are linked. Freedom presents us with a paradox: the experience of freedom becomes most apparent when our stance to 'what is there for us' is to embrace it, accept it, 'say yes' to it, rather than adopt an attitude that pretends and deludes itself into believing that 'something *else* is there for me'. This understanding of freedom has nothing to do with any passive or un–reflected submission to that which might be interpreted as wrong or undesirable or unjust. Rather, as with the previous discussion on choice, it situates the possibilities of freedom *within* the actual – as opposed to imagined – conditions that exist. Consider, for example, the unforgettable image of freedom revealed in that lone and anonymous Chinese student's placing him self directly in front of the tanks that rumbled into Tiananmen Square in 1989. Such a stance was not about any future *possibility* or gaining of freedom; it *was* freedom being lived.

Again, as with the view of choice discussed above, an existential phenomenological focus on freedom emphasises its experiential foundations in the Principle of relatedness: experiences of freedom are not solely contained within an individual. Rather, individual acts of freedom resonate with, and remind one and all, of our capacity to experience freedom. For example, what touched and remains with those of us who viewed that face-off between the lone student and the tanks was not a detached (if still respectful and admiring) awareness of his own personally lived freedom, but a connected experience of, and with, freedom that all could experience regardless of the plethora of differences in our life events both before and subsequent to that moment. This is not to remove the power and impact of that student's singular choice. How the student experienced freedom, and the unique invocation of freedom contained in his act, is being neither minimised nor disputed. But that those who witnessed it were drawn to the act, and through it experienced their own freedom, however momentary, must also be recognised. To quote Merleau-Ponty: 'One is not free alone' (1962: 142). Which is not to say that freedom is always and necessarily 'good' or 'benevolent'. We might point to moments of freedom encountered when meditating, or running, engaging in sexual activities or being moved by music. But, equally, we might experience such moments through the denial of food or the ingestion of vast quantities of alcohol. And as well, those who murder wantonly, for its own sake, have also expressed views suggesting experiences of profound freedom. What may be so disturbingly attractive about the question of evil, for instance, may well be its link to the possibility of unbounded freedom (May, 1990; Spinelli, 2001). And here, as well, the experience of connection through the Principle of relatedness comes to the fore. In contrast to the image of the young man facing up to tanks, consider that of the joyous laughter and spontaneous dance enacted by people all over the world in response to the images of airplanes flying into the World Trade Center towers. Here, too, was unbounded freedom carried out by a small group of individuals but experienced by hundreds of thousands who, for a few moments, felt their oppressor being brought to heel. This alternative view of freedom reveals its more disturbing qualities – and, once again, may assist us in comprehending the divided stance many therapeutic clients take toward its possibilities.

In common with instances of single-option choice, when we consider those moments in our lives when we experienced our selves as being most free we are likely to have discovered, somewhat paradoxically, that in the engulfment of freedom no genuine alternative 'way to be' seems possible, much less desirable. In freedom, we accept that which is there in the way it is being experienced. Once again, this experience of acceptance extends beyond the boundaried being and embraces *all **being*** as it is.

An Exercise Exploring the Theme of Existential Freedom

1.　Think of one example when you have felt most free in your life.
2.　Examine and explore your felt experience of that event.
3.　Think of one example when you have felt least free in your life.

(Continued)

(Continued)

4. Examine and explore your felt experience of that event.
5. Compare and contrast your felt experiences of the two examples. What, if any, experiences were similar? Different? Surprising?
6. Consider how your responses might clarify or raise new questions for the discussion on the theme of existential freedom.

Responsibility

And when we say that man is responsible for himself, we do not mean that he is responsible only for his own individuality, but that he is responsible for all men. Jean-Paul Sartre

Dominant views regarding responsibility would have it that our responsibility is bounded within personal confines: I am responsible for my actions just as you are responsible for yours and they are responsible for theirs. Responsibility neatly divided. This view runs through a great deal of therapeutic thinking as well. Many models rely upon precepts that are grounded in this segregated, boundaried responsibility and view any statements that extend beyond such boundaries as problematic and 'irrational' (Ellis & Ellis, 2011). Equally, responsibility is usually understood as a judgement of right or wrong, good or bad, or is equated with notions of fault and blame, praise and credit.

Both these perspectives can be challenged by an existential phenomenological approach to responsibility. Once again, it proposes an alternative that extends each individual's responsibility beyond the boundaried self so that it includes others and the world. From the standpoint of the Principle of relatedness, no demarcation between self, others and/or the world can ever be completely separate. As such, each individual's experience of his or her own responsibility cannot be individualistically maintained. If, for example, my experience includes the structure of 'slavery', even as an imagined experience that has not been lived by me and which I find repugnant, simply that I include slavery into my experience makes me responsible for the existence of slavery. This is not to suggest that this responsibility has anything to do with matters of origination or culpability. In this existential phenomenological sense – and *only* in this sense – those who label themselves as 'slaves' are as responsible for the existence of slavery as are those who act to enslave. Again, the issue here is exclusively concerned with experience, not origination. Does this suggest that had I no experience of slavery, it would not exist for me? In theory, yes. But once again, such a possibility assumes an experience that is not grounded in relatedness. Cut off from all, or at least most, others, it is remotely conceivable that I might never experience the possibility of slavery. Other than that, however ... And again, even if I were to deny its existence, the very act of denial highlights that slavery exists in my experience, even if it exists as a denied experience, and therefore I am responsible for it.

As human beings we are responsible not merely to self, our family or selected others, or our faith or the achievement of 'the good life'. All of these responsibilities are contained in, but also distort, that for which we are responsible – which is to *being* as it is expressed and reflected through any particular being. But how can one act responsibly toward *being*? While we may be unable to quite grasp the answer to such a vast question, nonetheless, we can 'feel' our way toward it. Consider, for example, the following passage from Henning Mankell's *The Fifth Woman*:

> When I was growing up, Sweden was still a country where people darned their socks. I even learned how to do it in school myself. Then suddenly one day it was over. Socks with holes in them were thrown out. No one bothered to repair them. The whole society changed. 'Wear it out and toss it' was the only rule that applied. As long as it was just a matter of our socks, the change didn't make much difference. But then it started to spread, until finally it became a kind of invisible moral code. I think it changed our view of right and wrong, of what you were allowed to do to other people and what you weren't ... A generation is growing up right now [who] have absolutely no memory of a time when we darned our socks. When we didn't throw everything away, whether it was our woollen socks or human beings. (Mankell, 2002: 224)

While the passage expresses nothing directly about responsibility in an existential phenomenological sense, it draws us toward an awareness that we are often less than that which we are capable of being. This view of responsibility serves to provide a *direction* to the choices available and reminds us that no expression of either choice or freedom can exclude responsibility to *being* in all its conditions and manifestations. This view also places responsibility within a spatio-temporal frame that extends beyond the boundaries of any one specific existence and widens its focus into a future beyond that life's ending. Responsibility, in this existential phenomenological sense, carries strong resonances with the ancient Hebrew notion of *Hochma* – the capacity to see and feel and then to act as if not the present but rather the future depended on us.

An Exercise Exploring the Theme of Existential Responsibility

1. Think of one example of something for which you feel responsible.
2. Think of one example of something for which you feel no responsibility whatsoever.
3. What factors or conditions create the distinction for you between these two examples?
4. What if that distinction was no longer possible for you to maintain? What, if anything, would change in your life? Stay the same?
5. If that distinction was no longer possible for you to maintain, what, if anything, would change in your relations with the significant others in your life? In your relations with others in general? In your relations with the wider world?

Authenticity and Inauthenticity

Half winged! Half imprisoned! This is man. Paul Klee

Of all the existence themes and concerns under discussion, those of *authenticity* and *inauthenticity* have probably generated the greatest confusions and disputes. In part, I suspect, this may be due to the terms themselves in that they appear to suggest appropriate and inappropriate, or superior and inferior, ways to be and, as well, imply a moral judgement. These conclusions are not what is intended by existential phenomenology.

Questions of authenticity and inauthenticity are most commonly approached from a subjectivist, or self-oriented, perspective. Such views consider the possibility of a truly substantive and unitary 'real self' and claim that 'authenticity is a direct experience of the real self' (Rowan, 2001: 458). Equally, authenticity is linked to an individual's self-congruence insofar as 'the person who is genuinely authentic ... is congruent within himself' (Bugenthal, 1981: 108). From such perspectives, authenticity is seen to reside within an individual, is an expression of that individual and is attained by that individual through various means that prompt him or her toward his or her true or genuine or real self. This is a perfectly acceptable way of understanding authenticity. However, it is also a view that is not – and if my arguments above are correct, *cannot* be – shared by existential phenomenology. Further, a darker, less considered, side to this view emerges. If authenticity is a boundaried experience centred upon 'being true to my self', then it must be conceded that it would be difficult, if not impossible, to distinguish the stance adopted by a sociopath, or at more extreme levels by a Hitler or a Pol Pot to one claiming to be authentic.

In my view, the critical difference is best illuminated in the now famous dialogue between Carl Rogers and Martin Buber (Kirschenbaum & Henderson, 1990). Rogers, taking a humanistic stance, attempted to argue that person-centred therapy encourages the establishment of an authentic I–Thou relationship. Buber's response, as I understand it, disputed this assertion and basically argued that any claim to the establishment of an I–Thou relationship actually revealed an I–It relationship in that the experience of I–Thou is not some 'thing' that is substantive and fixed in time (much less permanent) but rather a 'flow' of being-always-becoming.

Authenticity, from an existential phenomenological perspective, is not a stance to being that can truly be 'worked toward' so that 'it is free from commonly recognised forms of ego-distorted cognitive and affective perception' (Wade, 1996: 160). Wrapped in paradox as it is, existential phenomenology argues that the enterprise of making one self authentic is itself a statement of inauthenticity. Instead, authenticity reflects 'an openness to existence, an acceptance of what is given, as well as our freedom to respond to it' (Cohn, 1997: 127). Authenticity involves and implicates each being with existence as it is being presented. In doing so, authenticity can be seen as an expression of choice, freedom and responsibility when situated within an indivisible grounding of relatedness. Inauthenticity, on the other hand, expresses freedom, choice and responsibility as containable within the isolated individual. At this inauthentic level, choice, freedom and responsibility are asserted 'as if' either the structured subject or those agents and forces alien to the person (what Heidegger refers to as 'the they' or what Kierkegaard labels 'the crowd' (Cooper, 2003)) held the reins. In other words, an inauthentic stance is not only one that cedes the power of choice, freedom and responsibility to 'the other'. It is equally inauthentic to place such control upon the isolated, non-relational 'I'. Viewed from Buber's perspective, from an authentic stance that which is 'my' choice, 'my' freedom and 'my' responsibility requires consideration not only at the 'I' level but also, and equally, at the level of 'Thou'.

To summarise, authenticity and inauthenticity are often expressed and understood as instances of either 'being true to your real self' or of adopting self-deceptive stances (Bugenthal, 1981; Rowan, 2001). While these views certainly make sense within a non-relational approach or one which places the isolated self as the starting point to lived experience, they are untenable from an existential phenomenological perspective. Instead, from this latter stance, authenticity is a challenge to remain open to and embrace *that which is there in the way that it is there*. This attempt to be true to **being** rejects the tendency to understand inauthenticity as being *solely* the outcome of 'the denial of authorship and personal responsibility' (van Deurzen & Adams, 2011: 92). While it can certainly be that, I am also arguing that the focus upon an *over*-personalised authorship and responsibility that can be bounded and compartmentalised as either 'mine' or 'not mine', or 'yours', or 'theirs' is equally a stance of inauthenticity. Inauthenticity is not only the denial of an authoritative self; it is also the *elevation* of that self to a non-relational individuality proclaiming occurrences as owned or disowned, mine or not mine, there or not there.

An Exercise Exploring the Themes of Authenticity and Inauthenticity

1. Think of one example from your own life experience that comes closest to your understanding of existential authenticity.
2. Think of one example from your own life experience that comes closest to your understanding of existential inauthenticity.
3. When you compare and contrast the two, what, if any, similarities and differences do you note between them?
4. When you consider the two from the standpoint of your 'self' (or 'I') what similarities and differences do you note between the presence or role of 'I' in each?

Isolation (Aloneness) and Relation

Think more than just I. Lou Reed

The inter-related themes of *isolation* (which some authors prefer to label as aloneness) and *relation* reveal an existential polarity that is often missed or obscured by commentators. Yalom has written extensively, and wonderfully, on the theme of isolation. From his perspective, isolation refers to the awareness that through our unrepeatable, unique embodiment of existence, we are each, individually, alone in the world. Our very individuality insists that every being experiences existence in a unique way (i.e. no other being can replicate exactly my way of existing) so that 'the individual is inexorably alone' (Yalom, 1980: 353) and 'each of us is permanently separate from the other' (van Deurzen & Adams, 2011: 18). At the same time, however, the arguments being presented in this text propose that the foundational Principles of existential phenomenology rest upon an indivisible co-presence of the singular being and the world. It would seem that we are being presented with a puzzle: Are we isolated beings identified through our aloneness? Or are we always beings-in-relation?

One possible solution to this question would be that of identifying self and other as separate entities, each definable within its own boundaries, who can engage in different forms of relationships with one another. Viewed in this way, self and other exist in experiential isolation or in their unique aloneness. At the same time, each experientially isolated being can still form relationships with other experientially isolated beings and, thereby, remain both alone in the world and engage in relations with others. This is undoubtedly a straightforward and attractive solution. However, it must be asked whether it is a solution that is consonant with an existential phenomenological perspective. I would argue that it is not, precisely because it rests upon the assumption of self-contained boundaried beings.

Instead, let me propose an alternative solution which, in contrast to the above view, locates the issues raised by isolation within the Principle of relatedness. In doing so, a very different conclusion, consistent with the view of existential phenomenology being presented, becomes possible. This alternate argument reminds us that the individual's ability to experience its isolation from all others is itself dependent upon a pre-existing relatedness. And, further, that the awareness of this foundational relatedness is at least partially available to each individual as he or she considers his or her experiential isolation. Let me attempt to make this argument explicit by considering a similar concern explicated by Sartre in his account of the conflictual relations between self and others.

In his analysis of the different attitudes that any individual can adopt toward the existence of others, Sartre points out that one such option is that of indifference (Sartre, 1991). He suggests that if an individual becomes indifferent to, or detached from, all relations with others this strategy would seem to succeed in freeing the individual to exist outside of the other's conflictual presence and influence. This indifference can be enacted in multiple ways. The individual could act in a manner that rejects all interest in, or concern for, others. Alternatively, the individual might literally create distance from others by isolating him or her self through hermit-like inaccessibility. Unfortunately, although these strategies offer the possibility of a disengagement from others, Sartre argues that they are doomed to fail. Why? Because the individual's very determination to maintain this indifference creates the very opposite – it ties him or her even more to others. The strategies associated with indifference demand an avoidance of others at all cost. But in order to maintain this avoidance, the individual must remain ever-vigilant to the possible intrusive appearance of others. That individual must be forever focused on strategies that attempt to out-think and out-manoeuvre the other. As a result, all thoughts, concerns, projects and behaviours become other-focused, even other-obsessed.

Sartre's account of the failed strategy of indifference provides the key to the alternate view on the question of isolation or aloneness that is being presented: *The self's experience of its own unique isolation is dependent upon the prior experience of relatedness.* How could a self be able to identify its isolation, or raise any questions concerned with isolation, other than through a prior grounding of relatedness? In order for me to reflect meaningfully upon my 'permanent separateness' and 'inexorable isolation', I must have concluded that no other exists exactly in the way that I exist and that *there* is my isolation and aloneness. My isolation does reveal my uniqueness, but isn't there a prior requirement of my awareness of others in order for me to become aware of my uniqueness? In order for me to have raised the question of my isolation in the first place, in order for it to be of any significance to me that no other exists in the way I exist, requires an *a priori* condition of relatedness. That I am concerned or saddened or troubled or desperate or relieved or ecstatic that no other exists as I exist and that I am alone in the world reveals me as a being founded in relatedness. How else could I conclude that I was isolated? My awareness of my experiential isolation requires a prior awareness of the existence of others whose experience differs from my own. And even then, it must be asked: Why should these isolating differences *matter* to us at all, other than because our awareness of the gulf dividing our experiences is equally an awareness of that shared foundational relatedness through which an isolationist divide arose?

Isolation cannot be truly separated from its co-constituted counterpart of relation. Common sense claims concerning the themes of isolation and relation represent them as separate and oppositional experiences of existence. In contrast, from the viewpoint of existential phenomenology being presented, the dilemmas raised by isolation/relation are more adequately viewed as expressions of an inseparable polarity continuum.

An Exercise Exploring the Themes of Relation and Isolation

1. Think of an event in your life where you felt isolated. What was the experience like? How, if at all, did you experience the missing presence of others?
2. Think of an event in your life when the presence of others, or another, was irritating or unwanted. How did you experience that presence?
3. Consider how your responses might clarify or raise new questions for the discussion on the themes of relation and isolation.

Death Anxiety

Receive every day as a resurrection from death. William Law

The existential theme of *death anxiety* at first seems quite straightforward. It requires no intermediary or meta-theoretical explanatory prompt for anyone to become directly aware of the temporal nature of his or her life and its inevitable movement toward death. At the same time, we also know that the conditions for death's occurrence (such as when and how it will take place, or what will kill us) remain uncertain. Our socio-cultural constituents and religious beliefs undoubtedly influence how each of us responds to our awareness of our eventual death. For example, the conviction that science is just one step away from discovering the secret of immortality or, equally, the certainty that I will continue to exist eternally in some disembodied fashion, can be seen as avoiding the anxiety accompanying the 'realization that life is inevitably moving toward death' (Cohn, 1997: 70). Although such strategies allow us to reduce or avoid this anxiety, their unforeseen consequences express themselves through the specific stances and attitudes we adopt towards our existence as a whole. This conclusion is best summarised by the existential psychotherapist Medard Boss, who wrote that 'people who are most afraid of *death* are those who have the greatest anxiety about *life*' (Boss, 1979: 112; emphases in the original).

As an expression of relational uncertainty, the focus of death anxiety extends beyond the boundaried individual self. Death anxiety is not concerned solely with the termination of one's own life. It can be just as powerful when reflecting upon the ever-possible cessation of one or several particular others' lives, or of the world's existence, or of ending of strongly held values or beliefs or hopes or aspirations. For example, the anxiety surrounding the possible death of a partner, a child or a parent, and the impact upon the individual who must contemplate an existence that continues beyond that other's death can be as great, if not more, as any anxiety raised by the contemplation of that individual's own temporality. This broader relationally focused grounding reveals death anxiety's wider dimensions grounded in relatedness.

Likewise, the uncertainty provoked by death anxiety need not be exclusively focused upon the moment of death itself, but on the wider uncertainties of lives moving towards their ending. Such uncertainties might propel the individual toward the avoidance of any risk so that his or her own – or another's – movement toward death can be protected against the unforeseen and unknown. Alternatively, an individual might insist that either facets or the whole of his or her life be on a constant risk-focused trajectory founded on the assumption that a defiant stance that opts out of security and stability will also best protect against the anxiety. This wider view reveals death anxiety's all-encompassing presence throughout our experience of living. On reflection, it can be recognised that our reflective experience of ongoing *change*, and our responses to it, is intimately tied to death anxiety in that any instance of change requires the 'death' of whatever – or whoever – had existed prior to having undergone that change.

An existential phenomenological understanding of death anxiety addresses both the human being's awareness of the inevitability of death (be it personal, or that of others or of the world) as well as the unpredictability of any temporal being's moment of ceasing to be. But this tension between the certain and the uncertain is also apparent in that interplay between disruption and continuity that infuses all embodied experiences of change. As will be discussed in more detail in Chapter 4, change is experienced as *a disruption whose consequences upon our continuity remain both certain (in their inevitability) and uncertain (in their experiential consequences)*. Considered in this way, every moment of change connects us to our death anxiety. Like (or, perhaps, through) change in general, death anxiety permeates our every moment of relational being. Although change also creates a new way of reflectively experiencing relational being, who this new being will be and what will be his or her experience of relational being, remains uncertain and unknowable. Our experience of change rests upon the existential death of the being-who-was. Repeated over and over again, throughout our lives, our experience of existence is shown to be in a perpetual dance with death anxiety.

An Exercise Exploring the Theme of Death Anxiety

1. Imagine that it was certain that you would die within the next 5 years. How, if at all, would this knowledge affect your plans and goals? What, if anything, would change about how you currently live your life? What, if anything, would change in your relationships with others?
2. Imagine that it was certain that you were immortal and no matter what the circumstances you would never die. How, if at all, would this knowledge affect your plans and goals? What, if anything, would change about how you currently live your life? What, if anything, would change in your relationships with others?
3. Consider how your responses might clarify or raise new questions for the discussion on the theme of death anxiety.

Temporality

> Each moment in time calls all the others to witness. Maurice Merleau-Ponty

For Husserl, our *temporality* was best expressed as *erlebnis*, which is to say 'the flowing process of lived experience' (Cohn, 2002: 65). Following this insight, Heidegger argued that this flowing process is always one of both anticipation and looking back. The currently existing being is always projecting towards a future and therefore always becoming (anticipation). At the same time, any current way of being came into being via a prior process of becoming (looking back). Anticipation is intimately linked to death anxiety: we experience our existence through our projecting towards a future which is finite. At the same time, this future-directed anticipation rests upon, or is guided by, the interpreting of 'what has been'. Temporality can therefore be seen as a constant conjunction of anticipation and looking back (more simply, between future and past) that permits the present. Temporality unifies past–present–future. It is 'a future which makes present in the process of having been' (Heidegger, 1962: 374).

Following Heidegger, what is being proposed is that the human experience of time is not linearly unidirectional from past to present to future. Rather, as the existential therapist Susanna Rennie has expressed, time-as-process calls forth images of

> unfolding and enfolding, changing, moving, flowing, constantly between past, present and future. So time stops being an independent time line, a series of nows between birth and death, but is an unfolding process of logos, a within-time-ness. (Rennie, 2006: 337)

These ideas suggest a temporal view being taken by existential phenomenology, which acknowledges a continuous interweaving of past–present–future. How we relate to time, our dialogue with it, reveals us as beings whose existence is 'captured' as essence *in* time and yet, just as significantly, it can also be said that time is *in* our being. The existential phenomenological reconfiguration of the past should help to clarify a number of these more general points.

The Past

> On beginning to project a different future, I come to have a different past.
> Betty Cannon

As I have discussed elsewhere at greater length (Spinelli, 1994), many therapists, in common with their clients, hold to a linearly causal, unidirectional view of the past and, through this view, assume the task of the therapist to be that of uncovering the issues and influences of their past upon their current lives so that the conflicts and concerns that have arisen from, or which have been aggravated by, the past can be at least partially resolved.

While Sigmund Freud is perhaps most closely associated with the above view and, indeed, is assumed by many to be its originator, it emerges that Freud can be interpreted as maintaining a far more complex position of the interaction between causality and the past. Yalom highlights this alternative perspective and proposes a vastly different reading of Freud's conclusions. According to Yalom, Freud suggests that an

> analyst who is not successful in helping the patient to recollect the past should ... nonetheless give the patient a construction of the past as the analyst sees it. Freud believed that this construction would offer the same therapeutic benefit as would actual recollection of past material. (Yalom, 1980: 347)

Viewed from this perspective, what Freud is proposing is that whether the constructed past event is or is not historically 'real' or accurate matters far less than the process of constructing a reliable and useful narrative of *a* past rather than *the* past. This revolutionary stance opens the way toward an understanding of the past-as-recalled as being essentially interpretative rather than historically fixed or real. The past, seen in this light, becomes a 'plastic' or flexible concept open to re-evaluation and re-creation dependent upon the current experience of the individual who recalls it. Freud's strategy permits the appearance of a past that corresponds more closely with current experience. This compatibility, in turn, strengthens these temporal links and their experiential associations so that a less fragmented focus on future possibilities becomes possible (Yalom, 1980).

Just as the remembered past is 'plastic' in its meaning, so, too, is the remembered past always the product of a *selective* process. Clearly, the remembered past makes up a minute percentage of the totality of sensory-derived events that we have perceived over the course of our lives. In addition, it is also evident that what we attend to or what stands out for us as being relevant, meaningful or significant within any memory of a past event is itself a highly limited selection of all the variables and constituents contained within that remembered event. Thus, we are left with the conclusion that the remembered past – even at the level of its content alone – is a 'plastic', selective (and, hence, incomplete) interpretation of the totality of any lived past event.

What then does this alternative understanding of the remembered past propose? Partly in agreement with Freud's conclusion, existential phenomenology argues that *the past exists in the present*. Specifically, what is being suggested is that *the remembered past exposes, reflects and validates currently lived experience*. If I state that 'I am always honest' or that 'No one can cook gnocchi as well as my mother did' or that 'Geology does not interest me, but astronomy does', how do I know that I *do* actually hold these views other than via some validating recourse to my remembered past? Considered in this way, it is apparent that the remembered past is so *relationally* tied to the present that it is more accurate to speak of 'the-past-as-currently-lived' than of the past in itself. On further consideration, this interrelation of past and present must also take into account the role and impact of the *anticipated finite future*. Just as the source of, or rationale for, a currently lived experience is validated via the remembered past, so too is that same currently lived experience shaped and defined by those assumptions, aspirations, goals, purposes and wishes that are directed towards future possibilities. Thus, it is far more adequate to see the past as 'the-past-as-currently-lived-and-future-directed' than to conceive of the past as a separate, fixed and unchanging event-laden moment in time.

As a concrete example of what is being suggested, consider the following. My contention that 'I am always polite' is so challenged by the impact of actual lived experience that I alter my statement to 'I am usually, but not always, polite.' At this point, a surprising (if therapeutically common) phenomenon occurs: I begin to remember seemingly forgotten or suppressed past instances of prior impoliteness. Why does this happen? While many explanations are available, my reading of existential phenomenology would suggest that this newly adopted stance toward politeness requires validation so that its truthfulness will hold and buttress – or comply more adequately with – both current and future challenges to my lived experience. Similarly, let us suppose that within the newly reconstructed stance of 'I am usually, but not always, polite' is the additional component 'But I will try to be, even though I know how difficult that is.' Now, those events from my remembered past that both confirm this contention as well as serve to assist (or resist) its achievement will become more prominent in my current memories. New, previously seemingly forgotten examples will arise or existing examples will take on novel or more powerful meaning and in this way serve, and validate the worth of, my future-directed aspirations.

In sum, the past, as it is remembered, has little to do with causal or determining factors that have in some way made, or influenced, us to be who we are today. Rather, the remembered past provides us with the means to maintain or validate who we claim to be today not simply in terms of who and how we define our selves and our lived experiences, but also with regard towards whatever future direction we aspire to for our lived experience. As Cohn summarised: 'the past is still present in a present that anticipates the future' (Cohn, 1997: 26).

An Exercise Exploring the Theme of Temporality

1. Think of a past event in your life that you consider being a significant cause to the person that you are now.
2. Think of one likely direction that your life might take at some point over the next three years.
3. Staying with the example of your past causal event, explore the existential phenomenological proposal that, rather than cause, this event validates your current experience of self. Can you find any evidence from your own life experience that would support this? What, if anything, about your current experience of self would be affected if the past event you have identified was not a cause but a validating reflection of your current experience of self?
4. How, if at all, does your exploration of the relationship between the past event you identified and your current experience of self shift either your example of your future direction or the way you related to that future-direction example?

Spatiality

> For the wise man looks into space and he knows there is no limited dimension. Lao Tsu

Spatiality expresses not only the proximity or distance between locations. More significantly, spatiality reminds us that we constantly 'act' our existence in space – we are always moving away or towards, or being still, both physically and metaphorically, in space.

As with time, existential phenomenology emphasises an inter-relational grounding in the human experience of space. As Cohn has observed, severe disturbances such as agoraphobia and claustrophobia were considered by Medard Boss to be 'obstructive impairments in the spatiality of people' (Boss, 1979: 216, as quoted in Cohn, 1997: 80) in that they reflect the unease of relatedness as experienced from the perspective of 'too much' or 'too little' space.

Ludwig Binswanger, a contemporary of Boss as well as a significant early exponent of existential analysis, argued that people's inter-relationship with physical space and environment revealed their fundamental stance, or dialogue, towards their existence (Binswanger, 1963). Our own experience of varied, often intense, moods and feelings depending on the space in which we find our selves – be it a building, a particular room, a busy city street, an empty beach, and so forth – makes plain how space can affect us. Just as significantly, how we, in turn, shape and re-shape space can reveal and define a great many of our values, aspirations, insecurities and concerns.

In a previous text, I provided an account drawn from my work as an existential therapist of the existential dimensions of space (Spinelli, 1997). In brief, my client, Russell, had constructed a closed, restrictive space whose physical barriers prevented entry by others without his assistance. For example, the floor to his office was piled up with books and journals and papers such that only a very confined, single-person path to his desk was navigable. In the course of our therapeutic sessions, Russell's relations with others began to undergo significant change and, in parallel, so too did his relationship to his physical environment such that he began to feel a growing unease and dissatisfaction with various aspects of the physical space that he inhabited. For instance, the colour of his walls, the 'fit' of his work-chair, his inability to quite literally stretch out in the room, no longer suited him. Russell's subsequent actions, which focused upon the opening up of his physical space, were accompanied by a movement toward greater openness to others. Though he valued such ventures and judged them to be beneficial, nonetheless he recognised how they also provoked experiences of confusion and bewilderment. His shift away from the creation and maintenance of a world-space that permitted him to shut out, and thereby control, the impact and presence of others forced him to begin to inhabit a new space within which some of that power had to be relinquished. Indeed, over time, he came to dislike, even loathe, his previous world-space. It provoked a queasiness that he expressed as an insistent skin irritation. In the end, he declared that the space no longer suited him, was not his anymore and that he could not imagine who would appreciate it.

Rather than view Russell's relationship to his world-space as being either symbolic or some sort of displaced expression of his tensions with others, existential phenomenology would view it *in its own right* as a particular focus point from which Russell's experience of his existence revealed and expressed itself. Indeed, Russell's shift in his relatedness to spatiality paralleled a wider experiential shift to the extent that his rejection of that space, and re-shaping of a new one, reflected his abandonment and re-structuring of his previous chosen way of engagement with the world. As well as regaining human contact and relationship, Russell was also forced to embrace ever greater degrees of uncertainty and risk.

While we exist in space, space is neither static nor separate from us; its dimensions and shape are not merely physical but also, and always, imbued with, and reflective of, our existence concerns. Although infrequently reflected upon directly, this experience is often noticed through our moods – the embodied stances we adopt and enact in space. We feel restricted in certain environments and liberated in others; we flinch from or revel in the closeness or distance of contact with another. Spatiality is our way of living in relationally uncertain space.

An Exercise Exploring the Theme of Spatiality

1. Think of how you experience different kinds of space. What spaces provoke a mood of comfort or peace for you? What spaces excite and stimulate you? What spaces provoke unease and discomfort?
2. Explore how your experience of being in the spaces considered above affects your relation to your self, to others and to the wider world.

Summary

> Man is the only animal for whom his own existence is a problem which he has to solve. Erich Fromm

This chapter has provided an overview of the major existence themes and concerns that have been advanced in existential phenomenological literature. Specifically, it has considered them from the context of the three foundational Principles of relatedness, uncertainty and existential anxiety. In doing so, hopefully, it has clarified somewhat the particular ways in which these themes can be understood from an existential phenomenological framework and how this may sometimes be similar to, but more often distinctly different from, the understanding given to these same themes by other systems and models. This comparison and contrast is not intended to promote the superiority of an existential phenomenological approach over any or all others. Nor is it the case that the interpretations I have given to the themes are shared by all existential phenomenologists. Instead, it has been my aim to offer a way of considering these themes from a perspective that is consistent with existential phenomenology's foundational Principles so that when the thematic interpretations are applied in the arena of therapy both the rationale and distinctiveness of existential therapy are made more evident.

The next chapter seeks to draw together the major arguments raised in the first two chapters. In order to do so, it introduces readers to the notions of worlding and the worldview – two inter-connected terms to which I have given distinct meanings and functions that must now be clarified.

3
Worlding and the Worldview

An Overview

Gratitude bestows reverence, allowing us to encounter everyday epiphanies, those transcendent moments of awe that change forever how we experience life and the world. John Milton

Sometimes dancers experience a shift as they are dancing so that 'I am dancing' becomes something more akin to 'dancing being'. Equally, people who exercise by running talk of those experiential moments when 'the runner who is running' seems to become 'running action'. Similar accounts are expressed by people who meditate, lovers caught up in ecstatic moments of sexual union, gardeners engaged in their planting or weeding. Moments in one's life that are both ordinary and extraordinary can evoke experiential shifts that unite the acting being with the action so that existence is experienced as unified, process-like action. Such experiences are often fleeting. As soon as the unified action being somehow 'notices' this shift, the action-focused experience seems to evaporate and the being is returned to an existence that divides the act from the being who enacts it, that separates self from other or self from world. And when, as discrete, essentialised beings, we attempt to express action experiences of this sort, our language fails us. We are forced to talk of 'dancing being' or 'running action' or some such terms that try to convey the experience and which, while not incorrect, also remain inadequate. Our reflections upon these experiences remain elusive and incomplete, reliant upon metaphorical 'pointing towards' rather direct 'pointing at'.

I employ the term *worlding* as that mode of existence which is always-becoming, ever-shifting, process-like and linguistically elusive. Worlding is the experience of existence at a pre-reflective level. As such, *any* attempts to convey worlding can only be indirectly expressed through allusion and metaphor. No direct means of expressing worlding is possible simply because whatever means were to be employed would be reflectively derived. Any discussion concerning worlding can only 'point towards' worlding rather than claim to have captured or contained the experience. Although the term worlding can be found in the English translation of Martin Heidegger's *Being and Time* (1962), the use I make of it should not be confused with Heidegger's, even though some points of similarity do arise. As inadequate and clumsy as it still is, worlding, as I employ the term, suggests an action rather than an essence and, in this way, may be more adequate than other terms that have tried to express this mode of existence.

In contrast, when, as human beings, we experience our existence reflectively, we do so through the imposing of linguistically derived, structural limitations so that our experience of existing is essentialised and appears as 'thing-based', and hence as separate and distinct, if still relational, constructs such as self and other and world. This structural 'thing-ification' of our experience of being is expressed via the term *the worldview*. Unlike worlding, the worldview's reflective experiences of existence are open to direct linguistic expression. However, in order to be able to do so, the worldview requires that our experience of existence must be split or separated into discrete entities or structures that retain an adequate degree of 'fixedness' or stability in space and time.

Figure 3.1 sets out a schematic way of considering some key distinctions between worlding and the worldview.

All of the terms employed on the worlding side of the diagram act as potentially helpful, but ultimately limited (and limiting) inferences of worlding. They seek to express existence-as-action, **being**-always-in-the-process-of-becoming.

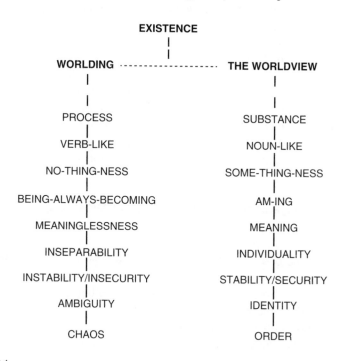

EXISTENCE

WORLDING ------------------ THE WORLDVIEW

PROCESS	SUBSTANCE
VERB-LIKE	NOUN-LIKE
NO-THING-NESS	SOME-THING-NESS
BEING-ALWAYS-BECOMING	AM-ING
MEANINGLESSNESS	MEANING
INSEPARABILITY	INDIVIDUALITY
INSTABILITY/INSECURITY	STABILITY/SECURITY
AMBIGUITY	IDENTITY
CHAOS	ORDER

FIGURE 3.1

This action-existence precedes any attempts at its becoming essentialised, and is therefore ambiguous and unstable insofar as its being 'captured' into a worldview structure has yet to occur. In this sense, worlding is chaotic in that its essence possibilities remain unclear and unpredictable, potential essences that do not as yet exist. Its 'not-yet-some-thing' reflectively derived meanings remain open, not yet structured in an essence that finds, or is bestowed with, meaning.

The worldview constructs a temporally and spatially essence-bound version of worlding. It creates reflectively derived structures that, at best, only partially express the flux of process-like worlding. Its attempts to reflect worlding are necessarily incomplete insofar as no worldview that exactly parallels worlding can be maintained. No matter how flexible the structures that make up the worldview may be, simply *that* they are structures imposes any number of limitations upon how the worldview can express the dynamic openness of worlding. Nonetheless, existence construed from the perspective of the worldview is no less an existence than that which infuses its worlding counterpart. The 'dualism' of worlding and worldview only emerges as a by-product of the attempt to express worlding from a worldview standpoint. Worlding and the worldview are always co-present and co-active and are perhaps most adequately considered as extremes in a unified polarity continuum.

At a worlding level, our existence is a dynamic, continuous *becoming*. The experience of becoming cannot be entirely grasped and maintained at a worldview level. The worldview reflects upon becoming from a structural focus that, in turn, allows any designated structure to 'stand out' or be identified, or compared and contrasted with any other. At the worldview level becoming is expressed as *am-ing*: 'I am Ernesto'; 'You are the person reading this text'; 'We are not citizens of the same country'; 'The world is experiencing dramatic weather change'; 'Gender and religion both unify and divide'. All these noun-centred statements – I, Ernesto, you, we, world, weather, gender, religion and so forth – express the structural 'am-ification' of becoming. But because the worldview cannot *fully* capture, contain, secure or stabilise the experience of worlding, its attempts can only, and always, allow for uncertain, open or incomplete reflective correlates. Karl Jaspers summarised this view wonderfully: 'Man is always something more than what he knows of himself. He is not what he is simply once and for all, but is a process' (Jaspers, 2009: 116).

An Exercise Exploring the Experience of Worlding and the Worldview

1. Try to describe one example from your life experience that approaches that of worlding.
2. How might you express this experience in non-verbal ways? Do these come closer to your memory of the lived experience?
3. Identify the worldview structures that you have relied upon in your attempts to describe your worlding experience.

Worlding and the Worldview: Existential Phenomenology's Foundational Principles

We are 'the be-thinged'. Martin Heidegger

In order to further clarify the distinctions being proposed between worlding and the worldview, it is helpful to consider these terms from the focus of the three existential phenomenological Principles – relatedness, uncertainty and existential anxiety – as discussed in the previous chapters.

The translation of process-like worlding through the essentialising structures of the worldview imposes an inevitable incompleteness in all worldview reflectively derived experiences of existence, including those centred upon relatedness. In addition, in order to be maintained, the worldview requires experiences of existence such as relatedness to be split or separated into discrete entities or structures. For example, I, as a worldview structure, require the existence of seemingly distinct others (i.e. alternate worldview structures) so that through comparison, contrast or correspondence I can make meaningful statements about my self. However, this split is only an expression of worldview-focused relatedness. From a worlding-focused perspective, no split in relatedness exists. At the same time, the worldview should not be seen as a lesser expression of relatedness in comparison to worlding. *Relatedness is* – regardless of the essence-like appearance imposed upon it by the worldview.

The worldview's structural expression of lived experience provides it with the means to contain and bound its reflections within a context of relative spatio-temporal stability, consistency, continuity, meaning and identity. Indeed, the worldview can only remain sufficiently secure, or fixed in time and space, if such attempts at certainty are part of its make-up. From the focus point of worlding, however, every moment of our existence is novel and unique, never to be repeated, never entirely identical to any other, never wholly predictable and, hence, perpetually uncertain. The interplay between worlding and the worldview imbues all the structural certainties that the worldview provides with a worlding-derived incompleteness, openness and uncertainty. At the same time, the worldview's structurally focused attempts to reflect upon worlding provides it with the means to withstand the full impact of worlding's chaotic uncertainty. If worlding offers us the certainty of uncertainty and the worldview provides us with uncertain certainties, then, together, worlding and worldview elicit *uncertain uncertainty*.

As was discussed in Chapter 1, existential anxiety is the experience of relational uncertainty. At a worlding level, existential anxiety is the response given to the experientially open possibilities of ***being***-always-becoming. This experience can be one of liberating acceptance of relational uncertainty that welcomes its de-structuring anxiety. But worlding experiences of existential anxiety can also be terrifyingly debilitating, as in those instances most commonly labelled as psychosis, when this experiential openness is an undesired outcome of the inability to generate and maintain sufficiently stable worldview structures. As an expression of the worldview, existential anxiety refers to the inevitable unease and insecurity that accompanies the worldview's partial and limiting attempts to reflect relational uncertainty from a structural, meaning-based perspective. As such, existential anxiety necessarily permeates *all* reflective experiences. It is neither avoidable, nor is it an aspect of pathology, but rather a basic given of our worldview experience of human existence.

An Exercise Exploring Worlding and the Worldview from the Focus of Existential Phenomenology's Three Principles

1. Return to the worlding experience that you attempted to describe in the previous exercise. Consider your description from the focus point of each of the three Principles.
2. How, if at all, does this focus serve to further clarify both your experience and the three Principles?

Worlding and The Worldview: Thematic Existence Concerns

> What oppresses us is not this or that, nor is it the summation of everything present-at-hand … it is the world itself. Martin Heidegger

In considering questions of existence from the combined focus of worlding and the worldview, existential phenomenology's conclusions regarding the various key thematic existence concerns, as have been discussed in the previous chapter, can be further clarified.

For example, existential phenomenology's central argument that 'existence precedes essence' can be understood from the dynamic of flowing process-like worlding being expressed as the am-ing of the worldview. Just as the worldview cannot ever fully correspond with the pre-structural potential of worlding, so, too, can no essence ever fully correspond with its 'no-thing' (or 'pre-thing-ified') existence possibilities. Recall that the 'nothingness' in the title of Sartre's most famous work, *Being and Nothingness* (Sartre, 1991), is not the equivalent of a lack, or emptiness, but rather points us to the primal 'no-thing-ness' of existence. Worlding, that process-like flow of ***being***-always-becoming, similarly attempts to capture this pre-thing-ifying aspect of our existence. Worlding points us to the open possibility that exists for the no-thing flow of being-always-becoming to essentialise, or thing-ify, as worldview. Equally, just as existential phenomenology argues that existence must precede essence, so too must worlding always precede whatever structural translations of worlding the worldview adopts.

Similarly, when considering the inter-related thematic existence concerns of meaning and meaninglessness, it is clarified that it is only at the worldview level that meaning is possible. At the level of worlding, our experience of being is meaningless, not in the sense of 'lack or emptiness of meaning', but rather that our experience is pre-essentialised, at best a potential 'not-yet-meaningful' and still unfixed in the necessary fixedness of structure that meaning requires. Meaning, in the sense being employed here, is not merely cognitive. Instead, that which is meaningful is experienced cognitively, emotionally and 'feelingly', as an overall 'mood' expressive of a stance taken towards currently lived existence. It is only when a 'mood stance' is experienced through the reflective structuring of the worldview that it can be said to be meaningful. In contrast, at the worlding level, 'mood stance' lived experiences are diffuse, not yet reflectively structured, open, not-yet-meaningful possibilities and, therefore, necessarily meaningless. In sum, from the viewpoint of worlding and the worldview, all instances of meaning reveal themselves to be captured, essentialised expressions of meaninglessness. Conversely, all meanings, as features of the worldview, must also retain some degree of incompleteness and openness – which is to say, all meanings remain inevitably open to novel interpretative, re-constitutive possibilities. In this sense of an ever-elusive finality, meanings are always open to the challenge of meaninglessness.

As a final example, let us consider how my notions of worlding and the worldview can further clarify existential phenomenology's interpretation of authenticity and inauthenticity. In their most general sense, authenticity and inauthenticity refer back to the degree to which the reflectively structured worldview corresponds to the perpetual becoming that is worlding. In its inevitable mismatch with, or incomplete 'trapping' of, process-like worlding into a worldview structure, our typical worldview engagement with our existence remains *inauthentic* simply because the worldview cannot fully express worlding. Further, it becomes evident that this inauthentic stance must permeate through any and all worldview-derived structures because in order for such structures to be identifiable, distinct, meaningful and sufficiently stable both temporally and spatially, they must stand out *as separate and boundaried structures* that engage in relationships of various kinds with other separate and boundaried structures as though their foundational relatedness was neither necessary nor evident. This view suggests that authenticity cannot ever be achievable at the worldview level, a conclusion very much in keeping with Sartre's stance on the inevitability of bad faith (Sartre, 1991). At the same time, the view under discussion also suggests that authenticity is possible, through those often fleeting and unexpected experiences of worlding. Further, even if the worldview cannot entirely correspond to worlding, it can attempt an increasingly adequate correspondence. In the same fashion, we are capable of approaching worlding authenticity through our inauthentic worldview stance. In linking authenticity with worlding, we are also able to clarify the existential phenomenological view that authenticity is neither a superior nor a necessarily desirable experience. As R.D. Laing, among others, demonstrated so vividly through his clinical case vignettes (Laing, 1960, 1967), worlding experiences can be terrifying and deeply disabling when their experiential openness (and, hence, their authenticity) arises through the worldview's inability to generate and maintain sufficiently stable structures. Worlding experiences can be exhilarating if the worldview is strong enough to cede to them only temporarily. When worlding overwhelms, it reveals the fragility or inadequacy of a worldview struggling to be maintained.

An Exercise Exploring Worlding and the Worldview from the Focus of Thematic Existence Concerns

1. Together with a partner, select one of the thematic existence concerns discussed in Chapter 2 and consider how it is further clarified through the focus of worlding and worldview.

Worlding and the Worldview: Disturbances in Being

Anxiety is the space between the "now" and the "then." Richard Abell

The dilemmas brought by clients often reflect experiential disturbances or clashes between worlding and the worldview. Most commonly, such dilemmas arise when the worldview is too distanced from its worlding counterpart such that its structures take on a rigidity that deflects any experiential challenges that might destabilise them. Instances of this can be noted, for example, when a mismatch is apparent between fixed beliefs and contradictory experience (such as, I believe my self to be caring towards my work colleagues, but my way of being with them is cold, dismissive and detached). However, too much consonance between worlding and the worldview may be as problematic as too little. Significant disturbances are provoked if the worldview is too structurally unstable. Statements such as 'I feel so fragmented', or 'I can't conceive of any worthwhile future' express something of this disturbance, as do any number of wider cultural concerns and social issues surrounding many individuals' sense of meaninglessness and anomie, civic and political apathy and the growing insistence upon immediate, present-moment satisfaction of desire.

It remains to be asked what purpose or function is served by both worlding and the worldview. All responses to such a question must remain speculative but if we consider the question from the standpoint of survival mechanisms, be they for any individual or for our species as a whole, then it can be argued that the interplay between worlding and the worldview enhances the likelihood of the continuation of *being*.

Imagine a life in which every single day demanded your following unalterable patterns of unrelenting ritual and habit. Alternatively, imagine how you might respond to a life where every day was marked by an unceasing, chaotic moment-to-moment bombardment of multiple novel possibilities at every level of your experience. Each instance, I suspect, would be experienced as intolerable, provoking a perpetual sense of unease centred upon either over-restrictive rigidity or overwhelming open–possibility. And, in turn, such unbearable circumstances might all too likely be responded to via various forms of numbing intoxication, or through abusive relations with self or others, or through disorders in thought, emotion and behaviour and diagnosed as instances of psychosis, or, at the most extreme level, through the enactment of the desire for the cessation of being. The combination of worlding and the worldview permits experiential strategies that navigate between the extremes of unrelenting Order and unceasing Chaos. When this navigation is inadequate or unsuccessful, we enact destructive strategies such as those highlighted above that would appear to be in the service of the cessation of being (or 'courting death' as Emmy van Deurzen-Smith has referred to it (1994)). However, as derived from the insights of R.D. Laing and his colleagues (Laing, 1960, 1967; Laing and Esterson, 1964), an alternative conclusion presents itself: The destructive acts may also have a constructive aspect to them so that they need not be seen to be *solely* as reactive responses expressing the desire to cease existing. Rather, they can also be seen to be attempts to either destabilise the too rigid worldview by inducing the experience of worlding, or to generate some temporary worldview stability that 'grounds' the overwhelming worlding experience. In short, such attempts can be seen as – admittedly desperate – ways to improve the likelihood of the continuation of being. Even in the extreme example of attempts at suicide, it can be argued that what propels the act is the desire to bring an end either to the rigid worldview or to the overly diffuse worlding experience rather than seek to extinguish life itself. Statements such as 'I can't go on *like this* any longer' or '*My* life's not worth living' or 'I can't take the pain any longer' commonly expressed by those who attempt suicide at least suggest that it is the particular conditions associated with living rather than the diffuse experience of life itself that are the basis to the suicidal desire. Of course, the risk is always there that the actions taken may very likely lead to the cessation of a person's existence. Nonetheless, the alternative view under consideration has the advantage of remaining consistent with the wider evolutionary aim of supporting the continuation of **being** rather than require the added explanation of how worlding and the worldview, as 'agents' of **being**, somehow switch their allegiance to that of the cessation of **being**.

An Exercise Exploring Disturbances in Being from the Focus of Worlding and the Worldview

1. Together with a partner, explore various forms of self-harm from the focus of worlding and the worldview. How, if at all, does this focus provide novel perspectives on the issues surrounding self-harm?
2. Together with a partner, discuss what might be the major factors leading someone to contemplate suicide. Consider these factors from the focus of worlding and the worldview. How, if at all, does this focus provide novel perspectives on what might lead someone to contemplate suicide?

Worlding and the Worldview: Embodiment

Let mystery have its place in you. Henri Frederick Amiel

The human experience of existence is always *embodied*. That is to say, we experience our being through our bodies. At a worlding level, our *embodiment* is pre-reflective and action-centred. It is, as far as our language can express it, the 'feeling-flow-of-action-being'. In this sense, the embodied experience of worlding need not be 'thing-like'. Instead, it is diffuse bodily experience prior to its being located within a structure labelled as 'the body'. At the worldview level, embodiment is an interweaving of thought, feeling and action (or, alternatively, of cognition, emotion and behaviour) reflectively structured within a discrete body. Worldview embodiment can be expressed as (take your pick) thoughtful-feeling action or feelingly thought action.

This clarification of the embodied status of both worlding and the worldview addresses a recurrent criticism of existential phenomenology, namely, that it is overly conceptual and insufficiently experiential. Recently, this view was summarised by Greg Madison, an existential therapist and trainer in Focusing (Madison, 2014). Focusing is a philosophically derived method centred upon the accessing of body experience, originally devised by Eugene Gendlin (Gendlin, 2003). Gendlin has argued that 'experience is not definable by concepts, rather, concepts get their definitions from bodily steps of experiencing' (Madison, 2014: 39). Focusing as a method 'keeps returning back to experience after it formulates something from experience' (ibid.). In doing so, what can be experienced is an 'unformulated experience … something that is not itself a "thing"' (ibid.). Although the terminology differs, what Madison is attempting to express is close to what I have termed as worlding's pre-reflective embodiment of existence.

In many ways, my response to the concerns summarised by Madison bears some resemblance to the research-derived conclusions set out by the Nobel Prize winning psychologist, Daniel Kahneman. Kahneman proposes that there exist two modes through which the brain forms thought: System 1, which is rapid, instinctive and emotionally centred, and System 2, which is more deliberative, slower and logically centred. System 1 thought is pre- (or sub-) conscious, whereas System 2 thought is conscious. Such conclusions share similar concerns with what has been set out in this text as worlding and the worldview. Of course, these latter terms are intended to convey more overall modes of experiencing our existence rather than being solely thought-focused. Nor does existential phenomenology suggest any actual systemic divide between worlding and the worldview as is implied in Kahneman's model. Nonetheless, at a wider level, the resonances are such that they will hopefully encourage further exploration by an interested follower of either viewpoint.

An Exercise Exploring the Experience of Embodiment

1. Make a brief statement about a topic or issue that is significant or matters to you.
2. Explore how you reflectively embody the statement in terms of cognition, emotion and action.
3. Make a brief statement about a topic or issue that is insignificant to you personally.
4. Explore how you reflectively embody this second statement in terms of cognition, emotion and action.
5. What, if anything, did you find similar in the exploration of your embodied experience of the two statements? Different? Surprising?

Exploring the Worldview

> From wonder into wonder existence opens. Lao Tzu

The worldview reconstitutes the dynamism of becoming within constructs or structures that can be defined and delineated as well as compared and contrasted with other structures. In order for the worldview to remain sufficiently distinct from worlding, each of its structures must be sufficiently stable and secure so that it remains relatively fixed in time and space as 'some thing'. Equally, in order to be meaningful, each structure must be sufficiently distinguishable from any other worldview structure. This relative fixedness in spatio-temporal and meaning stability opens the way for the worldview's am-ing statements of existence to be experienced as the expression of 'some-thing meaningful'. The standing out of any particular worldview structure as 'some-thing meaningful' is dependent upon the presence of all other structures. As with the figure/ground phenomenon of perception, any specified structure (the Figure) can only be identified, made meaningful, or be distinguished via its inseparable relationship with all those structures which it is not (the Ground) (Spinelli, 2005).

What is often missed or insufficiently addressed through structural analogies such as the Figure/Ground is that any statement about or identification of 'the Ground' is also relationally dependent upon the specific 'Figure' that has been identified. Any change in the specified Figure also changes the Ground. If we consider this from the perspective of worldview structures, we can see that the worldview as a whole from which any specific structure is said to emerge cannot be the worldview *that is as it is* without the presence of each particular structural focus point *that also is as it is*. If either is altered, so too are both. For example, if the 'Ernesto who hates eggs' were to become 'Ernesto who loves eggs', not only would the structure identified as 'Ernesto who hates eggs' be altered; so, too, would the whole worldview structure identified as 'Ernesto' be altered in all manner of currently unpredictable ways. It might, for example, logically alter those structures concerned with Ernesto's eating habits. But it might also affect those structures whose meaning associations with 'eating eggs' have no immediately predictable connection. Perhaps in his shift from hating to loving eggs, Ernesto's evaluation of his relations with his parents might alter significantly or he might discover that his experience of being in open space has changed. In general, viewed from its grounding in relatedness, *a change in any structural component of the worldview will alter the whole of the worldview in currently unpredictable ways.*

In addition, from an existential phenomenological perspective, it is pivotal to also recognise that the worldview structure meaningfully identified as 'Ernesto' is also a structural component of a wider 'world' worldview structure. As such, any change in the 'Ernesto structure' must also change the wider world worldview of which it is a structural part. For instance, Ernesto's shift from hating to loving eggs alters the number of eggs that are consumed in the world. This shift might be infinitesimally minor in its impact, but still a shift nonetheless. Alternatively, Ernesto might have a substantial Twitter following such that his announcement of his change in attitude towards eggs sets off a ripple effect leading to significant worldwide changes in egg consumption which, in turn, influence all manner of farming policies, the price of eggs, increases or decreases in the purchase of other foods, and so forth. And, as well as these more obvious relational impacts, any number of less obvious, but meaningfully associated world worldview-changing consequences are possible. Again, *a change in any structural component of the worldview will alter the whole of the worldview in currently unpredictable ways.*

An Exercise Exploring the Impact of Change on the Worldview

1. Together with a partner, take turns in recounting one instance of significant change in your life that you enacted willingly (for example, you decided to stop smoking).
2. With the assistance of your partner, explore how, if at all, this change affected your worldview in ways that were both expected and surprising (for example, when I stopped smoking I noticed changes in my eating habits and also in the music I enjoyed listening to).
3. Consider how, if at all, your examples help to clarify the contention that a change in any particular worldview structure impacts upon the whole worldview in currently unpredictable ways.

The Worldview: Embodied Existential Insecurities

> There are no whole truths; all truths are half-truths. It is trying to treat them as whole truths that plays the devil. Alfred North Whitehead

It can now be seen that the worldview is subject to two competing demands. First, it must reflect worlding in as adequate a structural fashion as possible.

Second, its structures must be sufficiently stable to resist the destabilising influence of worlding. In order to address both these demands simultaneously, the worldview must be sufficiently balanced, or 'good enough' so that it can generate reflections on its embodied existence that come close enough to their worlding origins *and* at the same time ensure that these reflections are sufficiently distanced from their worlding origins so that they retain their structural stability. This attempted balance of competing demands cannot be achieved on an ongoing, much less permanent, basis simply because the perpetual challenges of worlding will destabilise the worldview so that it continually reconstitutes itself in unpredictable ways.

In the same way as a photograph of an action-based event expresses something of, or points the viewer towards, an awareness of action, the captured 'stillness' of the photograph can only imply or allude to that action. Indeed, even the cinematic projection of a sequence of photographs at a speed that suggests action and movement remains an illusion since the 'moving film' is, after all, a collection of still images. If the stability of the worldview is an attempt rather than an achievement, then our worldview experience is *existentially insecure*. For example, I define my self as 'good'. You experience me as 'bad'. Our interaction provokes worldview insecurity: Am I as good as I thought I was? Am I as bad as you think me to be? Are you good or bad for thinking me to be bad?

You say that you are someone who doesn't 'do' love. In my presence, however, you experience feelings that you can only identify and associate with notions of love. Who are you now? How do you define and express your relation to me? How do I experience our relationship via your loveless stance? Or via your novel, possibly loving, stance? And how do each of these insecurity-provoking stances affect my relationship towards my self?

We experience a specific area of the world as being dangerous to the point that we avoid going there. For reasons necessary to our continuing employment, we are obliged to go to that part of the world and live there for a period of time. We feel insecure, on edge. Our lives are felt to be constantly at risk. No one around us seems truly trustworthy. Perhaps even the motives of our employers in having obliged us to move there require more careful analysis. Perhaps, if we had not been 'we', we would not be in this situation.

All these examples, and the many more that can be conjured up, reveal worldview insecurities. As will be discussed in Part Two, these insecurities inform many of the issues that clients bring to therapy.

Worldview insecurities have tended to have been most commonly identified from three points of focus: insecurities concerned with matters of essence (i.e., *that* the worldview (or any of its structures) is), existence (*in what way* the worldview (or any of its structures) is) and identity (*who or what* the worldview (or any of its structures) is) (Laing, 1960; Spinelli, 2005). My own preference is to restate these in terms of *embodied existential insecurities* focused on concerns surrounding *continuity, dispositional stances* and *identity*. My emphasis on the embodied status of these insecurities seeks to ensure that they are not misunderstood to be exclusively conceptual or cognitively focused. Rather, as embodied constituents of the worldview, they always interweave thought, feeling and action (or cognition, emotion and behaviour).

Embodied existential insecurities focused on *continuity* centre upon issues and questions dealing with the worldview's conviction of its own reality and presence and what it must do or be to ensure its ongoing reality and presence. How do I know that I am truly present and alive? What is real? Who (else) is real? What do I have to do or be in order to continue to exist? What threatens my continuing existence? What protects it? What needs to be done to protect it more or better? Just what defines my continuity? Is it my life? My partner? My children? My work? My achievements? My mind? Although I have posed the concerns surrounding continuity insecurities from the focus of the self, they can be equally centred on the continuity of another, or particular others, or others in general. In the same way, they can be directed upon the world such as via a specified object, or a company or organisation, or on the wider physical world itself in terms of environment or population issues or the quality of life.

Embodied existential insecurities focused on *dispositional stances* centre upon issues and questions regarding the worldview's values, meanings, beliefs, hopes, aspirations, expectations, assumptions, statements and demands regarding self, other/s and the world. They might arise when values are challenged, meanings questioned, beliefs lost or new competing beliefs adopted. They might be expressive of a conflict between any disposition that the worldview seeks to maintain and behaviour which contradicts that disposition. Or they might reflect a change in focus or definition that has been associated with a central worldview dispositional stance. Again, existential insecurities addressing dispositional stances can focus on self, other/s or the world and the interaction between them.

Embodied existential insecurities focused on *identity* centre upon issues and questions that arise regarding the worldview's ability to identify and define 'who I am (or am not)', 'who another or others are (and are not)' and 'what the world is (and is not)'. These insecurities focus upon the worldview experience of connection, fit-ness and comfort with that which it denotes as integral to, or is expressive of, self, another or others, or the world. Statements such as 'I don't know who I am anymore', 'Is he who he claims to be?' and 'China has now become the economic engine of the world' capture various worldview insecurities concerned with identity.

Of course, while the worldview insecurities focused on continuity, dispositional stances and identity can be separated and made distinct from one another for purposes of clarification, in actual lived experiences they are likely to be much more enmeshed and inseparable. Nonetheless, acknowledging the artifice of such divisions, it is through these that we can tease out and clarify more adequately the dominant or preferred focus point through which the worldview tends to express its insecurities.

An Exercise Exploring Embodied Existential Insecurities in the Worldview

1. Identify a recurring or persistent concrete concern in your own life experience.
2. Consider how this concern expresses itself, if at all, with regard to each of the three embodied existential insecurities (i.e., continuity, dispositional stances and identity).
3. What, if anything, has emerged that provides a new or alternate perspective on your concern?

The Worldview: Primary Structures

'I' is someone else. Arthur Rimbaud

So far, I have written about the structures of the worldview in a general way. It is now necessary to specify three of its primary structures: the self-, other- and world-constructs.

The *self-construct* reflects worldview experiences from the structural focus of 'self' or 'I'. For example: 'I need to binge in order to feel alive', 'I'm not allowed to make mistakes. Ever', 'I'm a cat-person'.

The *other-construct* reflects worldview experiences whose structural focus is either concerned with

a. that which is about or directed to 'an other' or 'others' in general. For example: 'You'll kill your self if you keep eating that junk', 'Young people today don't seem to hold any values', 'You're a complete stranger'; or
b. the ways in which 'an other' or 'others' impact upon the self-structure. For example: 'Your look just destroys me', 'You have no clue as to what I believe', 'You think I'm a saint'.

The *world-construct* reflects worldview experiences whose structural focus is either concerned with

a. that which is about or directed to the 'world', be it in terms of its living and non-living components and/or its physical, environmental, biological, social, cultural, moral and spiritual dimensions. For example: 'Mother Earth is dying', 'Bodies have no moral qualms', 'Reality is a particle thinking it's a wave. And vice-versa'; or
b. the ways in which 'the world' impacts upon the self-structure. For example: 'An apple a day keeps me healthy', 'Thatcher's Britain shaped the person I've become', 'No genome chart is ever going to define me'.

Examining the worldview from its primary structures should serve to clarify existential phenomenology's avoidance of any subjective or intra-psychic statements that do not overtly acknowledge their foundational relatedness. In addition, by extending the worldview's dimensions so that they express overtly the self-construct's inseparable relatedness to the other- and world-constructs, existential phenomenology raises an implicit critique of the great majority of personality theories within contemporary Western psychology, viewing these as being too restrictive and limited in their definitions because of their isolationist focus upon the subjective 'self'. In addition, in considering self, others and the world as primary structures of the worldview, it becomes clearer that, as structural outcomes of worlding experience, each provides the means of expressing the process-like quality of existence from an essence-based, structural perspective. In each case, the construct that emerges at any given instance of reflection is a spatio-temporal narrative incorporating past experience, current mood-stance and future expectations or goals. At the same time, as a construct, it is at best only a partial or selective focus point through which worlding is expressed at a structural level. Hence, the emphasis on *construct* articulates with greater adequacy that which everyday statements concerning the self, other/s and the world attempt to communicate and locates these statements within the worldview.

An Exercise Exploring the Primary Structures in the Worldview

1. Return to the recurring or persistent concrete concern in your own life experience that you identified in the previous exercise.
2. Consider how this concern expresses itself, if at all, from the focus of each of the three primary structures (the self-construct, the other-construct and the world-construct).
3. What, if anything, has emerged that provides a new or alternate perspective on your concern?

The Worldview: Embodied Existential Insecurities and Primary Structures

Too often we hold fast to the clichés of our forebears. We subject all facts to a prefabricated set of interpretations. We enjoy the comfort of opinion without the discomfort of thought. John F. Kennedy

Readers may have noted that the statement examples provided to clarify each of the worldview's primary structures allude to the embodied existential insecurities concerned with worldview continuity, dispositional stances and identity. This was intentional in that the examples can be used as a means to demonstrate how the structures and insecurities can be 'mapped' onto a schematic diagram.

TABLE 3.1

	SELF-CONSTRUCT	OTHER-CONSTRUCT	WORLD-CONSTRUCT
INSECURITIES CONCERNED WITH CONTINUITY	I need to binge in order to stay alive.	You'll kill your self if you keep eating that junk. Your look just destroys me.	Mother Earth is dying. An apple a day keeps me healthy.
INSECURITIES CONCERNED WITH DISPOSITIONAL STANCES	I'm not allowed to ever make mistakes.	Young people today don't seem to hold any values. You have no clue as to what I believe.	Bodies have no moral qualms. Thatcher's Britain shaped the person I've become.
INSECURITIES CONCERNED WITH IDENTITY	I'm a cat-person.	You're a complete stranger. You think I'm a saint.	Reality is a particle thinking it's a wave. And *vice-versa*. No genome chart is ever going to define me.

Table 3.1 presents a schematic diagram of the existential insecurities as reflected through the three primary structures. As can be seen, any experiential statement expressed by the worldview can be examined from the standpoint of its embodied existential insecurities concerning the worldview's continuity, dispositional stances and identity. Equally, the insecurities being expressed can be located within any of the three primary worldview structures – the self-, other- and world-constructs. Further, schematised in this way, the inter-relation between all the insecurities and the primary structures reveals how the worldview's reflective embodiment of any experience can hold shared, competing, complementary or even contradictory experiential stances so that, for example, the statements 'I'm a cat-person' and 'Thatcher's Britain shaped the person I've become' can be considered in relation to one another and thereby draw out a more adequate understanding of the particular worldview that is being maintained. Through such examples, the diagram makes much more evident how structurally complex the worldview is and how specific are its associated meanings. I will return to this diagrammatic representation of the worldview in Part Two in order to demonstrate how it might be employed therapeutically. For now, readers are invited to explore it by attempting the exercise at the end of this section.

An Exercise Exploring the Worldview via Embodied Existential Insecurities and Primary Structures

1. Return to the recurring or persistent concrete concern in your own life experience that you identified in the previous two exercises.

(Continued)

(Continued)

2. Using the material that you explored in the previous two exercises, place it in the schematic diagram above as far as is possible (not all sections of the diagram need be filled in and some sections may contain more statements than others).
3. What worldview 'picture' of your concern emerges? What shared, competing, complementary or even contradictory experiential stances, if any, emerge that provide a new or alternate perspective on your concern?

The Worldview: Sedimentation and Dissociation

> Dogmatism and skepticism are both, in a sense, absolute philosophies; one is certain of knowing, the other of not knowing. What philosophy should dissipate is certainty, whether of knowledge or ignorance. Bertrand Russell

In its embodied response to the experiential challenges of existence, the worldview may either be open and flexible to its reconstitution or may resist restructuring and continue to maintain the existing structure's experiential inadequacy or inconsistency. Those instances of structural inflexibility can be said to be *sedimented*. Worldview statements such as: 'I can't tolerate making mistakes', 'You must always trust others', 'Full moons generate temporary madness' can all be examples of sedimentation if they remain fixed, or inflexible, to those lived experiences that amend or contradict the sedimentation. In order to achieve their inflexibility, sedimentations must override any experientially derived challenge that is construed as threatening or destabilising of their certainty, security and fixedness. On reflection, without sedimentation the primary constructs that make up the worldview – the self-, other- and world-constructs – could not be construed or defined as (relatively) fixed and permanent essences. *How* sedimentation occurs currently remains an open question, whether considered from the perspective of philosophical, psychological or neurobiological investigation. *That* sedimentation occurs, on the other hand, is evident.

Sedimentations in the worldview can only be maintained via the strategy of dissociating the challenging experience either from the whole of the worldview or from that structural component whose sedimentation is under threat. *Dissociation*, in this sense, refers to the worldview's maintenance of a sedimentation by its distancing from, denial or disownership of the impact and consequences of experiential challenges upon it.

For example, in order to continue to hold her sedimented worldview claim that she had never experienced any form of anger towards her parents during her childhood, my client, Rosa, was forced to dissociate any contradictory challenges to this claim. In order to do so, she usually suppressed any counter-examples either by claiming to have no memory of them or by denying their occurrence. Equally, she explained many similar challenges as expressing something other than feelings of anger. Not uncommonly, she resorted to statements of temporary 'possession' that acknowledged the challenge ('Yes, they were angry feelings') but which disowned it and exculpated Rosa of any responsibility for their appearance ('When those feelings manifested themselves, I wasn't being "me" in some way'). Forces of some kind, be they chemical, environmental, circumstantial or supernatural temporarily took over Rosa and it was due to them that this false/possessed version of Rosa experienced anger towards her parents.

The value of sedimentation and dissociation is that, together, they maintain the relative certainty and continuity of the worldview. As will be discussed, some sedimentations can be challenged and redefined. It is likely, however, that some sedimentations are so deep-rooted in their fixedness and resistance to redefinition that only the most extreme challenges, or no amount of challenge, will alter them. The most rigidly maintained and deepest (or foundational) sedimentations provide the worldview with its structural bases. Examples of these deep sedimentations are not readily accessible, but I would suggest that they are likely to be expressed as brief, highly charged and emotive relational statements such as 'Don't hurt me', 'I'm a good person', 'Love me', 'I must make you love me', and so forth. My personal suspicion, based on informal discussions with therapists and trainees, is that these foundational sedimentations influence all other later sedimentations. In my opinion, these deep sedimentations cannot ever be fully de-sedimented, although they may be opened to taking on a greater complexity. For example, a deep sedimentation such as 'I'll show you' may initially be embodied through expressions of anger, aggression and the rejection of others. However, it might become open to novel possibilities of relatedness that focus on demonstration, education, self-revelation and the like.

De-sedimentation of inadequate fixed stances and re-ownership of dissociated experiences might logically appear to be attractive and sensible options. But what is being missed is that the consequence of such strategies is the destabilisation of the worldview as well as the unpredictability of the extent and duration of that destabilisation. For instance, consider the following example: I maintain the sedimented stance that 'I could never find pleasure in killing another human being'. Now imagine that such a sedimentation is, somehow, challenged enough so that the likelihood of de-sedimentation is high. In such circumstances, the destabilising of the currently embodied worldview might well be such that the embracing of some form of oblivion (whether focused on the destruction of the worldview or on the being's 'courting' of non-being) emerges as an option preferable to that of de-sedimentation. Any number of other, less extreme, examples, I am sure, should now readily spring to mind for readers. In general, a more flexible worldview receptive to the challenges of life experiences is also a worldview riddled with ever increasing levels of uncertainty, instability and complexity. Sedimentations and dissociations allow the worldview to appear to be unified and coherent; their removal confronts us with a worldview that is all too clearly chaotic and contradictory, and which is moving towards ever-increasing consonance with worlding.

As a summary of what has been discussed, consider the following example: As an aspect of my current embodiment, I claim that 'I am Ernesto who always systematically plans and prepares his lectures'. Unexpectedly, this claim is challenged in that I am placed in a position where I must deliver a lecture that has not been systematically planned and prepared. If the position 'I am Ernesto who always systematically plans and prepares his lectures' reflects a flexible worldview structure, I am not only able to deliver the lecture but, more importantly, my structure is altered in various ways and, in turn, so, too, is my worldview: 'I am now Ernesto who *usually* systematically plans and prepares his lectures and who also delivers unplanned and unprepared lectures.'

Worldview flexibilities such as in the above example make it plain that existential phenomenology rejects any entirely static definition of the worldview. Instead, it acknowledges the possibility of a continuing dynamic restructuring of the worldview throughout one's life. At the same time, however, existential phenomenology recognises that the consequences of this worldview shift cannot be entirely predictable. Equally, it acknowledges the difficulty, if not the likely impossibility, of a total flexibility as this would be too threatening to, or destabilising of, the maintenance and continuity of the worldview.

Let us now return to the example under discussion, but this time considering it from the perspective of sedimentation. In this instance, 'I am Ernesto who always systematically plans and prepares his lectures' is an inflexible embodied stance that is resistant to its being altered or amended in any way. Let us suppose, as before, that the circumstances of the challenge are such that the 'Ernesto who always systematically plans and prepares his lectures' actually does deliver an unplanned and unprepared lecture. If so, then the stability and continuity of the inflexible sedimentation is threatened. How can this threat be allayed or removed? Via dissociation. For example: Ernesto might insist that what he had delivered could not justifiably be labelled 'a lecture' but rather was more akin to a set of informal and somewhat spontaneous statements. Equally, Ernesto might claim to have 'forgotten' that he had, in fact, previously prepared a lecture on the self-same topic and that his ability to deliver this one had rested upon that earlier planning, so that the challenging event is defused of its de-sedimenting potential through the explanation of a timekeeping confusion or a prior forgetting of an earlier arrangement. In this way, the challenge to Ernesto's sedimented stance is suppressed and, as a consequence, the sedimentation can continue to be maintained.

An Exercise on Sedimentation and Dissociation

1. Identify a sedimentation that you adopt concerning your self-construct. Stances that maintain a fixed demand (i.e., I must/must not ever, I have to be/cannot ever be) will help you to identify the sedimentation.
2. Focusing on your sedimentation, explore how it is expressed through, or impacts upon, the three existential insecurities (i.e., continuity, dispositional stances and identity) from the focus of the self-construct.

(Continued)

(Continued)

3. Focusing on your sedimentation, explore how it is expressed through, or impacts upon, the three existential insecurities from the focus of the remaining two primary constructs (i.e. other-construct and world-construct).
4. Taking into account what you have clarified about your sedimentation, what dissociations from your lived experience can you now identify that are necessary in order for the sedimentation to be maintained?

Sedimentation and Dissociation as Strategies for the Maintenance of the Worldview

Life does not proceed by the association and addition of elements, but by dissociation and division. Henri Bergson

Sedimentations permit not only some degree of fixedness, certainty and continuity in the worldview itself; they also provide it with its very 'structuredness'. Without sedimentations, the maintenance of a worldview through which existential insecurities are expressed and contained as relatively fixed constructs that are able to extend through time and space would be untenable. While a worldview with few, if any, sedimentations might initially appear as being desirable or healthy, it should be apparent that it would be decidedly limited in its ability to generate and maintain sufficient stability and continuity. If the worldview is too open in reflectively experiencing its embodied insecurities focused on continuity, dispositional stances and identity, the persistent and inescapable unease and uncertainty being generated would likely be intolerable both for the person who embodies that worldview as well as for those others with whom that person interacts. The continuing ability to maintain the worldview *requires* sedimentation and dissociation. Without such, the worldview will not be able to withstand the full impact of the perpetual deconstructive challenges of worlding. As was discussed earlier, the worldview faces two competing demands. First, it must reflect worlding in as adequate a structural fashion as possible. Second, its structures must be sufficiently stable to resist the destabilising influence of worlding. *It can now be understood that sedimentations and dissociations provide the worldview with the means to adjust or calibrate the worldview's relation with worlding.*

If the worldview is experientially too consonant with its worlding counterpart, its structures will be too unstable. As a consequence, although the worldview will contain fewer sedimentations and dissociations, it will also be too limited in maintaining those reflective structures that sufficiently stabilise its structural insecurities. Examples of this might well be expressed as 'I'm completely lost', 'No one is trustworthy', or 'The world is just too frighteningly confusing and chaotic for me to feel able to relate to it'.

On the other hand, if the worldview is experientially too distant from, or dissimilar to, its worlding counterpart, the structures it generates will be too rigid and, hence, inflexible to those possibilities and demands for structural reconfiguration.

In this instance, the worldview will be over-sedimented and dissociated. Examples of this might well be expressed in phrases like 'I feel so empty or dead inside', or 'Others are just robots going through the motions', or 'Don't rock the boat'.

The experiential limitations apparent in both of the above options serve as a particularly pertinent reminder that existential phenomenology favours neither the openness of worlding nor the stability of the worldview. Its concerns lie with the possibilities that emerge when both are viewed in conjunction with one another not as separate agencies but as extremes of a unified polarity. Each of us seeks to find the means through which we can navigate as adequately as possible between these polar extremes. Veering too close to one extreme and too far away from the other generates levels of disturbance that are expressed in embodied stances enslaved to either chaos or order.

Most of us, thankfully, find some reasonably adequate navigational route. Never ideal, and constantly requiring calibration, the worldview either de-sediments or demands further dissociations. While neither option emerges as being inherently preferable over the other, nevertheless it does appear to be the case that our more typical chosen stance relies upon the strategy of dissociation. Why should this be so? Why, for instance, as in my earlier example above, would Ernesto wish to evoke dismissal or forgetfulness? What would be so terrible about de-sedimenting one's sedimentations?

Such questions return us to the three key Principles of existential phenomenology – relatedness, uncertainty and anxiety. If we assume relatedness then we are forced to accept that the exposure of any particular sedimentation to a de-sedimenting challenge will open the *whole* of the worldview to that challenge. Further, the extent to which the worldview will be affected and altered, how it will be altered and whether the consequences of this alteration will improve or worsen the calibration between worlding and the worldview remain uncertain. For instance, what might initially appear to be a relatively minor de-sedimentation in one construct may have vast and unpredictable consequences and repercussions upon any of the remaining constructs or upon the worldview as a whole. We cannot know these effects and consequences of de-sedimentation in advance, only once they have been enacted. Finally, if the effects of de-sedimentation cannot be predicted before they occur, then the willingness to de-sediment opens us to the anxiety that arises when we choose in advance the responsibility of acceptance and ownership of unpredictable outcomes. If the effects of de-sedimentation could be revealed prior to their being undertaken, as generating improvements in the adequacy of existing calibrations, then the anxiety linked to the action would be substantially reduced. But because we do not, and cannot, know the consequence in advance, the anxiety that comes not only with the taking of the action but, as well, with the owned responsibility of the action, provokes levels of unease that might easily seem too disabling to pursue or permit.

Of course, the attempt to remain with the existing sedimentation will further distance the worldview from its worlding counterpart. This, too, will also provoke relational uncertainty that intensifies the experience of anxiety. But here is where the power of sedimentation and dissociation comes into play: maintaining the sedimentation brings to it an increased rigidity, stability, security, and, hence, a certainty that is 'housed' in the sedimentation. In turn, relational uncertainty, and its accompanying anxieties, is located within that which has been disowned and dissociated. Through the rigidified sedimentation, I continue to experience existential anxiety, but in a detached manner, as though it did not belong to me, existing beyond my choosing and responsibility, housed in dissociation. As an example of this, consider my client, Aretha, and the dilemma she presents below.

Aretha holds the sedimented perspective that she is exclusively heterosexually oriented. However, she awakens one morning to find her self in bed and in the embrace of another woman, Cynthia. As well as this, Aretha remembers a night of exciting and thoroughly satisfying sexual abandon with Cynthia. But how can this be? Aretha views her self as being exclusively heterosexual. In order to maintain the sedimentation and reject the challenge of her de-sedimenting lived experience, Aretha 'explains' the events that had occurred as being due to the substantial amounts of alcohol and cocaine that she and Cynthia had taken. Further, she claims that she had been pushed or forced into such behaviour by Cynthia's powerful presence, her persuasive abilities, and unrelenting demands. Dulled by alcohol and drugs, overwhelmed by Cynthia's power over her, Aretha concludes that what has occurred was due to forces beyond her control and therefore that it was not truly 'Aretha' who had participated in, or so enjoyed, the previous night's sexual encounter, but rather it had been a 'false' or 'possessed' or 'manipulated/non-free-will' Aretha who had done so. In brief, Aretha's dissociative strategy allows her to maintain, perhaps even further rigidify, her sedimentation while at the same time the challenging experiences can be disowned, existing beyond her choosing and responsibility. Equally, when Aretha recalls the events in question, she recalls them in a detached or dissociated manner. They do not belong to her, the Aretha defined through her sedimentations, but to another, separate, Aretha – an Aretha whom she may not recognise, or feel little, if any, connection to, other than that, temporarily, this 'alien Aretha' possessed the 'real' (i.e. sedimented) Aretha. However, this alien Aretha has come into being as a result of powerful forces – drink and drugs and Cynthia's persuasive powers – and may yet return to possess once more. But even if – or when – she does, the Aretha who maintains a rigid sedimentation as well as an equally necessary set of dissociated experiences, can continue to claim ownership of, responsibility for, *only* for that which aligns with her sedimentation. This does not mean that Aretha experiences no anxiety. She clearly does, and it is this anxiety of alien possession, of being made to think and feel and act in ways not of her choosing and responsibility, that has brought her to therapy. But there is another anxiety that Aretha's sedimented stance permits her to disavow. It is the anxiety that would be there were Aretha to begin to question her sedimentation, to reconsider her definition of her self as exclusively heterosexual. And it is the wider anxiety being provoked by such questioning that taps into and challenges every inter-related facet of Aretha's worldview. What has become of that anxiety? It has been 're-located' and belongs solely to that which Aretha has dissociated and which manifests itself as 'the alien Aretha'. By so doing, Aretha is able to maintain the sedimentation while rejecting via dissociation that which threatens its maintenance and whose ownership by her would generate unbearable anxiety.

Of course, there is another means by which Aretha could maintain her sedimentation. She could claim to have forgotten the challenging experience, either in whole or in part, in all manner of ways. And this, too, can be seen as a dissociative strategy that, in turn, re-locates the anxiety that would be raised were she to question her sedimentation to that dissociated existence which, though not belonging to her, nonetheless Aretha continues to access.

Aretha's narrative, while uniquely hers, is also a more universal one. It is that narrative whose basic elements must be present in all instances of sedimentation and dissociation. It is that narrative which, from a psychoanalytic perspective, is called 'the unconscious', and which from an existential phenomenological perspective, is the narrative of divided consciousness – sedimentation and dissociation (Spinelli, 1994, 2001). Its value, ultimately, is that it obscures, rather than fully removes, the anxiety that appears when the worldview is challenged by those confrontations with the relational uncertainties of existence that threaten to destabilise its very structuredness by making it too consonant with worlding. Under such circumstances, it is not surprising that our most commonly chosen course is that of maintaining the sedimentation.

An Exercise Exploring the Maintenance of a Sedimentation

1. Return to the sedimentation that you identified in the previous exercise and review those dissociations from your lived experience that you identified as important to its maintenance and stability.
2. Imagine that you choose to attempt a partial de-sedimentation. What is the impact of this upon the dissociation?
3. What is the impact of this attempt on the three existential insecurities (i.e., continuity, dispositional stances and identity) from the focus of the sedimented self-construct?

Worlding and the Worldview: A Summary

That which is in opposition is in concert and from things that differ comes the most beautiful harmony. Heraclitus

Whatever the worldview adopted, no matter the extent of its openness or rigidity, it will impose a necessary structure upon worlding. A requisite dissonance between the two therefore emerges simply through this act of construing process-like experiencing as a structure. It is this very divide that allows the worldview to maintain its structuredness. Indeed, its structuredness rests upon how adequately the worldview is able to both reflect worlding and to resist the destabilising influence of worlding. However adequate its resolution, a divide is demanded.

Bearing this in mind, readers may now better understand the insistence running throughout existential phenomenological literature of the human tendency toward *inauthenticity* (Heidegger, 1962), or *bad faith* (Sartre, 1991) or *I–It* relations (Buber, 1970), and the like. The discussion on worlding and the worldview reveals that the various expressions of 'fallen-ness' (or existing in ways that are 'less than' that which is possible for us to be) occur simply through the act of construing structure upon that which is process-like. Those readers who are students of the teachings of The Buddha as interpreted by various schools of Buddhism may find interesting resonances with this conclusion (Siderits, 2003).

Existential therapy is itself a 'fallen' attempt to apply the Principles of existential phenomenology. It is 'fallen' in the sense that existential therapy, as a therapy, even if one that is critical of therapy, must adopt various structures that serve to identify it as a therapy as opposed to anything else which it might be. A question arises immediately: what therapeutic structures must existential therapy adopt? Can any be amended or rejected? And equally, how and to what extent, if at all, can practising existential therapy remain at least in adequate harmony with the key foundational Principles of existential phenomenology?

Although this and the previous chapters' discussions of existential phenomenology's key Principles and its ways of considering recurring thematic existence concerns do not begin to do justice to their richness and diversity, I hope that readers will at least have become sufficiently acquainted with the major issues they raise so that their influence upon existential therapy will be obvious. One such overriding issue is perhaps best summarised by Ronald Valle and Mark King:

> From an existential perspective, human existence reveals the total, indissoluble unity or interrelationship of the individual and his or her world ... In the truest sense, the person is viewed as having no existence apart from the world and the world as having no existence apart from persons ....
> (Valle & King, 1978: 7)

This foundational assumption of relatedness underpins all of the considerations given by existential phenomenology to the question of existence. Some of these considerations were subsequently reformulated so that they might be addressed from an applied perspective, be they that of psychology (Ihde, 1986a, 1986b; Spinelli, 2005), research methodology (Crotty, 1996; Spinelli, 2006), or, central to our concerns, as therapy (Cohn, 1997, 2002; Spinelli, 1997; van Deurzen-Smith, 1988; Yalom, 1980). But in joining ongoing therapeutic discourse, existential therapy has had to address the major topics and concerns which infuse that discourse – topics centred on therapeutic views and assumptions regarding change, causality, conflict and symptomatology. The following chapter provides a brief overview of the most pertinent of these topics as interpreted by existential phenomenology.

4

Existential Phenomenological Critiques of Therapy

An Overview

We all know how little skill avails, how ineffective are its artifices, in filling the lack of true artistic motivation. Mark Rothko

In an age and a culture that so values 'the expert', it is hardly surprising that in response to the numerous discontents of existence, more and more of us seek out *experts in living*. Perhaps it has always been so. Every culture has its wise men and women, its priests and shamans, its holy and enlightened beings who might point out 'the way' for us when it seems as though we are lost or in need of illumination. In contemporary Western culture, although the influence of religion has never fully died (and, in some cases, such as in what has become known as 'Middle America', continues to retain a significant socio-political influence), some part of this expertise has been assumed by therapists. But just what is the expertise being provided?

Overall, our culture's answer, which, not surprisingly, is shared by many who label themselves as therapists, centres on issues of specialist techniques, skills and know-how. Unfortunately, as has been debated and demonstrated all too often by now, it seems evident that the methods identified by experts as leading to a beneficial therapeutic impact upon the lives of clients tend to remain empirically unproven (Ablon & Jones, 2002; Longmore & Worrell, 2007; Luborsky et al., 1999, 2002; Messer & Wampold, 2002; Piper, 2004).

This is not to say that therapeutic interventions have no value. On the contrary, there is evidence that at both outcome and process levels therapeutic interventions are substantially effective and are more often beneficial than disruptive (Cooper, 2008; Howard, Moras Brill, Martinovich & Lutz, 1996; Howard, Orlinsky & Lueger, 1994; Spiegel, 1999). Clients' reported experiential accounts and evaluations of therapy suggest similar conclusions (Sherwood, 2001). However, just what the specific factors might be that provoke this overall positive evidence remain unclear. In short, *that* therapy 'works' for most people seems clear; *why* it does so, however, remains an open question. Currently there is a clear divide between what therapists assume to be important and what clients report as having been of significance to them. In brief, while many therapists tend to emphasise techniques and skills – the specific model-led *doing factors* of therapy – clients instead place the greatest significance upon their experience of being in a therapeutic relationship and, more broadly, upon the *being qualities* that they experience as in some way having been generated within the encounter (Anderson and Goolishian, 1992; Howe, 1993; Sherwood, 2001).

The stance taken by therapists arises in part from an assumed set of philosophical precepts to which most therapists subscribe, though sometimes not explicitly. Alvin Mahrer's ongoing research has been significant in exposing many of these assumptions to critical examination (Mahrer, 2000, 2004, 2006). Mahrer, in common with the view taken herein, has argued that just about 'every field of study has its basic propositions, its fundamental starting points' (Mahrer, 2000: 117) which can be characterised as that field's *foundational beliefs*. With regard to therapy, Mahrer proposes, it becomes apparent that 'the field is rife with foundational beliefs that are generally presumed, assumed, implied, taken for granted, and occasionally spelled out' (ibid.). Mahrer criticises therapy for relying far too much on foundational beliefs that serve as pleasing ideas (or what Jerome Kagan has referred to as 'seductive ideas') which can be immunised against critical analysis simply by their being assumed to be correct by the majority of therapists (Kagan, 2000; Mahrer, 2000). For example, most therapists would agree with the belief that depression distorts individuals' views such that they generate systematic logical errors in appraising themselves, the world and the future. But, some doubt has been thrown on this. One analysis of the empirical evidence for this pleasing idea found instead that 'depressed peoples' ratings of their own social performance were more in accord with the views of independent judges than are those of the non-depressed' (McGartland & Polgar, 1994: 23) and that the general logical problem-solving capability of depressed individuals remains largely unimpaired while non-depressed individuals may demonstrate quite marked errors in logical reasoning (McGartland & Polgar, 1994).

Many of these questionable assumptions are underpinned by a key (or deeply sedimented) foundational belief to which the majority of therapists subscribe – whether they ally themselves to seemingly vastly different and competing models such as psychoanalysis and CBT, or claim no allegiance whatsoever to any one particular model and instead adopt eclectic or integrative approaches. This belief expresses a philosophically derived assumption that views the world, and the relations that exist within it, from a perspective that divides and isolates subject and object (or investigator and participant) such that the latter may be named, studied, analysed, manipulated and altered by the former, who remains scientifically detached from the enterprise.

This is not to say that the investigating therapist claims to feel nothing whatever for the participant or that moral or ethical considerations do not exist. Contrary to the popular stereotype of the distant and aloof investigator who cares only for his or her project or for the results to be gained from it, the vast majority of therapists are, I believe, greatly concerned for the overall well-being of their clients. Rather, it is through this assumption of separateness that it becomes possible for many therapists (and particularly those oriented toward CBT) to claim that it is largely the investigator's skills in themselves which generate the impact and effects of the investigation. And that, if so, then anyone who is able to apply these skills appropriately will provoke the same, or at least highly similar, impacts and effects. This view is highly appealing to our culture and runs rampantly throughout it. It may well be the source of the great success we have had in advancing our selves in all manner of ways, not least technologically. But, as some have suggested, it may also be the basis of our culture's increasingly experienced malaise. Heidegger, for example, taking his lead from the work of Søren Kierkegaard and Friedrich Nietzsche, railed against the 'technologisation' of human beings and the limitations upon human relations that these permitted as attacks against *being* itself (Heidegger, 1977). Nonetheless, the reliance upon a philosophical stance promoting a divided view of existence remains dominant within Western culture and continues to exert its influence upon how knowledge is acquired and interpreted.

Existential phenomenology challenges this dominant view, as well as its varied implications, not so much by rejecting them, but rather by repositioning them as consequences of relatedness. In this way, rather than create yet another contrasting duality (which would be contradictory to its own Principles), existential phenomenology is able to subvert the assumption of dividedness without dismissing its felt experiential qualities and implications. Further, as well as subvert, this alternative reformulates therapists' recurring assumptions regarding the *doing of* therapy and, ultimately, therapists' assumptions regarding what therapy *is*. Both sets of assumptions rely on a number of foundational beliefs among which, I suggest, the most notable focus is on questions of change, causality, conflict and symptomatology. A summary of existential phenomenology's stance regarding these can now be provided.

An Exercise Exploring Foundational Beliefs in Therapy

1. Focus upon one example of a foundational therapeutic belief *to which you subscribe*.
2. What allows you to maintain this belief? What, if anything, would threaten it?
3. Imagine that you no longer subscribed to this belief. How, if at all, would it affect the way you understand and practise therapy?

Change: An Existential Phenomenological Perspective

> If my devils are to leave me, I am afraid my angels will take flight as well.
> Rainer Maria Rilke

The assumption of change – its avoidance and possibilities, its limits and potential – is foundational to the therapeutic enterprise. Yet the experience of change confronts us with an immediate paradox: we single out experiences of change as though they were in some way special or different or unusual while at the same time we recognise that change is a constant of lived experience. To exist is to change. But if this is so, how could therapy *not* change anyone? What are therapists claiming or offering when they present themselves as 'experts in change'? Clearly, they are not referring to change in general, but to certain specific ways in which change is experienced.

At the level of worlding, the experience of change is an expression of that flow of **being**-always-becoming. Equally, at the worldview level, change is experienced through its disruptive impact upon some or all of the worldview's structures. In those instances when change is reflectively accepted, the novel potential it offers to the worldview's ability to maintain its stability and continuity is judged to outweigh whatever disturbing insecurities might be generated. For instance, the change that Janet experiences in moving from her parents' suburban home to a small North London flat provokes all manner of insecurities for her yet she still accepts this change in that it confirms her worldview that she is capable of taking care of her self, is more engaging with other people when she feels an edge to her life and that living in the city is exciting.

However, in those instances of reflectively troubling change, the worldview attempts to reject or deny the unpredictable and destabilising impact of change via both sedimenting and dissociative strategies that attempt to neutralise the impact of change. For example, the change that George experiences in moving from his parents' suburban home to a small North London flat provokes all manner of insecurities for him that threaten the maintenance of his current worldview in various ways, including George's sedimented view of him self as a 'kith and kin' sort of person. In seeking to maintain his sedimentation, George's experience of living in North London is made up of various detachments – from his environment, from the others in that world, and from the George who lives in North London. These detachments, in turn, provoke experiences of falseness (whether focused on the North London self, others or world) that further confirm the genuineness of the worldview he continues to attempt to maintain as well as permit any challenges to it to be dissociated as 'alien experiences' belonging to false or unreal versions of others, the world and of George him self.

Experiences of change at both worlding and worldview levels can be seen as movements-towards-death. From a worlding focus, the experience of change lies in the perpetual flow from current being to becoming. At a worldview level, any structural alteration, no matter how minute or seemingly insignificant, impacts upon the current worldview such that it can no longer be maintained *exactly* as it had been prior to the change experience. For instance, in the examples of Janet and George, as discussed above, the worldview that each manages to maintain in response to change resembles their prior, preferred, worldview in many ways, but is not an exact replica of it. In this way, change brought the previously maintained worldview to an end. The experience of change and the experience of what is usually termed as *death anxiety* go hand-in-hand.

At the worldview level, the disruptive aspects of change are obvious. Change is the movement from 'what was or was not' to 'what is or is not'. This reflective experience of change also requires *continuity*. Without continuity, we could never make statements like: 'I have changed' or 'You are different' or 'The world is no longer as interesting as it used to be'. We would just be constantly changing beings with no reflective awareness at any point of who we/others/the world had been or who we/others/the world might become. *From a worldview focus, therefore, change always expresses an inter-relation between disruption and continuity.*

The dilemma of change, as encountered and addressed within therapy, is not with instances of change in general, but rather with those reflective change experiences whose impact is deemed to be too threatening or too dangerous to the maintenance and stability of the currently lived worldview. What is different about this experience of change as opposed to all other instances? I would suggest that the crux of the issue lies in worldview's acceptance or rejection of the inter-relation between disruption and continuity. *Unwanted and unaccepted change experiences deemed to be disturbing, divisive and dangerous separate disruption and continuity and treat these as though they were* not *inter-related.*

The maintenance of a non-relational response to change can be seen if we return to the example of George's dilemma as discussed above. George's various dissociations allow him to adopt a non-relational stance between the disruptions he experiences to his worldview and his desire to maintain its continuity. In part, George is able to maintain sufficient continuity in the worldview by dissociating the disruptive impact of the change experience upon it. However, this solution has its price: in its dissociation of experience, it provokes the dividedness of 'not-quite-being' the George who was and 'not-quite-*not*-being' the George who was. This divided stance is experienced as a lifeless sort of life, a perpetual 'in-between' experience of being.

But why turn to this solution when it would be so much the better to shift towards reflectively accepted change? While other models of therapy view the question from the perspective of exclusively negative, destructively tinged tendencies such as, for example, irrational beliefs, unconsciously derived eradicative instincts or manifestations of false self deviations in living, existential phenomenology reminds us that as limiting, debilitating and divisive as it may be as a solution, the in-between strategy offers a means to neutralise the impact and effects of change *without* the need to resort to, or embrace, the unknown and unknowable consequences that any fully committed reflective acceptance of change would impose. By remaining in-between disruption and continuity the most troubling consequences of experienced change can be denied, diluted or dissociated.

Recall that existential phenomenology argues that any particular structure of the worldview is inseparably entwined and inter-connected with every other structure. Thus, a disruption to any particular structure will impact upon *the whole* worldview. If this were not provocative of unease in itself, it is also the case that, at present, no one, and certainly no model of therapy, has the ability to predict with any significant degree of accuracy in what way and to what extent any particular worldview structure disturbance will affect the whole worldview. Regardless of how seemingly insignificant or minor is the 'tweaking' of one structure, the change to the whole worldview can be subtle or hardly notice-able or can be dramatic and wide-ranging. In similar, if opposite fashion, major alterations to a single structure may have either enormous or barely notable worldview-wide effects. Our openness to the experience of change reflects an openness to the unknown and uncertain. It risks 'the death' of all that the world-view maintains.

Thus, when confronted with what we deem to be undesirable or threaten-ing disruptions to our worldview experiences of stability and continuity, we are likely to make attempts to off-set, reject or deny those disruptions, even if those attempts generate a great deal of pain and suffering. Unfortunately, although these strategies can partially and temporarily achieve their intended purpose, their exis-tential cost is that of eliciting embodied experiences of dividedness and dissocia-tion. Nonetheless, as awful as this in-between existence can be, viewed from the standpoint of the attempt to off-set the consequences of uncontainable disruption and to maintain worldview stability and continuity, it remains a strategy that makes a great deal of sense.

In its various ways, every therapeutic approach challenges its clients to embrace the unexpected and unwanted consequences of change. From an existential phe-nomenological perspective, this shift requires a fundamental willingness to risk the stability and continuity of the whole worldview *without* the security of knowing beforehand what new worldview will emerge. It is a shift that demands the accept-ance of disruption and continuity as inseparable worldview polarities simultane-ously present and having equal value.

But by what mechanism or through what step-by-step manualised set of inter-ventions do clients find the means to attempt such shifts? Here, like all current models of therapy, existential therapy has no single, satisfactory all-inclusive answer. Its primary concerns lie with its attempts to clarify descriptively that which the client experiences as disruptive to the continuity of the worldview so that its sedimentations and dissociations can be explored inter-relationally. This is not to suggest that existential therapists remain naive to the change-provoking effects that their mere presence, much less any verbal statements they make, might well have upon the client. Rather than view themselves as being non-directive, existential therapists attempt to remain focused upon the elucidation of the client's world-view as it presents itself in the therapeutic relationship. This stance on directivity frees them from the task of setting the direction or content of the discourse itself. Instead, their focus addresses what is revealed of the client's worldview through and within the direction that the encounter itself finds and directs in its own way (Gadamer, 2004). Rather than focusing upon 'who the client might become', existential therapists concentrate upon 'who the client is being' and how that way of being is inter-relationally experienced and expressed. Paradoxically, existential therapy argues that it may be via the very process of assisting clients to 'stay still' with their experience of problematic change that the possibility of a beneficial shift is more likely to occur. Interestingly, this same view informs recent developments in what has been labelled as Third-Wave CBT (Claessens, 2010; Hayes, Stroshal & Wilson, 2011).

An Exercise Exploring the Experience of Change

1. Describe one example of change in your life to which you were welcoming and receptive.
2. Describe one example of change in your life that you attempted to resist or reject.
3. Describe one example of change in your life that you could not bring about.
4. Compare the felt experience of each of these instances of change. What differences, if any, did you notice in how you embody these changes?

Causality: An Existential Phenomenological Perspective

> The law of causality, I believe, like much that passes muster among philosophers, is a relic of a bygone age, surviving, like the monarchy, only because it is erroneously supposed to do no harm. Bertrand Russell

Most everyday notions of *causality* adopt a linear approach (from cause to effect) that is also, implicitly, uni-directional (i.e., causes generate effects, but effects do not generate causes). This uni-directional linearity continues to dominate many contemporary models of therapy. It is perhaps most apparent when therapists consider the role of the past in the client's current set of difficulties or disturbances. Specific (if, at times, unknown) past events are understood to be the uni-directional causes to the client's present set of circumstances (the effect). As has already been discussed in Chapter 2, existential phenomenology rejects this view of the relation between past and present (and future) and, in doing so, also rejects linearly causal explanations as inadequate.

As will be briefly discussed below, existential phenomenology is far from alone in raising such concerns. The appeal of linear causality may lie in much of therapy's continuing dependence on nineteenth century models of physics for many of its underlying assumptions concerning human behaviour. The great success of linear causality in nineteenth century physics rested upon its proven ability both to accurately describe and to predict certain kinds of behaviour – such as that of the swings of pendulums or the motion of balls rolling along a surface – broadly speaking, those movements and behaviours that are orderly and regular. However, does this linear view of causality fit the behaviour of human beings? Apparently, numerous therapists would like to think so – and linear causality allows them to do so. But how adequate is this assumption?

Consider the following example. You and a friend have just been engaged in a conversation. When reflecting upon it, or summarising its content and movement from one topic to another, it is recalled and presented as orderly, segueing smoothly from topic to topic almost as if each bit of content leads into the next in what would seem to be a linearly causal flow, each part of the conversation eliciting the next topic's appearance. Now, imagine that the conversation had been recorded. Playing it back, you would likely be surprised to note how much more haphazard and disordered were its shifts in topics and its directional flow. The causal links between topics would be seen as much more complex in that their movement was dependent at least as much on mood and pauses, mishearing and side-stepping of topics as it was on any orderly sequencing. Far from being so straightforwardly linear and uni-directional, the causality required to adequately express the changes in your conversation would need to be multi-directional and non-linear (or multi-linear) as it would include all of the innumerable and minute changes taking place within the whole complex conversational system as its causal influences.

Within contemporary physics, a mathematically derived model generally referred to as *dynamical systems theory* is increasingly employed in the study of complex, irregularly behavioural – or chaotic – systems. Causality, as understood within dynamical systems theory, is non-linear and multi determined. It is shaped through the interaction between multiple event components with no component viewed as being more causally significant than any other. Seemingly minor events are viewed to be as equally causally significant to any changes in the system – even the most dramatic – as are major events. In general, dynamical systems theory's emphasis on sudden, often powerful shifts in the system stands in contrast to the more traditional perspectives of a steady, linearly directed, build-up of causal events leading up to change (Al-Khalili, 2012; Feldman, 2012).

Perhaps most paradoxically, dynamical systems theory argues that the complex, chaotic interactions within the system are *self-organising* in that their interplay is itself the basis to the system's organised patterns and order (ibid.). With regard to this self-organising precept, if we return to the example of a conversation, dynamical systems theory would argue that the smooth flow and orderliness which characterises the reflective experience of conversation is a self-organised causal outcome of the complex and chaotic interplay between the sum total of all the conversation's components.

In recent years, the conclusions drawn from dynamical systems theory have been applied to psychological models. For example, within debates surrounding the understanding of child development, dynamical systems theory has challenged models that promote a generalised, stage-like process of development. Although stage models of development have dominated child psychology, their limitations with regard to linearly regular, compartmentalised modes of understanding development have become increasingly apparent (Burman, 2008). In contrast, among researchers who have pursued this critique, Esther Thelen has proposed a developmental model derived from dynamical systems theory (Thelen, 2005). Thelen's approach attempts to encompass multiple factors that may be in operation for an individual at any given developmental moment. From this perspective, human development emerges as a constantly fluid, causally non-linear and multiply determined interaction between any particular person and the world. In addition, Thelen's model combines previously opposing notions of stability and instability (or continuity and disruption) into an ever-shifting emphasis continuum whose self-organised constancy lies not in stasis but in the very motion between temporary states of stability and instability. Novel circumstances provoke novel 'self assemblies' that are not solely the result of a combination of genetics and culture but are, just as importantly, also influenced by the 'interweaving of events at a given moment' (Thelen, 2005: 271). In this way, issues of human development reveal unique chaotically derived patterns of self-organisation arising from the interaction of time, body and experience that cannot be truly generalised nor open to rigidly linear causal prediction.

The conclusions drawn by existential phenomenology on issues of causality reveal a fascinating resonance of thought (albeit arrived at from differing directions and employing different terminology) to that of dynamical systems theory. Through the foundational Principle of relatedness, existential phenomenology proposes a view of causality that is non-linear, and equally multi-determined. In addition, from a perspective that is somewhat startlingly akin to that of self-organisation within complex systems, existential phenomenology argues that chaotically experiential worlding is the basis for the organisational structuredness of the worldview. Such proposals suggest a causality that is mutually generated and maintained by what, from a linear perspective, would be labelled as separate cause and effect.

In his text, *Relational Being,* Kenneth Gergen makes the point that linear causal explanations arise as a consequence of prior assumptions regarding bounded (or boundaried) being that 'split the world into independent entities' (Gergen, 2009: 51) and which can be labelled as distinct causes and distinct effects. He proposes an alternative view focused on 'co-active *confluence*' (Gergen, 2009: 49; emphasis in the original). As an example of this, he writes:

> Have you truly 'helped someone in need' if the recipient detests your action? Can you 'help' another without his or her affirming that it is help and not hindrance? Within this question ... we shift our gaze from singular entities to conjunctions .... More specifically, let us explore the potentials of a co-active process in which 'help' is located within a conjunction of actions. (Gergen, 2009: 31)

As summary, Gergen's conclusion can be re-phrased from an existential phenomenological perspective as: causality is located within a conjunction of actions.

An Exercise Exploring the Experience of Causality

1. What are your assumptions regarding causality? What example would you identify from your own life experience that confirms your assumptions?
2. Identify a view of causality that is different to yours. Consider the above example that you provided from this alternate causality perspective.
3. How, if at all, does the consideration of causality from this second perspective affect your allegiance to the first perspective?

Conflict: An Existential Phenomenological Perspective

Conflict is the beginning of consciousness. M. Esther Harding

The differences between varied approaches to therapy are reflected in the diversity of ways by which *conflict* is understood and, through that understanding, what it is that therapists attempt to provide in order to address, reduce or remove it. From my understanding of it, existential phenomenology proposes that, at its most foundational level, conflict arises from the currently maintained worldview's structurally derived expressions of, and inadequacies in reflecting, the lived experience of worlding. The worldview, of necessity, must adopt some fixed, structurally reflected stances, or sedimentations. In doing so, it must experientially split off – or dissociate – those experiences that are too threatening to its overall structural maintenance. As a consequence, the experience of conflict becomes inevitable.

In the earlier discussion on change, it was argued that change arises through the co-action of disturbance and continuity. Only in those instances when the disturbance is too threatening to the worldview's continuity is change experienced as being problematic. Similarly, existential phenomenology views conflict in general as being neither necessarily constructive nor destructive, positive or negative, good or bad. Considered from this perspective, instances of conflict reflect the worldview's (usually temporary) sense of disturbance that can be experienced as either stimulating or disquieting (May, 1983). This clarification highlights that to associate issues of conflict *solely* with experiences of debilitation and disorder is far too limiting a perspective to take. The felt experience of unease, disturbance and tension which is so characteristic of conflict can be as much the source point for creativity, possibility, novelty and engagement as it might be about distress and suffering. Like so much else expressive of human experience, it is the particular stance adopted toward the conflict that determines the degree to which it is experienced as being constructive or destructive.

From this perspective, the client's problematic presenting disturbances cannot be isolated, or considered as distinct from that of the currently maintained worldview. In general, I have proposed that existential phenomenology highlights two significantly different conditions that express how conflict is being perceived, namely, conditions of dissonance (dissonant conflict) and conditions of consonance (consonant conflict) (Spinelli, 2014b).

Dissonant conflict arises from those instances of conflict that provoke the experience of a lack of fit, or tension, or contradiction in the currently maintained worldview. For example, dissonant conflict is the conflict that arises when my certainty about my belief in a benign god is eroded by the nightly television images of slaughtered innocent civilians; or, the conflict that arises when the dominant view I hold about my self as being a bad and unlovable person is confronted with the felt genuineness of another's statements about how good I am and the strength of positive feelings towards my self that this other's approval provokes for me. In each example, a dissonance exists between the maintained worldview and actual lived experience. This dissonance provokes the experience of conflict.

Consonant conflict arises from those instances of conflict that expose previously unforeseen or insufficiently considered aspects of a currently maintained worldview. Unlike dissonant conflict, which reflects a lack of fit with lived experience, consonant conflict originates from the unexpected or undesired implications that accompany the continuing maintenance of a particular worldview. Consonant conflict may be disorienting and undesirable, but its basis rests on the challenging event's compatibility with the currently maintained worldview. For example, consonant conflict is the conflict that arises when my fixed certainty about my belief in a god creates serious obstacles in my relationship with my best friend who is an atheist; or the conflict that arises when the dominant view I hold about my self as being a bad and unlovable person leads me to experiences of unwanted loneliness or seemingly uncontrollable self-harm. In each case, the conflictual experience confirms the sedimented stance but in ways that are unexpected or undesirable.

The resolution of dissonant conflict requires structural de-sedimentation. For example, my resolution of the dissonant conflict that arises when my certainty about my belief in a benign god is eroded may require me to acknowledge my uncertainty about the existence of a deity or, alternatively, may require the re-defining of my concept of god. Equally, my resolution of the dissonant conflict that arises when the dominant view I hold about my self as being a bad and unlovable person is challenged may require re-evaluation of my self as *always and only* a bad and unlovable person.

Consonant conflict, on the other hand, is an expression of the additional, previously unforeseen, consequences of a sedimented stance whose maintenance continues to be desirable. The possible resolution of consonant conflict requires the embrace and acceptance of the existing worldview from a more adequate, complex or truthful standpoint, such that the uneasy or unwanted consequences of that worldview are as fully owned as those deemed to be desirable and acceptable. For example, I might have to extend my belief in a god to include the challenge that this belief can be maintained in an ongoing relationship with my best friend who is an atheist. Or that my dominant views about my self as being a bad and unlovable person can also permit an embracing of the social world and a concern for the physical well-being of all humankind, including my self. If the sedimented stance cannot incorporate these novel adjustments, its risks de-sedimentation.

Different as they are in their direction and in the ways in which they are experienced, nonetheless dissonant and consonant instances of conflict both provoke unpredictable levels of disturbance in the continuity of the worldview. Many therapists have a tendency to consider and seek the resolution of conflict only from the perspective of dissonant conflict; rarely is consonant conflict given adequate consideration. In taking this position, therapists may, in some instances, inadvertently exacerbate the risk that the attempted resolution of a client's conflict will, instead, generate unexpected and unwanted shifts in anxiety far more debilitating than any being provoked by the presented issues.

Viewed in this way, existential therapy's approach to conflict is not primarily about its alteration, reduction or removal. Instead, it suggests that the therapist's task is to assist the client in focusing upon, and connecting more adequately the perceived source of conflict with the worldview that shapes and defines it. In this way, the possibilities, limits and consequences of any attempt at conflict resolution are more likely to be experienced as beneficial rather than disruptive shifts in the worldview.

An Exercise Exploring the Experience of Conflict

1. Describe one example of dissonant conflict from your own life experience.
2. Describe one example of consonant conflict from your own life experience.
3. What felt differences, if any, do you notice from the comparison of the two?
4. How, if at all, does the distinction between dissonant and consonant conflict add to your understanding and ability to work with conflict?

Symptoms: An Existential Phenomenological Perspective

The human condition is such that pain and effort are not just symptoms which can be removed without changing life itself; they are the modes in which life itself, together with the necessity to which it is bound, makes itself felt. For mortals, the 'easy life of the gods' would be a lifeless life. Hannah Arendt

As I write, the debates surrounding the problems and limitations of the newly published 5th edition of the *Diagnostic and Statistical Manual of Mental Disorders* (DSM-V) show no sign of being resolved. The DSM is a manual used mainly by North American psychiatrists and GPs in order to diagnose symptomatically various states of mental distress and disorder. A similar manual, the *World Health Organization's International Classification of Diseases (ICD)*, encompassing mental disorders is the preferred choice of British medicine. Both manuals tend toward providing descriptive forms of symptomatic categorisation associated with various disorders of thought, emotion and behaviour as understood within a medical model. It is this medical model emphasis that has provoked related therapeutic debates. Is therapy a quasi-medical enterprise concerned with diagnosis and cure or is it primarily an undertaking centred upon an inter-relational engagement that can reveal patterns of experienced unease and disturbance? Strong arguments continue to be made for either perspective as well as for perspectives that seek to conflate the two. Existential therapy, as will be discussed below, places itself firmly within the inter-relational, non-medical position. In doing so, it has remained suspicious of all manual-derived symptom diagnoses (Langdridge, 2013). This is not to suggest that no attention is given to felt experiences of disorder and disturbance. On the contrary, influenced by the path-finding work of Karl Jaspers (1963), existential therapists have sought to focus upon the clients' felt sense of disabling unease by way of their self-reports as well as through various descriptive methods of exploration. In many ways, these efforts express a different concern to that of psychiatric diagnosis that was aptly summarised by David Pilgrim: 'The psychiatric question "Is this person suffering from a mental disorder or not?" becomes transformed ... into "How do we account for this person's actions and experience in this particular context?"' (Pilgrim, 2000: 302). In addition, existential therapy's adoption of the foundational Principle of relatedness challenges implicit assumptions of isolated abnormal factors and variables and seeks to reconsider such within the inter-related context of the client's worldview. This attitude allows existential therapists to 'assume a continuity between the normal and the abnormal' (Pilgrim, 2000: 302). In short, diagnoses as provided by the *DSM-V* and the *ICD* are psychiatric, not therapeutic, diagnoses. Just as current debates rage as to diagnostic alterations and amendments in the *DSM-V*, a related debate has been taking place within the Division of Clinical Psychology of the British Psychological Society (BPS). Although not renowned for their radical attitude, BPS clinical psychologists have questioned psychologists' very use of, and reliance upon, psychiatric disorders as defined and named in medical manuals. Further they have argued that psychiatric symptom diagnosis is not the same as a psychological diagnosis (Johnstone, 2013). However, a medicalised symptomatology is so deeply embedded in psychological language that it continues to dominate.

Existential phenomenology considers the question of symptoms by returning the term to its original meaning. A symptom is that which 'befalls' upon a person such that it is experienced as an atypical disturbance in thought, feeling and behaviour *as subjectively experienced by that person*. In this definition, symptoms of mental disorder or instability are subjectively derived and not open to another's direct measurement. From this perspective, in therapy it should only be the client who diagnoses his or her symptoms. The clarification of the client's disturbing preoccupations must remain attuned to the client's own descriptions and evaluations of his or her experience.

Viewed in this way, symptoms are considered to be principally rooted in socio-ethical tensions arising from the dilemmas of relatedness. *Every symptomatic disturbance is also an attempted solution to the irresolvable 'problem' of existential anxiety.* The client's presenting symptoms, therefore, are the starting point for the existential therapist's investigations in that they are the way in to the client's presenting worldview, rather than alien obstacles that attack it and which require expulsion. Any attempt to remove, reduce, amend, or re-shape the presenting symptoms will have its unpredictable impact upon the whole of the worldview. Consequently, any enterprise of symptom removal should be avoided without prior clarification of the co-maintenance of symptom and worldview. As disturbing as the symptom may be, it may also be the one available means by which either the worlding openness of **being**-always-becoming or the structural security and continuity of the worldview, or both, can be either accessed or adequately maintained. As such, symptom manipulation or its attempted removal may generate a far greater degree of unbearable disturbance and disorder.

Such views remain deeply indebted to the still revolutionary work of R.D. Laing (1960) and the studies that he undertook together with his colleagues Aaron Esterson (Laing & Esterson, 1964) and David Cooper (Laing & Cooper, 1964). In brief, Laing argued that symptoms were most adequately understood as expressions of deeply felt and ·divisive unease, conflict and fragmentation of various facets of one's experience of one's own being, as expressed through one's relations with one's self and with others (Burston, 2000; Laing & Esterson, 1964; Spinelli, 1994, 2005). These various expressions of existential disturbance – or, to employ Laing's preferred term, *ontological insecurities* – can be seen to be consonant with the previous chapter's discussion focused upon the embodied existential insecurities surrounding continuity, dispositional stances and identity as they are expressed and located within the primary structures of the worldview – the self-, other- and world-constructs.

To summarise my position, existential therapists attempt neither to isolate nor pathologise the various symptoms that are expressed by the client via his or her worldview. Nor do they take the amelioration or removal of symptoms to be their primary task. Rather, together with the client, they attempt to expose and consider these symptoms as inter-related expressions of the client's worldview so that the implications of their maintenance, reduction or removal upon that worldview can be considered and evaluated.

An Exercise Exploring Symptoms

1. What, if any, is the role and function of symptoms in your work as therapist?
2. What, if anything, do you find valuable or helpful about working from a symptoms-focus?
3. How, if at all, might your approach to therapy change if you could no longer rely upon a generalised language of symptomatology?

Sexuality and Spirituality: An Existential Phenomenological Perspective

Buddhatvam Yosityonisamasritam (Enlightenment is sexual). The Buddha

So far, this chapter has sought to explore existential phenomenology's stance toward a number of fundamental assumptions within therapy: notions of change, causality, conflict and symptomatology. These notions, and the concerns they raise, are not experienced abstractly. Rather, they are identified through various broadly identifiable topic areas which form the focus of a great deal of therapeutic discourse. Two such topic areas are sexuality and spirituality. Both raise a vast range of important issues and questions that are beyond the confines of this text. However, because of their extensive influence upon therapeutic discourse, it is necessary to provide some general, and all too brief, existential phenomenological perspective.

Being Sexual

Existence permeates sexuality and vice versa, so that it is impossible to ... label a decision or act 'sexual' or 'non-sexual'. Maurice Merleau-Ponty

In his series of dialogues with groups of psychiatrists and psychologists, Heidegger reminded them that it is not so much *what* we talk about but rather *how* we talk about it that is pivotal to the possibilities of change (Heidegger, 2001). Considering the issues surrounding sexuality, it can be argued that we in the West, and increasingly throughout the world, are bombarded by incessant discourse and chatter surrounding sexuality. Not surprisingly, therapeutic discourses reflect this situation through their emphasis upon a particular *way* to talk about sexuality. Following Heidegger, I have argued elsewhere that existential phenomenology can challenge the dominant discourse on sexuality that has been adopted and, by so doing, can reveal several significant limitations that this mode of discourse has imposed upon the experience of being sexual (Spinelli, 2013, 2014a, 2014c).

With Heidegger's injunction in mind, exposing how we talk about sexuality immediately brings to question not only several seemingly 'natural', culturally embedded assumptions that were elaborated as key elements of modern sexology from its beginnings during the mid–nineteenth century (Foucault, 1979). What is also highlighted is how difficult, if not impossible, it is to define sexuality (Sears, 2010). Such definitions, as well as being somewhat limited (i.e. sexuality is the quality or state of being sexual) also have a tendency to consider sexuality as both a verb (a way of being or doing) and a noun (the 'thing' that is experienced or done) thereby highlighting the elusive quality of the topic under focus.

Addressing this definitional dilemma, Maurice Merleau-Ponty warned that sexuality, like existence, cannot be 'pointed to' in any direct way. To do so would be to limit it so that it could only be thing-ified, encased in a structure. Thus, in any discourse on sexuality, all that the discourse can truly address in any directly reflective fashion are the *expressions* of sexuality – that upon which we imbue – or impose – a sexual meaning. If, on the other hand, we de-structure – or perhaps more accurately, pre-structure – sexuality, so that, again like existence, its process-like (or worlding) possibilities are also acknowledged, then it becomes more 'like an atmosphere' (Merleau–Ponty, 1962: 168). Simply in the attempt to define sexuality, its 'atmospheric' quality is restricted, limited by the constraints of language and the necessary structuring or thing-ifying of ***being*** that language demands. This dilemma should by now, hopefully, sound familiar to readers of this text. In an attempt to remain as open as possible to its definitional tensions, my own preference is to avoid the use of the term human sexuality and replace it with that of '*being sexual*'.

In previous writings on this topic, I have argued that dominant discourses on being sexual reveal three persistent assumptions (Spinelli, 2013, 2014a, 2014c). In brief, these are:

1. that being sexual can only be understood as a biological activity whose originating aim is that of reproduction and hence serves as *the* key mechanism for the survival of our species;
2. that seen in this way, it becomes possible to identify 'normal' or 'natural' expressions of being sexual which can be contrasted with 'abnormal' or 'unnatural' deviations from, or perverted expressions of, being sexual;
3. that being sexual is a key component of a person's identity, such that who one is as a person can to a significant degree be described, labelled and judged by what one does or does not act out in sexual relations. This third point also holds numerous corollary assumptions regarding the fixedness of one's identity and, through it, the fixedness of one's sexual orientation as well as debates as to whether such fixedness is predominantly inherited bio-genetically or acquired through lived experience.

Although existential phenomenology challenges each of these assumptions, it is the third in particular upon which it has primarily focused its critiques. On reflection, the assumptions can be seen to be grounded in an exclusively essentialist perspective. Essentialising being sexual provides the means to identify and label. If these attempts were solely concerned with the categorising of difference from an equal status standpoint, then essentialist perspectives would not be so dominated by the plethora of rigid value judgements that divide and mystify experiences of being sexual. Unfortunately, divisive mystification is precisely what this mode of discourse has created and continues to promote. Among its many consequences is the persistent view adopted that to belong to one distinctively labelled group allows its members to claim knowledge or awareness that is available only to that group and which cannot be shared by members of alternately labelled groups. This argument would have it, for example, that 'being sexual heterosexually' is a distinct given that can be fully discernible only to those who are so identified. Similar arguments arise at the level of gender wherein essentialist discourses impose an unbridgeable divide between male and female consciousness. Essentialist arguments retain an appeal not only for those who employ such in order to diminish and ostracise but as well for those who have been, and continue to be, ostracised. It is the separatist, essentialising consequences of such arguments that are of concern to existential phenomenology and while its investigations must respect essentialist-derived statements of experience, these must also be considered within the framework of its foundational Principles.

Existential phenomenology's challenge seeks to reconfigure the issues surrounding being sexual such that they are no longer so dominated by stances and conclusions based upon essentialist dominated perspectives. Instead, existential phenomenology initiates its discourse on being sexual at a pre-essentialist level. In brief, it argues that if we start from the general assumption that 'existence precedes essence' (as was discussed in Chapter 2), then so too must this hold for issues concerned with being sexual. This 'existential turn' can re-instate a felt sense of ownership and connectedness to our experience of being sexual such that it *includes* us as active agents of our lived experience rather than as victims to possessive forces. In doing so, it highlights the divergent experiences of being sexual that exist not only between demarcated groups but between persons. Equally, it addresses those existence insecurities that are present for all persons with regard to being sexual. As with the argument presented concerning isolation/relation in the previous chapter, existential phenomenology argues that each of us is alone in our experience of being sexual and this aloneness arises as a direct consequence of our shared grounding in relatedness. Essentialist stances provide certainties that also require dividedness. While these might serve the agendas of those who, for whatever reasons, insist upon segregated groups of consciousness, this view remains incompatible with existential phenomenology's conclusions.

Without doubt, with the challenge of an existential perspective on being sexual, the multiple experiential possibilities of being sexual are inevitably placed within a context of uncertainty and anxiety. Is such a trade-off any sort of improvement to that which currently exists as the dominant mode of discourse? Insofar as it can challenge recurring dilemmas centred upon essence, choice and difference as expressed via concerns surrounding gender, identity and normality, existential phenomenology, in my view, offers a more adequate set of Principles with which to clarify the human experience of being sexual.

An Exercise Exploring the Experience of Being Sexual

1. What does being sexual mean to you?
2. When you compare your own lived experiences of being sexual to those lived experiences that you would identify as 'not being sexual', what differences and similarities, if any, emerge?

Spirituality

There's a blaze of light in every word. Leonard Cohen

Multiple, and contradictory, definitions of *spirituality* confuse our discourse. At times, spirituality is employed to express matters or concerns that stand in opposition to the physical or the material such that 'spiritual values and pursuits' can be contrasted with material ones. On the other hand, spirituality may also refer to the quest or attainment of states of being that are characterised by experiences of an unbroken communion or belonging – whether it be focused upon self, another or others, the world, values or precepts, a chosen deity or life itself. In therapy, and particularly in various humanistic and transpersonal traditions, spirituality is often seen as a step towards personal growth, well-being and development which, paradoxically, is experienced during instances when the self seems somehow to have been transcended (Moss, 1999). Somewhat obviously, spirituality is concerned with the spirit. But there appears to be a dichotomy between when spirit is intended to denote non-material being and, on the other hand, when it seeks to express the foundational 'breath' that animates all living beings.

In her various texts on existential therapy, Emmy van Deurzen has proposed a model centred upon four existence dimensions: the physical, the social, the personal and the spiritual (van Deurzen & Adams, 2011). She argues that it is primarily through the spiritual dimension that human beings confront the unknown and respond to it through their construction of meanings, values and ideals. This interplay between the unknown and meaning imbues the spiritual dimension with inevitable tensions between 'our need for ultimate meaning and purpose ... [and] ... the relativity of our existence' (van Deurzen & Adams, 2011: 22). Van Deurzen's emphasis on a spiritual dimension makes clear that the issue of spirituality is not one that existential phenomenology shuns or dismisses. Indeed, from her model's perspective the human insistence upon meaning-making is directly related to the spiritual dimension.

At the same time, this dimensional approach remains problematic. However inadvertently, it compounds the tendency to view as distinct and separate that which is physical or material from that which is spiritual. Once again, the spiritual is implicitly 'other-worldly', not belonging to, nor an expression of, the social and the personal. I don't think that such divides are necessary in order to clarify that, at times, whether by technique or happenstance, we are pulled out of our habitual, everydayness and are presented with an altogether different experience of our existence. Considered within the terminology of worlding and the world-view, we access our spirituality not in spite of our material being, but through it. Those experiences that we might label as spiritual arise as consequences of temporarily closer conjunctions in the interplay between worlding and the world-view. During these often unexpected and surprising instances, the structures that maintain the worldview appear to dissolve and permit a worlding experience to take precedence. This is most obvious in the impact such experiences have upon primary worldview structures such as the self-, other- and world-constructs. In these moments of embodied spirituality, not only the separateness of these structures, but also the structures themselves are difficult, if not impossible, to maintain.

This existential phenomenological interpretation of spirituality steers clear of any assumptions having to do with dis-embodiment or 'the beyond'. If anything, its stance asserts quite the opposite. Or, perhaps more accurately, its stance is one that considers the experience of spirituality as being simultaneously up-lifting and grounding. It is not so much that these moments we label as spiritual take our breath away; rather it is that we experience a different way of breathing.

Why do such shifts occur? It would seem, as many others have concluded, that they are in some way related to matters of meaning. But perhaps it is not so much that these instances serve to maintain our meanings but rather that they act to challenge them. If spirituality is linked to a temporarily closer consonance between our experiences of worlding and the worldview, then structured patterns of meaning are temporarily opened to their counterpart of meaninglessness. In turn, this allows novel, perhaps more adequate, meanings to emerge once the worldview is re-stabilised. What we call creativity is one outcome of the interplay between meaning and meaninglessness. Another, I am suggesting, is what we identify as spirituality. The extra-ordinary permits us a different view of the ordinary. This view may excite, arouse, fill with awe, horrify, terrify, take us away from our selves, put us closer in touch with our selves, make life worth living, or further destabilise our existential insecurities. All of such, however contradictory, coincide under the label of spirituality as proposed by existential phenomenology. As confusing and confounding as the label may be, in its openness to its meaning it remains in harmony with those experiences towards which it points us.

An Exercise Exploring the Experience of Spirituality

1. What would you identify as a spiritual experience in your life?
2. What is it about the experience that, for you, makes it spiritual?
3. What meanings, values or significance, if any, do you attach to the experience you identified as spiritual? How do these differ, if at all, from the meanings, values and significance you give to non-spiritual experiences in your life?

A Very Brief Note on Consciousness

The history of the world is none other than the progress of the consciousness of freedom. Georg Wilhelm Hegel

The recurring, deeply embedded therapeutic assumptions that have been discussed in this chapter themselves rest upon the bedrock of *consciousness*. All contemporary models of therapy begin with the premise that we, as human beings, are conscious beings. As well, many models assume the existence of a separate, distinct mental system, usually referred to as either non-conscious or unconscious. Daniel Kahneman's dual-system model of thought provides one example of the former (Kahneman, 2012). Psychoanalytic theories, even if disagreeing as to how to understand the unconscious, nonetheless view it as a foundational Principle to their model (Frosh, 2012). However, regardless of these therapeutic assumptions, it remains the case that consciousness is the focus of a series of ongoing, perhaps irresolvable, debates. What is it to be conscious? How does consciousness arise? These and numerous related questions remain major concerns to philosophy, psychology and neuroscience. No straightforward, or universally accepted, theories exist. Instead, radically different views compete to provide the most adequate answers. Any analysis of these debates, as fascinating as they are, lies far beyond the boundaries of this text. I encourage interested readers to pursue and keep up to date with these interdisciplinary discussions by reading the *Journal of Consciousness Studies*. For the purposes of this text, all that remains possible is to provide an all-too brief and undoubtedly inadequate existential phenomenological account of consciousness as relevant to therapeutic practice.

Descartes' famous conclusion 'I think, therefore I am' is not entirely disputed by existential phenomenology. What can be said, however, is that this conclusion may only be correct insofar as it addresses consciousness from the standpoint of the worldview and, even then, solely from a cognitively dominated focus. Nonetheless, an existential phenomenological re-statement of Descartes' argument would be along these lines: The act of reflecting upon **being** requires thoughtfully feeling (or feelingly thoughtful) structures. Viewed from a worlding perspective, however, Descartes' conclusion is far more problematic. If worlding is pre-reflective then the experience of being from this standpoint must precede any reflectively substantiated being, much less a thinking one. At this worlding level, we can only speak – and even then hypothetically and inadequately – of a foundational pre-reflective consciousness which is not directly accessible through reflection but which provides the experiential basis for all reflectively conscious activity. Even then, existential phenomenology proposes no actual split or distinction between the pre-reflective and the reflective. Instead, as I understand it, it argues that views of consciousness suggestive of dual, or multiple, mental systems can only be seen as outcomes of a worldview perspective. In other words, existential phenomenology assumes a single system – consciousness – that, reflectively *appears* as dual or multiple. For instance, as was discussed in the previous chapter, in order to maintain its embodied stability and continuity, the worldview requires internalised divisions expressed as sedimentations and dissociations. Dissociations, of necessity, are experienced as being separate from, or alien to, the owned structures of the worldview. But that they are experienced as divided does not mean that they are actually separate and distinct. The worldview makes them appear to be so. In this way, as I have elaborated more fully elsewhere, existential phenomenology is able to address the phenomena associated with psychoanalytic notions of the unconscious without requiring the existence of a separate mental system (Spinelli, 1994, 2001).

This is not to suggest that existential phenomenology makes any claims to having solved some or all of the recurring debates surrounding consciousness. All it can claim, at least with regard to how consciousness tends to be understood within therapy, is that it is able to address a great deal that appears to require dual or multiple systems from a single system perspective. Given that our current understanding of consciousness is so limited, it seems sensible to consider the questions it raises as expressions of a single, largely unknown, system rather than insist upon the separate existence of other, equally unknown, systems.

An Exercise Exploring Consciousness in Therapy

1. How do you understand and work with issues of consciousness in therapy?
2. If you adhere to dual or multiple systems, what convinces you to keep doing so? What, if anything, would change your view?
3. If you adhere to a single consciousness system, how have you come to understand and work with clients' experiences suggestive of dual or multiple systems?

Having now highlighted a number of the major existential phenomenological concerns and critiques surrounding therapy, the following chapter will provide an overview of the principal qualities and conditions underpinning the practising of existential therapy.

5

Existential Therapy:
An Overview

Historical Background

It is the task of existential phenomenology to articulate what the other's 'world' is and his way of being in it. R.D. Laing

As Mick Cooper has argued in *Existential Therapies* (Cooper, 2003), no single form or interpretation of existential therapy derived from existential phenomenological ideas has emerged. Rather, there currently exist various approaches to, or schools of, existential therapy. Often reflecting both a primary allegiance to a major contributor to existential phenomenological thought and practice as well as unique cultural emphases, most now have established strong relations with other national and international organisations. Increasingly, questions concerned with what unifies and distinguishes these schools from one another have begun to be addressed.

The psychiatric work and philosophical ideas of Karl Jaspers can be considered to be among the earliest direct attempts to apply existential phenomenology to therapy (Jaspers, 1963; Misiak & Sexton, 1973). Jaspers was deeply influenced by Martin Heidegger's philosophy and maintained an ongoing correspondence with him. Nonetheless, in spite of (or perhaps due to) the range and originality of ideas to be found throughout Jaspers' work, the origins of a designated existential approach to therapy are more commonly linked with the contributions of three other internationally renowned psychiatrists. Ludwig Binswanger's Existential Analysis (Binswanger, 1963), Medard Boss' Daseinsanalysis (Boss, 1963, 1979) and Viktor Frankl's Logotherapy (Frankl, 1988) each pioneered a school of existential therapy that continues to attract substantial numbers of adherents and trainees (Cooper, 2003; Valle & King, 1978). Both Binswanger's and Boss' approaches have the added authority of Heidegger's direct − though sometimes critical − involvement (Valle & King, 1978). Frankl's model was initially developed outside the broad influence of existential phenomenology and more as a 'meaning-focused' response to Viennese psychoanalysis. Its relation to other existential approaches has not always been so evident. In recent years, however, mainly through the ongoing theoretical and practice-based papers emerging from the International Society for Logotherapy and Existential Analysis, the links with other existential therapies has become far more apparent (Längle, 2005).

More recently, North American and British expressions of existential therapy have been established and have revitalised interest in the approach as well as inspiring closer contact between international organisations. Though still deeply indebted to the philosophical underpinnings of existential phenomenology, these newer American and British Schools are also substantially influenced by later developments in both philosophy and psychology and by the relational, social-constructionist and narrative theory movements that have arisen within other contemporary therapeutic models. The American School is closely identified with the work of, among others, Rollo May (1969, 1981, 1983), Irvin Yalom (1980, 1989, 2001) and James Bugenthal (1981, 1987). R.D. Laing (1960, 1967, 1982), Emmy van Deurzen (-Smith) (1988, 1997), Hans W. Cohn (1997, 2002), Freddie and Alison Strasser (1997) as well as the present author (Spinelli, 1994, 1997, 2001, 2005) are all regarded as major contributors to the development of a British School of existential therapy (Cooper, 2003).

This text presents my own understanding of existential therapy as an applied expression of key foundational Principles that underpin existential phenomenology. Although it has been developed under the aegis of the British School, it does not seek to represent it as a whole, but rather as one strand of its thought and practice whose primary focus is concerned with the implications of relatedness rather than the transposing of various significant existence themes onto therapeutic discourse. As such, the description of existential therapy as discussed below follows *a* path rather than *the* path developed by the British School.

Existential Approaches: An Exercise

1. What is your understanding of existential therapy?
2. What, for you, are the main concerns of existential therapy?
3. What, for you, distinguishes existential therapy from other therapeutic approaches?

Existential Therapy: Relatedness

> Unity can only be manifested by the Binary. Unity itself and the idea of Unity are already two. The Buddha

Existential therapy's adoption of the Principle of relatedness, as has been discussed in previous chapters, is crucial to its practice. From the standpoint of relatedness, the problems presented by clients can no longer be seen as being solely their own, in any exclusively individualistic sense. Perhaps the most obvious implication of this shift is that existential therapy cannot concern itself solely with the uniquely subjective experience of the individual client. Instead, its focus rests upon that foundational relatedness through which the client experiences his or her unique way of being. At a practical level, this stance emphasises an *inclusive exploration* of all the primary structural constituents of the worldview rather than seeking to isolate and elevate one constituent (the self-construct) over others. Equally, in terms of the encounter between client and therapist, the emphasis of relatedness reveals that existential therapy is as much 'about' the therapist as it may be 'about' the client. While the primary focus of this enterprise obviously remains with the unease, travails and disturbances in living experienced by the client, nonetheless the exploration of such centres itself upon that which emerges experientially *between* therapist and client and what is revealed about the client's disturbances through that particular encounter. From this perspective, existential therapy is not merely practised; it is embodied through the unfolding and enfolding interaction of therapist and client.

Existential Therapy: Uncertainty

> The quest for certainty blocks the search for meaning. Uncertainty is the very condition to impel man to unfold his powers. Erich Fromm

In being more relationally attuned, the therapeutic encounter itself becomes an expression of uncertainty. In their willingness to remain with that uncertainty, existential therapists encourage a dialogue that finds its own direction and thereby opens the possibility of change whose direction and impact is indeterminable. Viewed from this perspective, existential therapists become 'agents' of uncertainty not only through their way of being with the client but also, as importantly, through their own willingness to remain open to the unpredictable consequences of encounter.

How the client responds to, or makes use of this willingness, is also unpredictable. Nevertheless, as the relational therapist Leslie Farber proposed, the client's recognition of, and willingness to engage with, the uncertain therapist was, for him, the most reliable indicator of a likely beneficial therapeutic outcome (Farber, 2000). Through the client's increasing willingness to 'meet' an uncertain – and hence imperfect – therapist, two significant relational shifts can occur. First, in reaching out to the therapist, the client simultaneously breaks out of his or her self-centred, self-focused, other-excluding stance and begins to recognise the existence of the present other (the therapist). Second, simultaneous to reaching out, the client 'reaches in' to find and accept his or her own uncertainty. In turn, both shifts invite an investigative approach that is more prepared to critically examine the client's currently maintained worldview.

Of course, this challenge to the client is dependent upon the therapist's own initial willingness to embrace uncertainty – not only as directed towards the client's way of being, but also from the therapist's own open stance toward the impact of encounter upon him or her self. As has been suggested by narrative and social-constructionist psychotherapeutic approaches influenced by existential phenomenology, therapy might be thought of as a co-creation of novel meanings via mutual dialogue (Kaye, 1995). If so, the Principle of uncertainty highlights a set of uneasy stances for the therapist to accept – what the emergent meanings may be, whether these will have perceived impact upon one or both of the participants, whether they may apparently resolve conflict or provoke new concerns and anxieties, and how they might reconstitute the worldview being maintained by either or both participants prior to the discourse. All of these issues and possibilities, at present, remain unknown and unpredictable.

Existential Therapy: Existential Anxiety

Courage resists despair by taking anxiety into itself. Paul Tillich

In his novel, *Rapids* (Parks, 2006), Tim Parks vividly encapsulates the Principle of existential anxiety as is often expressed by the concerns brought to therapy by clients:

> [S]o many of these people who do dangerous things on rivers and mountains are afraid .... Afraid of dying, afraid of settling down. Afraid of life beginning really, and afraid it will never begin. These sports are something you do instead of life .... To feel they're really living, when they're not in danger of living at all. (Parks, 2006, quoted in Alvarez, 2006: 40)

Existential therapy argues that the experience of anxiety is neither the consequence of insufficiently met instinctual demands, nor the product of opposing drives, nor the outcome of inadequately established infantile relations, nor the distillation of misunderstood, incomplete or improper learning experiences. Rather, the problematic existence concerns and insecurities presented by clients can be considered as the consequences of attempts to cope with, reduce or avoid the inevitable existential anxiety that accompanies human existence.

Considered from this perspective, the task of existential therapy is not that of providing further means to reduce the experience of anxiety but, rather, to disclose and explore the sedimented stances and dissociated experiences through which clients have *already succeeded* in distancing themselves from the existential anxiety arising out of relational uncertainty. In this way, the co-dependence between the debilitating disturbances identified by clients as being problematic and their currently maintained worldview can be further clarified. In exploring the client's presenting disturbances as expressions of the worldview rather than as external, alien disruptors of it, they can be viewed as being not solely problematic, but also as the consequence of partially successful attempts to reduce or deny existential anxiety. If existential therapy can be said to 'treat' anxiety, its treatment has less to do with the reduction or eradication of anxiety than with finding a more adequate and courageous way to acknowledge and live with its inevitability.

In his influential text, *Existential Therapy* (1980), Irvin Yalom explores at length the various problematic concerns that might arise in response to attempts to evade existential anxiety. For example, in his analysis of death anxiety, Yalom posits two general modes of response that can generate numerous problematic disorders. The first of these rests on clients' sedimented conviction of their 'specialness and personal inviolability' (Yalom, 1980: 115). This stance, Yalom argues, can provoke a variety of disturbances ranging from clients' compulsive reliance upon death-defying behaviour designed to prove their specialness and personal inviolability through to the workaholic's need to push him or her self beyond ordinary temporal, mental and behavioural limits so that the conviction of personal indispensability can be maintained. In like fashion, current problematic 'addictions' focused upon health, virility and the denial or arresting of physical ageing can be considered as further examples of this first response to death anxiety. The second response suggested by Yalom relies upon 'the Ultimate Rescuer', who may be an omnipresent supernatural entity or force or, alternatively, another, albeit superior or charismatic, human being such as a religious or political leader (Yalom, 1980). In all instances, the Ultimate Rescuer guides, watches over and protects, and often bestows ultimate reward or punishment, thereby fulfilling the function of rule-maker, law-giver and meaning-constructor. In this way, the belief in an Ultimate Rescuer imparts certainty and security of meaning and purpose upon one's life and, as well, minimises the power of death, often by reducing its finality to a mere turning point toward another (typically more elevated) realm of existence (ibid.).

The unforeseen problems arising out of an embrace of either of these anxiety-reducing strategies centre upon the necessity of maintaining inflexible worldview sedimentations that, in turn, require dissociative responses to a multitude of lived experiences. Both such solutions rely upon worldviews that cannot easily maintain stances of questioning and doubt. Their rigidity of thought and behaviour can extend to more problematic obsessions, fanaticism, and ritualised patterns of social and sexual behaviour, which are then taken to therapy.

An Exercise Exploring Three Foundational Principles as Applied to Practising Therapy

1. On the basis of what you have read about relatedness, uncertainty and existential anxiety in this text, explore how, if at all, these three foundational Principles influence your own preferred approach to practising therapy.
2. How, if at all, do these three Principles challenge your own preferred approach to practising therapy?

Existential Therapy as an Investigative Enterprise

> The phenomenological project continually resolves itself before our eyes,
> into a description – empirical despite itself – of actual experience and into
> an ontology of the unthought that automatically short-circuits the primacy of
> the 'I think'. Michel Foucault

As an investigative enterprise concerned with the descriptive clarification of the client's currently lived experience, existential therapy shares a common undertaking to that of Human Science Research in general and phenomenological research in particular in that each requires '[a]n empathic and imaginative identification with the subject ...' (Gillett, 1995: 112). As I have argued elsewhere, viewing existential therapy as a form of structured investigation immediately frees it from the more quasi-medical dictates and assumptions adopted by other models (Spinelli, 1994, 2006). In addition, this view allows existential therapy to remain more consonant with the investigatively focused aims of existential phenomenology (Crotty, 1996). As well, it permits existential therapy to return therapy to its original meaning and purpose centred upon the attempt to illuminate or clarify a being through another's willingness to 'stand beside' that being in such ways that open the worldview to more adequate descriptive clarification (Evans, 1981).

As a form of structured enquiry rooted in the Principle of relatedness, existential therapy *implicates* the presence of the therapist/investigator as an unavoidable and uncertain variable upon the direction, focus and consequences of the investigation. Further, the method of investigation it adopts attempts to remain within a broadly *descriptively focused* framework which is equally open to the competing, complementary and contradictory stances that, together, structure and maintain the worldview.

In its focus upon matters of *understanding* rather than being predominantly concerned with issues of *explanation,* existential therapy promotes human-centred investigations, thereby maintaining distinctions in enquiry first identified as pivotal differences between Natural Science research and Human Science research (Hodges, 1952; Karlsson, 1993; Kvale, 1994). The avoidance of any use of, or reliance upon, psychiatrically derived diagnostic categories and typologies highlights one significant example of its human-centred allegiance.

Finally, as a therapeutic enterprise that acknowledges the significance of change – however generated – existential therapy takes, as one of its most basic guiding assumptions, the view that *to describe is to change.* In other words, unlike many other therapeutic models' assumptions that description is a first step towards the establishment of conditions that may lead to (hopefully beneficial) change, existential therapy argues that the descriptive enterprise *in itself* generates change. First, by focusing on the person who is present rather than the person who might one day become or who once was. And second, through this focus, via its adoption of temporary non-judgemental acceptance of the person who is present. In this latter emphasis upon acceptance, existential therapy shares Carl Rogers' conclusion that: '[t]he curious paradox is that when I accept myself as I am, then I change' (Rogers, 1990: 19).

Existential Therapy as an Investigative Enterprise: An Exercise

1. If you accepted existential therapy's view of therapy as an investigative enterprise how, if at all, would your definition of therapy and your way of practising therapy be affected?

Existential Therapy and the Therapeutic Relationship

Kinder the enemy who must malign us than the smug friend who will define us. Anna Wickham

In recent years, the critical importance given to the therapeutic relationship itself as a major variable influencing beneficial outcomes for the client has been so well established that hardly any model of contemporary therapy exists that does not include the establishment and maintenance of an appropriate therapeutic alliance as a necessary condition for its effectiveness. In 2011, the published findings of an American Psychological Association (APA) interdivisional task force on evidence-based therapeutic relationships concluded that:

> The therapy relationship makes substantial and consistent contributions to psychotherapy outcome independent of the specific type of treatment ... The therapy relationship accounts for why clients improve (or fail to improve) at least as much as the particular treatment method ... [And that] [e]fforts to promulgate best practices or evidence-based practices (EBPs) without including the relationship are seriously incomplete and potentially misleading. (Norcross & Wampold, 2011)

Not surprisingly, given the centrality of existential phenomenology's Principle of relatedness, existential therapy remains in broad agreement with this conclusion. In general, existential therapy considers the therapeutic encounter as the microcosm through which the macrocosm of the client's stance toward the possibilities and limitations of inter-relational being in the world is both explored and expressed (Cohn, 1997; Spinelli, 1997, 2001; Strasser & Strasser, 1997). This focus on the co-active presence of therapist and client alike permits a mutual attunement to the client's continuing maintenance of worldview-derived problematic stances – no matter how debilitating, restrictive, limiting and irrational these may appear to be to the therapist (if not all others in the client's world, as well as the client him or her self).

From the existential therapist's end of this co-active attunement, several attitudes or 'being qualities' stand out as expressions of the therapist's willingness and ability to remain present in the encounter. A summary of these key qualities is discussed below.

An Exercise Focused on the Therapeutic Relationship

1. How, as a therapist, do you understand and work with the therapeutic relationship?
2. What, for you as a therapist, are the key qualities and functions of the therapeutic relationship?
3. What, for you, distinguishes a therapeutic relationship from a non-therapeutic one?

The Existential Therapist as the Present Other

Everyone is the other and no one is himself. Martin Heidegger

The existential therapist is *the present other* to the client. As this other, the therapist acts as both the representative of all others in the client's wider world relations and, just as importantly, is also the other who challenges the client's primary worldview constructs simply through the inter-relational impact of his or her presence. For example, the present therapist-as-other may both clarify and challenge any number of the client's worldview sedimentations concerning others, how others expect the client to be, and how the client expects others to be with him or her. In this way, in contrast to many other therapeutic models, explanations regarding the therapeutic impact of the therapist's presence as other upon the client are not reliant upon assumed mechanisms of transference or counter-transference (Spinelli, 1994).

Any existential phenomenological discussion on the topic of 'the other' – including the other who is the therapist – is bound to be indebted to the work of Jean-Paul Sartre (Cannon, 1991; Sartre, 1991). Through his analyses of conflict, often lucidly brought to life through the struggles of the characters in his novels and plays, Sartre returned again and again to the theme of the other as the antagonist to one's life project. For Sartre, the presence of the other signals the clash of competing ways of being. If a solution to their conflict exists for Sartre, it cannot be through its being resolved or transcended, but rather *through the mutual acknowledgement of its inevitability.* Via this acknowledgement, a reciprocal co-operative possibility emerges which, while not avoiding the different and competing elements that distinguish one person's life project from that of the other, also acknowledges the similarity of their aim in that all life projects seek to create and maintain the deceptions of security, definability and certainty and, by so doing, hold transformative possibilities for both self and other. This reciprocal possibility involves both parties' switching their relational focus from one that seeks to dominate the other so that he or she becomes that other whose existence is in the service of my interests and objectives to that which is founded on our mutual *attempts* to be in the service of the other's project. In turn according to Sartre, these attempts to assist, rather than undermine, the other's aims reveal that the other is not only an external entity but is also the other who, as an alien, detached or contradictory presence, also resides within each being.

Following Sartre, the existential therapist's presence as the other becomes the catalyst to the client's confrontation with his or her own experience otherness – for instance, via the client's willingness to recognise dissociated experiences (i.e. experiences identified as disowned, or belonging to an 'other') as being relationally connected to his or her worldview maintained sedimentations. In acknowledging the otherness of the therapist, existential therapy includes the role of conflict and competing strategies as inevitable aspects of the therapeutic encounter. What distinguishes its attempts at encounter is not the *lack* of such conflict, but rather this very willingness to recognise and work with it rather than seeking – or proclaiming – its eradication. As the other who is currently present, the existential therapist provokes the client's experience of being with others in the immediacy of the therapeutic encounter. In this way, the client's experiences of being-with-the-other-who-is-the-therapist can be compared and contrasted to the more general way of being with others that he or she adopts and, with this, to the investigation of how these similar or differing ways of being-with-others might be related to the client's presenting concerns.

As an expression of the Principle of relatedness, it is evident that the therapist's presence as the other is contingent upon the therapist's openness to, acceptance of, and willingness to remain with the client's currently presenting worldview. To adopt any other stance which intends a directive or manipulative change in the client's way of being, no matter how benevolent or concerned to ameliorate the client's distress, will only serve to maintain the client's view of the-other-who-is-the-therapist as antagonist rather than as a co-operative presence. In turn, this will serve to maintain the client's disconnected and conflictual stance towards the other within his or her worldview. While therapeutic benefits can certainly arise through strategies that strengthen the client's ability to improve conflictual superiority over the others in his or her life, the benefits being sought by existential therapy are more concerned with the possibilities arising out of improved connection and co-operation with both external and internal others.

An Exercise Focused on the Therapist as the 'Present Other'

1. What sort of therapeutic 'other' do you attempt to be with your clients?
2. How, if at all, do you, as therapist, work with the conflict or differences liked to being 'the other'?

The Existential Therapist's Acceptance

Out beyond ideas of wrongdoing and rightdoing, there is a field. I will meet you there. Jalal ad-Din Rumi

Acceptance requires of existential therapists the abdication of the assumption that the trained and expert professional who is the therapist can know and direct the means by which the client is to be helped. Rather than focus upon notions of problem-solving, goal-setting, educating, establishing programmes for change and directing discourse, existential therapists attempt a stance of *acceptance* which can be defined as the reflective openness both to who is there in the encounter and how it is to be in the encounter as it is being lived.

This acceptance is neither about approval or disapproval of what the client does or does not do. Rather, acceptance enjoins the existential therapist to assume no initial understanding of any aspect of the client's worldview. Instead, its clarification becomes the focus for descriptive investigation. But, in order to be able to engage in this enterprise, the therapist must be both willing and able to stay with what is being presented, rather than moving on to alternative ways of being that may appear to be preferable to either or both participants in the encounter. Thus, existential therapists avoid adopting the role of a superior, objective instructor who distinguishes for the client what is assumed to be unreal, false and/or irrational and who attempts to replace this with real, true and/or more rational ways of being. Similarly, rather than present themselves as quasi-medical symptom-removers and treatment-providers, existential therapists return therapy to its original enterprise of attempting to stay with, stand beside and accept the otherness of the being who is present (Evans, 1981).

In general, the existential therapist's stance of acceptance toward the unknown and alien worldview of the client requires the abdication of the security that comes with assumptions such as 'doing it right', or directing change, or of the expert's superiority of knowledge and status. This stance has nothing to do with any perverse belittlement or rejection of more typical therapeutic enterprises; rather, it is a necessary constituent of the specific form of human-centred investigation being undertaken.

An Exercise Focused on the Therapist's Acceptance

1. How, as a therapist, do you understand and work with your acceptance in the therapeutic encounter?
2. How, if at all, does your way of being therapeutically accepting compare or contrast with an existential perspective?

The Existential Therapist's Experiential Immediacy

> A good therapist must create a new therapy with every person they see. Irvin Yalom

Once the existential therapist's presence becomes acknowledged as being in the service of a more open, truthful, clarifying process of worldview investigation, a sufficient degree of trust can be established between client and therapist. This trust is felt in the *experiential immediacy* of the current encounter and is often mutual. Although the client's experience of being with a particular other (the therapist) remains the primary focus for descriptive investigation, it is also the therapist's experience of being with a particular other (the client) that can be addressed and employed as part of that client-focused investigation.

Existential therapy emphasises the experiential immediacy of the client's *conscious* experience. It acknowledges that a great deal of experience remains non-conscious. Equally, it recognises that much of our conscious experience is insufficiently brought to awareness so that it remains largely implicit, peripheral or insufficiently reflected. Nonetheless, existential therapy remains cautious as to the necessity of invoking or working with what is often referred to as *unconscious* material. Some existential therapists retain this latter term in order to express the idea of potential awareness upon which persons cannot, or will not, allow themselves to reflect consciously (May, 1983). Others, as was discussed in the previous chapter, have re-stated the question of the unconscious from the standpoints of worldview dissociation and sedimentation (Spinelli, 1994, 2001; Strasser & Strasser, 1997). In either case, while not denying the human ability to distort, deny or suppress conscious experience, existential therapy seeks to demystify many of the underlying ideas associated with psychoanalytic notions of the unconscious that have been embraced by numerous models of contemporary therapy. Lengthier discussions on this issue can be found in Boss (1963), Condrau (1998) and Spinelli (1994, 2001).

An Exercise Focused on the Therapist's Immediacy

1. How, as a therapist, do you understand and work with your immediacy in the therapeutic encounter?
2. How, if at all, does your way of expressing therapeutic immediacy compare or contrast with an existential perspective?

The Existential Therapist's Dialogical Attitude

In true dialogue, both sides are willing to change. Thich Nhat Hanh

This attention upon the conscious aspects of existence is further reflected in existential therapy's *dialogical attitude*. Martin Buber's notion of *inclusion* addresses significant aspects of this attitude (Buber, 2002), as does the work of the relational analyst Leslie Farber, who was deeply influenced by Buber's ideas. For example, Farber's emphasis on a dialogical attitude was guided by his overarching intent to shift the central enterprise of therapy away from a set of inflexible methodological conditions and to re-focus it towards a *morally derived attitude* expressive of the therapist's attempt to achieve a particular way of being with others. One critical implication of this can be noted in Farber's insistence that the topic (or the 'what-ness') of therapeutic dialogue could be about anything – that is to say, the content of the discussion did not truly matter. Instead, Farber's dialogical concerns centred on *a way of talking* that led both therapist and client toward a truthful dialogue with themselves and one another (Farber, 2000).

This notion of a truthful dialogue parallels the ideas put forward by the phenome-nologist George Gadamer (2004). Gadamer contrasted the truthfulness that emerges via a dialogue that is not pre-set in its focus and intent by any of the participants to one that has been pre-set in its intention or direction by at least one of the par-ticipants. All dialogues, Gadamer acknowledged, have – or more accurately – *find* a direction, but there exists a truthful quality to a dialogue that shapes its own content, direction and focus which cannot be ascertained – or experienced – in a dialogue that is being actively directed toward a certain pre-set goal. One consequence of this, as Gadamer wrote, is that 'the way one word follows another, with the conversation taking its own twists and reaching its own conclusion, may well be conducted in some way, but the partners conversing are far less the leaders than the led. No one knows in advance what will 'come out' of such a conversation' (Gadamer, 2004: 383). Paradoxically, this abdication of control over the directive aspects of dialogue permits a greater sense of its ownership by its participants.

In many ways, the views expressed by Farber and Gadamer concerning dialogue hark back to Martin Heidegger's own injunction to therapists that they focus less on the content of any discussion and more on *the way* content is discussed and expressed (Heidegger, 2001). Heidegger's concern addresses questions regarding whether what is stated is being presented from an owned or dis-owned perspec-tive, such that '[i]dle talk is the possibility of understanding everything without previously making the thing one's own' (Heidegger, 1962: 213). Various existential therapists have tended to interpret Heidegger's statement as a command to avoid therapeutic discourse that is not in some way directly significant to the client's pre-senting issues and concerns but which, rather, takes the form of some sort of gossip, chatter or everyday discourse. For example, they might dismiss the client's state-ments concerning the previous evening's television programme, or a news item, or the weather as some sort of evasive mechanism. I believe that in doing so they have seriously misunderstood Heidegger's point, as Farber makes plain. It does not matter whether the content of the client's discourse is focused on philosophy or on *The Simpsons*. It is *how* such topics are addressed – which is to say, how 'owned' they are as expressions of the client's currently maintained worldview that is the critical factor. In addition, for the existential therapist to take control of the client's subject matter by determining its appropriateness and judging its relevance not only blocks the possibility of dialogue-directed dialogue as suggested by Gadamer, but, more tellingly, contradicts the very method of investigation being espoused.

In related fashion, the therapist's over-emphasis on a discourse that directs the client to the contemplation and assimilation of assumptions and conclusions that express the theoretical aspects of the therapist's preferred approach can also be rec-ognised as an expression of Heidegger's 'idle talk'. Although existential therapists tend to be highly dismissive of any formal technique, it must be acknowledged that attempts to educate clients directly about the Principles and thematic concerns of existential phenomenology is as much a technique as is the assigning of homework or the training of clients to regulate their breathing. Once again, Heidegger made this point clear in his discussions with Medard Boss and his colleagues, alerting them to the fact that existential therapy's attention was not to be placed upon the elucidation of the underpinning Principles of existential phenomenology, but, rather, that its 'way of talking' was consonant with, and reflected, those Principles (Heidegger, 2001).

An Exercise Focused on Therapeutic Dialogue

1. What distinction, if any, do you make between a therapeutic dialogue and a non-therapeutic dialogue?
2. Consider a recent therapeutic dialogue that you have engaged in. What made it so? What would have prevented it from becoming so?

Un-knowing

> To know what you do not know is best. To not know of knowing is a disease.
> Tao Te Ching

As this brief overview discussion has hopefully highlighted, existential therapy is in broad agreement with current evidence-based conclusions regarding the centrality of the therapeutic relationship (Mearns & Cooper, 2005; Norcross, 2002; Norcross & Wampold, 2011). However, many differing expressions of relationship exist. What is existential therapy's 'way'? Although this question will be explored and developed more fully in Part Two, what can be summarised here is perhaps best expressed through what Karl Jaspers called the existential therapist's relational enterprise of *not-knowing* (Jaspers, 1963) and which I have referred to as *un-knowing* (Spinelli, 1997). In either case, the terms express the attempt to remain as open as possible to that which presents itself in the current and ongoing encounter and to treat the seemingly familiar, assumed to be understood or understandable, as novel, unfixed in meaning, and, hence, accessible to previously unexamined experiential possibilities. The attempt to un-know suggests the therapist's willingness to explore the world of the client in a fashion that not only seeks to remain respectful of the client's unique experience of relational being, but also to be receptive to the challenges that this unique way of being creates for the therapist's own biases and assumptions – be they personal or professional or both (Spinelli, 1997). In striving to un-know, existential therapists attempt to accept client values and beliefs that may appear to be either similar or alien or contrary to their own by remaining receptive to their novelty and mystery as expressions of the client's way of being. This shift toward a *phenomenological attitude* of initial openness and naivety requires the therapist to abdicate, at least for the time being, a great deal of that which might, from the standpoint of other therapeutic models and approaches, be taken as the therapist's authority, expertise and interpretative power. Perhaps most significantly, the existential therapist's attempts at un-knowing parallel processes very much akin to the client's ongoing experience of descriptive investigation. The following quote from Dave Mearns and Mick Cooper's recent text *Working at Relational Depth in Counselling and Therapy* (2005) provides a sound parallel means with which to summarise the idea of un-knowing. Arguing against the focus and emphasis given to technique, they write:

> [T]echnique can make it more difficult to meet clients at a level of relational depth ... This is for a number of reasons. First, if we try to implement a technique, our attention is likely to be on what we are doing to our client and its outcome, rather than on the particular human being present to us. In other words, our relationship with the client is no longer im-mediate [sic], but mediated by certain plans and actions. Second, if we relate to our clients through techniques and therapeutic strategies, we are less likely to be open to them as the unique human beings that they are, but will be looking for particular responses and outcomes from them across particular dimensions. And third, the more we are relating to our clients in a technique-based way, the more we lose our own naturalness, spontaneity and uniqueness and start to relate in formulaic and rehearsed ways. This, again, reduces the possibility of an immediate and direct human encounter. (Mearns & Cooper, 2005: 117–18)

An Exercise Focused on Not Knowing/Un-knowing

1. What would be the impact, if any, upon your way of practising therapy if you adopted a stance of 'not knowing' or 'un-knowing'?

Summary of Part One

> Nothing is perfect. Life is messy. Relationships are complex. Outcomes are uncertain. Hugh McKay

From its origins as a philosophical movement, existential phenomenology has provided a radical and at times disturbing view of human existence. Although its ideas confront many pivotal Western beliefs, it is only through one's attempts to engage experientially with these views that their impact upon the 'flesh and blood' of lived existence comes to the fore.

Part One of this text has attempted a brief, and necessarily incomplete, overview of what I suggest are the three essential underpinning Principles of existential phenomenology: relatedness, uncertainty and existential anxiety. Each of these Principles has been examined from the perspective of its significance to, and implications for, any attempt to apply existential phenomenology to therapy. In doing so, Part One has also provided a discussion of several related thematic existence concerns relevant to any general understanding of what it may be both to practise existential therapy and to 'be' an existential therapist.

I have proposed that existential therapy is best understood and practised as a predominantly descriptively focused investigative enterprise rather than a primarily curative one. Further, this enterprise centres upon the elucidation of the client's experience of 'existing in the way that he or she exists' via the inter-relational enterprise of the therapeutic encounter itself. This last aspect of the investigation highlights the presence and role of existential therapists as implicated constituents of the investigation, rather than assuming their detachment from both the act and the consequent meanings derived from the investigation. Equally, it follows that existential therapy does not merely tolerate but, more correctly, values and embraces the diversity of client worldviews as expressed in terms of culture, race, gender and sexual orientation.

Any investigation that is situated within this set of arguments reveals further implications for existential therapy. Not least among them is the recognition that in its complexity and uncertainty the client's experiential world can never be captured in a final or complete fashion. As a consequence, while acknowledging that the therapist's own way of being will always in some manner resonate with and stand revealed through the attempted disclosure of the client's worldview, just what will be disclosed or how this disclosure will occur remains both unknown and uncertain. This realisation can be both liberating and disturbing for the therapist, let alone the client. Under such circumstances, the injunction that it is not *what* you talk about but your *way* of talking that matters becomes particularly relevant for the existential therapist.

Just what this particular way of talking may be provides the *structure* or set of conditions for the therapeutic encounter to which existential therapists aspire. Equally, it provides the basis for all the *practice-based interventions* that the therapist might initiate or offer in response to the client's challenging presence.

In addressing these questions, I have presented views and conclusions that are representative of my own attempts to grapple with, understand, apply and communicate a number of ideas that have led me, in line with a great many other authors and therapists, to declare an allegiance with existential phenomenology and the practice of existential therapy. As well, throughout Part One, I have employed a terminology that makes sense to me, both personally and professionally, but which I recognise may be viewed as alien or inadequate to other authors and practitioners. For example, my distinction between worlding and the worldview, and the related discussion on worldview sedimentations and dissociations of reflective experience are attempts on my part to interpret various pivotal insights of existential phenomenology so that I can communicate as adequately as I can to my self and others both that which has inspired me about, and *the way* I have been inspired by, these insights. Debates will always exist as to the relative adequacy of the terminology chosen and I do not ask that others employ my personally preferred terms. If I have avoided the more commonly employed terminology that the majority of existential therapists prefer to emoloy, I have done so in order to minimise the confusion of meaning that long-accepted nomenclature often contains. Ultimately, it is what terms point us toward rather than the terms in themselves that marks their value.

In similar fashion, unlike many other authors who have sought to provide a way in to both existential phenomenology and existential therapy, I have purposefully avoided extensive summaries of the works and ideas of its principal philosophers and practitioners. I remain aware that this strategy might be interpreted by some as reflective of my philosophical naivety or, worse, of my dismissive arrogance. I am in no position to comment on the former possibility, but as to the latter I can state without qualm my deepest indebtedness to, and respect for, these authors. To any-one who has been the least bit intrigued by what they have read in this text I offer my unhesitant encouragement to initiate their own encounter with them. Rather than seek to denigrate or diminish, I have attempted to explore those underlying Principles that I think provide a unifying strand to the diversity of themes and concerns to be found in the major writings on existential phenomenology and its therapeutic applications. In doing so, my hope has been to provide readers with an encounter focused on how it might be to practise therapy from an existential phenomenological focus rather than to simply read about existential approaches to therapy.

In line with this aim, Part Two offers a structural model concerned with practis-ing existential therapy through which its Principles and its way of working with the thematic concerns of existence can find their expression.

PART TWO
Practising Existential Therapy: A Structural Model

TABLE 6.1

Phase	Therapist	Client	Key focal points

Phase One: co-creating the therapy-world	*The therapist as idiot*: investigative focus is on the clarification of the relationship between the client's presenting problems and his/her worldview as experienced in the therapy-world and contrasted with wider-world worldview experiences	The client hears his/her own voice more accurately and truthfully	Settings
			  contract
			  frame
			Conditions
			  magic feathers
			  placebo effects
			  client's journey
			  greetings
			  initial narrative
			Descriptive attunement
			  being-with/being-for
			  other-focused listening
			  un-knowing
			Descriptive enquiry
			  phenomenological method
			  noematic/noetic challenging
			  strategic questioning
			  body-focused description
			  metaphorical attunement
			  narrational scene-setting
			Indications of shift from Phase One to Two
			Obstacles to shift from Phase One to Two

Phase Two: exploring the therapy-world	*The therapist as fool*: investigative focus is on the clarification of the client's presenting problem as they are being reflected in the encounter with the therapist	The client hears the voice of the other (who is the therapist)	Listening to and challenging the client's narrative through:
			  shifts between particular/general
			  shifts from explicit to implicit
			  therapist's use of self-as-other
			Working with existence polarity tensions
			Exploring the primary structures and core existential concerns of the client's worldview
			Exploring sedimentations and dissociations in the client's worldview

| Phase Three: closing down the therapy-world | *The therapist as executioner:* investigative focus is on the client's new-found relational wider world possibilities | The client hears the voice of the world | Working with the inter-relational realism of encounter
Working with intimacy
therapist disclosures
the present moment in therapy
general and erotic attraction
differences in gender and sexual orientation
the daimonic
dreams
Reconfiguring setting, contract and frame conditions
unexcepted encounters outside the therapy-world
Indications of shift from Phase Two or Three
Obstacles to shift from Phase Two or Three
Working with the They-focus
Possibilities and limitations in bridging
The therapy-world and wider-world
assignments
Endings
gift-giving/receiving
Post-therapeutic relations |

6

A Structural Model for Practising Existential Therapy: An Introduction

Introduction

The structural model being presented is derived from, and is an attempt to explicate, *my own* current way of understanding therapy and working as a therapist from an existential perspective. This perspective emphasises existential phenomenology's key foundational Principles of relatedness, uncertainty and existential anxiety, as have been discussed in Part One. Nonetheless, although these Principles will, I hope, be seen by the reader to underpin all of the specific components of the structure under discussion, I make no apology for the fact that none of them is ever addressed *explicitly* within the context of the therapeutic encounter. In this, I am, I believe, adhering to an important position addressed by Martin Heidegger in the course of his *Zollikon Seminars* with Medard Boss and his psychiatric colleagues. Heidegger states:

> The decisive point is that the particular phenomena, arising in the relationship between the analysis and the analyst, and belonging to the respective, concrete patient, be broached in their own phenomenological content and not simply be classified globally under existentialia. (Heidegger, 2001: 124)

This statement, as I understand it, highlights Heidegger's concern that the practice of existential therapy should refrain from educating the client toward the direct and explicit understanding and acceptance of its Principles. Rather, Heidegger argues, existential therapy's focus lies with a descriptive investigation that is grounded in these Principles and, through which these Principles may reveal themselves 'as belonging to the actual patient' (Cohn, 2002: 83).

In previous chapters, I have employed the terms *worlding* and *worldview* in order to convey the human experience of our existence as the perpetual interplay between process (worlding) and essence (the worldview). The worldview is the outcome of an attempt to essentialise worlding. Its resulting structures, simply because they are structures, cannot express directly *all* of the process-like aspects of worlding. In addition, in order to retain some adequate degree of spatio-temporal stability and continuity, the worldview must both sediment and dissociate worlding-derived experiences of embodied **being**. *The disturbances in living with which we all must contend are consequences of the degree to which the worldview is able to be both consonant and dissonant with worlding. The disorders and dilemmas brought by clients to therapy reveal how the client is currently experiencing this interplay.*

It may be that the client's experience of unease and conflict arises from too great a *dissonance* between worlding and the currently maintained worldview. In such instances, the structures being maintained within the worldview are revealed as being too limiting and rigid in their sedimentations and, in turn, demand ever-increasing dissociations.

But it is also possible that the presenting disorders are expressions of too great a *confluence* between worlding and the worldview. In these instances, the worldview structures are experienced as being too unstable and fragile, and hence inadequate in their ability to sustain the worldview against insecurity-provoking challenges to its continuity, dispositions and identity.

Both possibilities may generate concerns and conflicts that are expressed in superficially similar ways. For instance, presenting statements such as 'I feel so lifeless and empty', or 'My partner says that she doesn't know who I am anymore', or 'If a god can allow these terrible things to happen, then I can't believe in a god any longer' can be expressions of either too great a dissonance or consonance between worlding and the worldview. Obviously, it is therapeutically vital to address the issues from the focus through which the client experiences them.

In order to minimise the likelihood of assuming an inappropriate focus, existential therapy attempts a descriptive clarification of the client's presenting issues in relation to that client's overall worldview. In doing so, it assumes that this exploration will expose in microcosm the client's wider, macrocosmic relational dissonances and consonances between worlding and the worldview. Further, existential therapy argues that this descriptively focused investigation is, in itself, a significant challenge to the client's currently maintained worldview. In short, existential therapy asserts that, rather than being seen to be the preliminary basis to any experience of change, or as an initial step that will set into place the conditions for change, *description in and of itself provokes change*. Thus, existential therapy denies the necessity of an explanatory clarification to the client of his or her presenting concerns for beneficial and lasting change to occur.

Precisely *how* existential therapy's descriptive focus elicits noticeable and beneficial shifts in the client's experience of being remains, at present, largely unknown. In this, it is no different from all other contemporary therapeutic approaches. There exists a good deal of firm, well-established evidence *that* therapy in general is most often beneficially effective (Cooper, 2008; Duncan, Miller, Wampold & Hubble, 2010). *Why* any particular therapy or therapies in general are effective remains a largely unanswered question (Norcross & Wampold, 2011). Far more than techniques employed in specific models, common and extra-therapeutic factors such as social support, expectancy effects, as well as the therapeutic relationship itself, have been identified as the major, pivotal, variables consistent with therapeutic effectiveness (Duncan et al., 2010). However, explanations as to what it is about these factors that make them so pivotal in generating beneficial outcomes are not easily forthcoming.

The structural model being presented addresses these various factors in a particular way. It proposes that the client and existential therapist enter into, and engage with each other within, a *therapy-world,* which can be compared and contrasted to the extra-therapeutic or *wider-world* that both client and existential therapist inhabit. From this perspective, the non-specific and relational factors identified by researchers as being among the principal determinants of therapeutic effectiveness emerge from the distinct spatio-temporal and relational boundaries and conditions set by the therapy-world.

Three Phases of Existential Therapy

The structural model of existential therapy that is being proposed demarcates a sequence of identifiable shifts or movements in the encounter between therapist and client that can be most simply expressed in terms of three distinct phases.

Phase One is largely concerned with the co-creation by the existential therapist and client of a therapy-world. This includes making explicit and respecting the boundaries, frame and inter-relational conditions that set its parameters. By so doing, Phase One permits the initiation of an open and truthful descriptive exploration of the parameters of, and explicit tensions in, the client's worldview as experienced relationally within the therapy-world. What is clarified through this exploration can, in turn, be compared with and contrasted to the client's wider-world relations.

Phase Two mainly focuses upon the descriptive investigation of the client's inter-relational experience of co-habiting this therapy-world together with the existential therapist. Often, this can be an intensely felt experience. As well as permit the investigation of the client's worldview as it presents itself in the therapy-world, Phase Two seeks to clarify the implicit or covert existential insecurities that maintain the explicit or overt tensions and disturbances being presented by the client within the experiential immediacy of the therapeutic encounter.

Phase Three puts into practice the possibilities of reconfiguring the client's experience of inhabiting his or her wider-world through the experiential alternatives provoked by the therapy-world. It focuses on the exploration of the possibilities and limitations in the client's attempts at *bridging* his or her therapy-world experience with that of living in the wider-world. By doing so, Phase Three also provides the means by which the temporary therapy-world is closed down and the therapeutic encounter concluded.

However useful it may be to identify and consider the proposed structural model from the focus of these three phases, it must be stressed that this is not intended to suggest a step-by-step, or 'one-two-three' rigid formulation of process. While a phase-focus holds substantial explanatory and instructive value for those wishing either to develop their practising of existential therapy or, equally, for those wishing to clarify, compare and contrast its practice to that of other therapeutic models and systems, nonetheless it cannot hope to express in full the dynamic experience of engaging in existential therapy. As with the worldview's necessarily incomplete affinity with worlding, this phase-focus reflects a truthful attempt to express existential therapy from a structural perspective. In the course of an actual therapeutic encounter, the phases' co-presence is far more 'fuzzy' in that some aspect or influence of all three will likely be present in every instance of encounter.

Existential Therapy: Inter-relational Implications

I have argued that existential therapy offers a descriptively attuned investigation centred upon questions of dissonance and consonance between worlding and the worldview. While the directed focus of this descriptive investigation is on the client, existential therapy recognises that, in entering the therapy-world, and engaging with the client within its confines and conditions, the therapist, too, is neither absent from, nor immune to, the impact of relational encounter. The strength, significance, direction and lasting effects of therapy-world encounters upon either or both participants cannot be predetermined.

In keeping with the implications of the three key Principles of existential phenomenology, as discussed in Part One, any calibration between the client's worlding and worldview, whether towards greater consonance or dissonance, will also impact upon the therapist. From their shared grounding of relatedness, every aspect of their encounter influences the interweaving between their own and one another's worlding and worldview experiences in ways that cannot be predetermined. From this standpoint, existential therapy reveals itself to be a relationally uncertain, anxiously experienced enterprise for therapist and client alike. Both experience alternate worlding/worldview possibilities that may be temporary or of lasting consequence and whose experiential reality may be restricted to the boundaries of the therapy-world or which may extend beyond them. *Whatever the case, as with all encounters, the encounter between therapist and client generates a worlding-derived, wave-like 'ripple effect' whose course runs through the embodied experience of both participants and flows across their wider-world relations so that its ultimate influence, whether subtle or obvious, leaves its trace upon all existence.*

7

Phase One: Co-creating the Therapy-world

Basic Structural Preconditions

Setting the Conditions for a Therapy-world

The *therapeutic contract* is typically concerned with the explication of statements and rules regarding the length, frequency and overall duration of therapy sessions; their location; financial arrangements; rules of behaviour; and so forth. The contract may be quite extensive or relatively brief, either written (and sometimes co-signed) or verbal (although, increasingly, professional bodies either encourage or require written documents). Taken together, the issues regarding settings and the contract can be viewed as the primary constituents for the establishment and maintenance of what other approaches in contemporary therapy refer to as a *secure frame* (Luca, 2004).

To a large extent, many of the commonly shared assumptions about contractual and frame conditions of therapeutic practice can be seen to have been derived from the stipulations originally set by psychoanalysis. Historically, psychoanalysis is acknowledged to be the earliest model of therapy that continues to be practised in the twenty-first century (Ellenberger, 1970). It appears to be the case that regardless of the concerns and critiques of psychoanalysis raised by competing contemporary approaches, the vast majority have adopted and adapted a good deal of the psychoanalytic structure. Although there is nothing inherently problematic about this, it reveals a certain degree of unquestioning adherence to a stance that, while entirely coherent and consistent within psychoanalytic Principles, may not make too much sense within the Principles espoused by alternative models. Nonetheless, detailed questioning of these shared assumptions by either therapists or their professional bodies remains a rarity.

From the perspective of existential therapy, so long as the contractual and frame settings remain within appropriate ethical guidelines and standards of practice set by professional bodies, there exists no generally specified set of conditions linked to its foundational Principles that provides a guideline for practice. For instance, the room in which therapeutic encounters occur would usually be the therapist's, but it might also be part of the client's living or work space, or different rooms and different locations might be set for meetings, or meetings might not take place within the confined space of a room but rather occur via telephones, Skype and in 'virtual' space. In similar fashion, the length and frequency of meetings, and whether they are open-ended, time-limited or a one-off event has no inbuilt fixedness. Of course, it remains the case that most existential therapists continue to follow 'therapeutic tradition' when it comes to such matters, if for no other reason than that of convenience as well as, increasingly, professional body expectation. But what is critical here is the awareness that alternatives *are* possible. Even if existential therapists wished to be guided by research findings dealing with such issues, they would be hard pressed to find any evidence either of beneficial consequences arising from the adherence to the more generally accepted assumptions or of the negative impact of alternative stances (Cooper, 2008; Duncan et al., 2010; Madison, 2002; Norcross & Wampold, 2011). As such, it would seem to me to make sense that, when considering the therapeutic contract from the standpoint of existential therapy, what is essential is that *whatever* the contractual conditions, and *however* these were derived, they are explicit, understood and agreed to by both therapist and client.

An Exercise Exploring Therapeutic Settings

1. As your point of focus, imagine that you, as an existential therapist, are at the very start of your very first session with a client.
2. Ask your self the following questions and note down your responses to them:

   o What preparations, if any, did I make as a preliminary to this session? Are they preparations I always make before the start of all sessions? What would it be like for me if I didn't or couldn't make these preparations before a session?
   o In what ways is this therapeutic encounter likely to be similar to other relationships in my life?
   o In what ways is it likely to be dissimilar?
   o What is attractive/exciting/fulfilling about being the therapist in the therapeutic encounter?
   o What is limiting/frustrating/infuriating about being the therapist in the therapeutic encounter?
   o What do I like about my self being the therapist in the therapeutic encounter?
   o What would I want to change about my self being the therapist in the therapeutic encounter?
   o What do I want my client to note and appreciate about me being the therapist in this therapeutic encounter?
   o What would I not want my client to know about me being the therapist in this therapeutic encounter?

The Therapy-world

The importance of the above discussion, as I see it, is that the conditions that are set and agreed to by therapist and client create the basic frame or boundary conditions of a distinctly experienced *therapy-world* which can be compared and contrasted to the extra-therapeutic *wider-world* that both therapist and client inhabit. The structural model being presented proposes that the very entry into, and exploration of how it is to exist within, the therapy-world permits the client to entertain and try out experiential possibilities that provide a means by which his or her worldview is temporarily reconfigured within the therapy-world boundaries. The extent to which this exploration can occur is, in part, dependent upon the contractual agreements that set the structural and relational conditions of the therapy-world.

As I have argued in Part One, existential therapy attempts to provide the means whereby clients can calibrate the consonance and dissonance between their maintained worldview and their experience of worlding. Although precisely *how* this adjustment occurs remains largely unknown, research evidence on the effectiveness of therapy in general has emphasised the overwhelming importance of both non-specific factors and the therapeutic relationship itself (Norcross & Wampold, 2011). What I am suggesting is that this evidence is consonant with the therapeutic objectives of the structural model being presented, namely that via the co-creation of a sufficiently distinctive therapy-world, the various similarities and differences between the client's therapy-world and wider-world worldviews can be opened to descriptively focused enquiry. In doing so, the client's presenting issues of disturbance and disorder can be explored within these worldview contexts and potentially reconfigured in ways that the client experiences as being beneficial.

Considered in this way, the importance of frame and contractual conditions for existential therapy should become more apparent. The contract sets the foundational boundaries – including those of its spatial and temporal setting – that permit the entry-point into the therapy-world that is being co-created. Whatever is contained in the contract, and how brief or detailed its specifically stipulated contractual conditions may be, are variables which, in themselves, are of far less significance than is their ability to convince the participants that they have entered and are temporarily co-habiting a distinct therapy-world.

Although largely co-created by the therapist and client, some of the stipulated conditions are likely to be non-negotiably imposed by the therapist. For instance, the therapist might insist that no extra-therapeutic contact is permissible or that the client must pay for missed sessions regardless of the circumstances that forced a cancellation. Such conditions might well strike the client as being unreasonable or undesirable. Nonetheless, what matters is that, together with the therapist, the client understands and agrees to the rules being set. In this, the therapy-world, like the wider-world, reveals itself as not always comprehensible with regard to the meaning and purpose behind its rules, nor is it always in agreement with personal views, preferences, desires and predispositions. Rather, the pivotal difference that the therapy-world can demonstrate is that at least one of its inhabitants – the therapist – remains consistent in honouring *all* of the explicitly agreed-upon conditions and who is, therefore, trustworthy 'as one who says what he or she means and does what he or she says'.

This effort should not be misunderstood as an attempt to exclude anxiety as a constituent of the therapy-world. Indeed, in many ways, the clarification of, and adherence to, the conditions of the therapy-world may well aggravate the client's experience of anxiety rather than diminish it. Critics of therapy have highlighted the artificiality of the therapy-world precisely because it seeks to avoid the chaos and confusion of the wider-world, wherein rules and agreements are repeatedly broken or opened to re-interpretation by any one inhabitant without any communication, much less negotiation, with any other. In response to this, I would suggest that although it may make sense to argue that the attempt to adhere to the contract-derived rules of the therapy-world is in various ways *different,* this is not sufficient reason to judge it as being artificial. Further, while critics have rightly pointed to the abundant evidence of some therapists' lack of adherence to their own set contractual rules and the serious consequences for their clients that the various forms of contract deviation have provoked, this undesirable state of affairs demonstrates that, if anything, the experience of inhabiting the therapy-world is hardly artificial (Alexander, 1995; Bates, 2004; Sands, 2000). Indeed, it is not unusual to come across statements by clients and therapists alike that their inhabiting and relating within the therapy-world provokes a deeply felt sense of 'being real' that can be contrasted with more common wider-world experiences (Gordon, 2000; Kirschenbaum & Henderson, 1990).

An Exercise Exploring the Significance of the Contract

1. From the standpoint of your 'being a therapist' what contractually is essential for you?
2. From the standpoint of your 'being a client' what contractually is essential for you?
3. What is or was made explicit in the contract with your own therapist?
4. Is there or was there anything implicit in your therapeutic contract that should have been made explicit?
5. How was your therapeutic contract communicated to you? Was there any discussion or negotiation regarding any of its stipulations?
6. Have you, as a therapist, ever deviated from your contract? If so, how did you alone or you and your client experience this deviation?
7. Have you, as a client, ever experienced your therapist deviating from the contract? If so, how did you alone or you and your therapist experience this deviation?

(Continued)

(Continued)

8. Following the discussion on the contract and what has emerged from doing the exercise so far, what views do you now hold with regard to the therapeutic contract?
9. Write out your version of a contract and present it to a colleague for discussion.

An Exercise Exploring the Therapy-world

1. Together with a partner, explore the idea of a therapy-world as it has been presented above. How, if at all, does it assist you in clarifying the importance of contractual and frame conditions? How, if at all, does it assist you in clarifying the existing evidence focused on the importance of the therapeutic relationship as well as general non-specific factors as determinants of beneficial outcomes?

The Dumbo Effect

As has been argued above, existential therapy offers the possibility of a far more flexible range of setting conditions that is worth acknowledging and considering – particularly if the therapist is principally working in the public arena where practical issues of spatial and temporal settings are of constant concern to units and their managers. However, it would seem to be the case that many existential therapists continue to practise from a more traditional set of conditions. Habit and convenience provide possible answers as to why they choose to. Let us consider another by exploring what I have somewhat facetiously termed *the Dumbo Effect* (Spinelli, 1994, 2001).

Anyone who has seen the Disney cartoon *Dumbo* (Disney, 1941) will recall that Dumbo the elephant is able to fly because he has convinced himself that he possesses a magic feather that grants him this ability. At first, Dumbo believes in the power and significance of the feather as the sole cause of his new-found ability and, as well, of his self-esteem. The loss of the magic feather during a critical sky-diving performance initially leads to Dumbo's panic. However, much to his astonishment, he discovers that he can still fly and, with that, the magic feather is recognised as possessing nothing that is inherently necessary or magical.

I would argue that therapists' reliance upon a particular and rigid pattern of contractual and frame related settings serves the same function as Dumbo's magic feather in that while such patterns have no special or magical qualities in themselves, it is therapists' *belief* in them as essential factors in their ability to 'be' a therapist and to 'practise therapy' that makes them significant. In addition, it may be the case that clients, too, hold values and beliefs about 'being a client' and experiencing the benefits of therapy that rely upon the Dumbo Effect as expressed through issues of setting, frame and contract. Indeed, as the evidence for the pivotal importance of non-specific factors in determining the effectiveness of therapy highlights (Duncan et al., 2010), there may be very little in, or about, the practice of therapy as a whole that is *not* a Dumbo Effect. This conclusion is not intended to suggest that, therefore, 'magic feathers' are unnecessary or even potentially problematic. However, what may be a challenge to existential therapists in particular is to question their reliance upon certain magic feathers to the extent that they may no longer consider them to be magic feathers at all, and instead have come to view them as rigid sedimentations that, in turn, rest upon unnoticed dissociations in their worldview definitions of 'who they are being when they are being existential therapists' and 'what they are doing when they are practising existential therapy'.

For existential therapists, the challenge being put forward is twofold. First, to attempt to clarify what magic feathers they require with regard to the overall contractual and frame-related setting issues necessary to the practice of therapy. Second, to challenge the necessity of those requirements. As the whole thrust of the existential enterprise is directed toward disclosing the structure-bound patterns of the client's worldview, it would follow that for the existential therapist it becomes particularly relevant to make clearer to him or her self what current magic feathers can be identified and, once identified, to consider the challenge of no longer requiring them. I doubt that any complete or final ridding oneself of the reliance upon *all* magic feathers is either possible or necessarily desirable. But the attempt to pursue such investigations with the aim of arriving at a more adequate worldview stance toward them would be in keeping with the existential enterprise.

An Exercise Exploring the Therapist's Reliance upon 'Magic Feathers'

1. Clarify what conditional 'magic feathers' you require with regard to questions of contractual and frame settings for the practice of therapy.
2. Challenge each of those requirements by considering: (a) what makes them necessary for you; (b) what would be the effect of and consequences to your ability to 'be' a therapist and to 'practise therapy' if each ceased to be a requirement.
3. Consider how the idea of a Dumbo Effect might serve to reveal the flexibility or lack of flexibility that you permit in your general assumptions about, and definitions of, therapy.
4. Together with a partner who has also carried out the same exercise, discuss your responses to these questions. How do you each react to the other's identified magic feathers? What, if anything, might they clarify for you about the Dumbo Effect?

Therapeutic Settings Issues Considered from the Perspective of Theatre

It is by no means a novel idea to suggest intriguing correspondences between therapy and theatre (Røine, 1997). For instance, one might ask: 'What are the preconditions that alert and prepare us for a theatrical experience?' In response, one might take a traditional position and argue that a theatrical event must take place within the confines of an enclosed space, perhaps include a stage that demarcates the actors from their audience, as well as being bounded by a specified time-frame, and so forth. Radical forms of contemporary theatre challenge such fixed assumptions by, for instance, removing the spatial barriers between audience and actors so that the space between them is fluid or uncertain, or by obscuring all clues as to when the play has begun or ended. The notion of 'suspension of belief' is usually presented as a necessary constituent in order to engage with a theatrical event. I would suggest that rather than beliefs being suspended, it is more a case of the co-creation, between performers and audience, of a unique and temporary 'theatre-world', entry to which is gained via the various agreed-upon settings and conditions which, taken as whole, serve as 'magic feathers' to all participants.

In this sense, therapy is akin to a theatrical event in that each requires the co-creation of a temporary 'world' – be it the therapy-world or theatre-world – which in various ways provokes participants to experience who and how it is to be within, rather than outside, it. Considered from this perspective, the value of magic feathers lies in their ability to create the magical conditions and constituents necessary for the co-creation of a distinct world within which all participants experience novel worldview possibilities.

An Exercise Exploring Therapy as Theatre

1. Explore how you, as therapist, create 'theatrical' conditions for therapy. For instance, what preparations do you make with regard to the room you use as well as its furniture and furnishings? How might these parallel the openness and boundaries between a theatrical stage and its audience?
2. How do you create your therapeutic 'character'? Do you, for example, wear particular clothing as your 'costume'? Do you adopt a particular stance or way of moving and sitting? Do you adopt a 'therapeutic voice' or way of speaking?
3. With such questions in mind, together with a partner, explore what correspondences, if any, exist between therapy and theatre both in general and in your own particular practising of therapy.

Therapy as Placebo

Contemporary medical researchers who have examined and studied the placebo effect have identified three key factors necessary to its success. The first of these centres upon the patient's *expectations* of the treatment – which is to say, the patient's belief in the potential effectiveness of the cure. The second factor emphasises the *relationship* between patient and care-provider in that it has been found that positive rapport between the two generates the patient's positive enthusiasm for treatment, which in turn generates positive outcomes. The third factor highlights the significance of a variety of *inter-relationally focused dispositional attitudes or qualities* that are ascribed by patients to their care-providers. These include the patient's perception of the care-provider's friendliness, interest in the patient and sympathy with regard to the uncertainty and suffering being provoked by the illness as well as the patient's evaluation of the care-provider's authority, know-how and prestige (Miller & Kaptchuk, 2008; Moerman & Jonas, 2002). These identified factors resonate closely with current research findings concerned with critical non-specific factors in clients' experiences of beneficial therapeutic outcomes (Duncan et al., 2010; Norcross & Wampold, 2011; Sherwood, 2001).

In addition, Daniel Moerman and Wayne Jones have argued that it is not the actual placebo 'object' itself, be it a pill or a specific physical manipulation, that provokes beneficial outcomes. Rather, it is the *meaning* with which such objects or actions have been ascribed that is the critical variable in determining its effectiveness. They write:

> Insofar as medicine is meaningful, it can affect patients, and it can affect the outcome of treatment. Most elements of medicine are meaningful, even if practitioners do not intend them to be so. The physician's costume (the white coat with stethoscope hanging out of the pocket), manner (enthusiastic or not), style ... and language are all meaningful and can be shown to affect the outcome .... (Moerman & Jones, 2002: 473)

However, in emphasising the question of meaning, an obvious conundrum arises: eliciting the placebo's meaning response appears to require remarkably little effort. Then why don't placebos work *all* of the time? An intriguing reply to this question has been put forward by the British psychologist Nicholas Humphrey, who has suggested that it is only when *another* who has been bestowed with some sort of authority – however illusory – provides the placebo constituents (for example, by prescribing a pill or performing a ritual) that the placebo 'works' (Humphrey, 2002). What this suggests is that successful placebo effects involve an interaction between persons. As such, the beliefs being engendered are of a particular *kind* or express a specific *way of believing or meaning-making*.

In an important article appearing in the *Journal of the Royal Society of Medicine*, its authors, Franklin Miller and Ted Kaptchuk, propose that a more accurate term for the placebo effect is that of *contextual healing*. Contextual healing refers to 'that aspect of healing that is produced, activated or enhanced by the *context* of the clinical encounter, as distinct from the specific efficacy of treatment interventions' (Miller & Kaptchuk, 2008: 224; emphasis in the original). Factors that play a role in contextual healing include the environment of the clinical setting, the cognitive and affective communications of clinicians, and the ritual of administering treatment (ibid.). Crucial examples of contextual variables include the self- and mutual labelling of doctor and patient; the gestures, communications and shared feedback the participants give one another; and the nature and quality of the relationship they are in. In addition, a variety of equally significant, though often overlooked, contextual factors exist: the look, lighting, and overall 'sensory feel' of the consulting room as well as the subtle cues surrounding the space as a whole (for example, the wall notices, information leaflets, and so forth) which, taken together, suggest that something particular, serious and important takes place in the specified location. Together, these variables act as critical contextual factors in the meaningful narrative that the patient and the healing-provider co-construct. This context is loaded and charged and often of momentous importance to patients and providers who together co-create a *healing drama* which acts to enhance the belief that this dramatic process will have beneficial effects upon the patient (ibid.).

Not surprisingly, it has been proposed that therapy *as a whole* can be best understood as a placebo effect (Evans, 2003). Such pronouncements are often read by therapists as critical statements if not outright attacks upon the profession. Nonetheless, as the brief summary provided on current medical research on placebos should make clear, the notion of the placebo is in many ways far more intriguing than it is threatening to therapists. For example, these new perspectives help to clarify the significance of non-specific factors in therapy by bringing in a much more subtle and extensive understanding of these factors as expressions of a particular *kind* of belief or *way of believing or meaning-making* that is centred upon the interaction between persons. This inter-relational focus highlights the power of context and content *that is jointly shared and which mutually affects both client and therapist alike.* In other words, it may be the case that the degree of efficacy of placebo-like phenomena rests on the effect to which *both* participants – the client/ patient and the therapist/medic – believe in who they are and what they do within a particular context, be it a hospital setting or a therapy room.

An Exercise Exploring Therapy as Placebo

1. Review the brief summary on placebo effects in medicine as provided above. In what ways might these same effects be seen to occur in therapy?
2. If non-specific factors in therapy outcomes were to be reconsidered as placebo effects, how would this impact upon how you define therapy and understand its practice?
3. Consider therapy as an expression of 'contextual healing'. How, if at all, might this help to understand the importance of therapists' 'magic feathers'?

Entering the Therapy-world

The Client's Journey to the Therapist

Perhaps surprisingly, it is unusual for therapists to pay much attention to the journey conditions negotiated by the client that enable him or her to appear at the
entrance to the therapist's consulting room. Such issues ask us to consider the
question: 'How did the client get to me?' As can be surmised, this question concerns itself not only with matters of geography and travel but also with the broader
issues of initial pre-therapeutic contact.

For those existential therapists who work privately, the issues here highlight
such matters as whether the client selected you on the basis of geographical
convenience or through some sort of personal recommendation or reference (for
instance by a colleague, or possibly one of your ex- or even current clients), or
whether your name and details were found in a professional register or on the
web. For those existential therapists working in the public sector, perhaps in a
hospital or educational setting or as part of a GP practice, the working-out of
the referred client's route to you, perhaps through a GP, a Psychological Unit, an
Assessment Process or some other information-based system could prove to be
of substantial value.

Whatever the conditions, I would argue that it would be worth having a
clear sense of the actual journey that the client makes to get from his or her
residence or work-place to your consulting room and then back to it once the
session is finished. This exploration could highlight how that journey is negotiated, for instance whether by car, public transport, or walking, and how long
this journey typically lasts. Further, such investigation might well consider the
physical and social environment through which the client's journey takes him
or her. Are there, for instance, any noticeable difficulties or dangers or tempting
locales for the client to fix upon? For example, if the client's issues have to do
with alcohol abuse, does the journey confront the client with numerous pubs
or wine bars?

Related factors dealing with the client's journey would include *the means* by
which first contact was made. Was it by telephone, letter, email or text message?
Was the contact directly with the therapist or indirectly through a GP or agency
or some other intermediary? And, equally, what was actually stated or agreed to by
the end of that first contact? If it was a direct contact, what was the therapist's felt
sense of that contact? Was that felt sense subsequently communicated to the client
or kept to one self?

Why should such matters merit so much attention? From an existential perspective, the way that the client progresses through the various steps to the start
of a session may offer valuable clues as to the client's presenting stance, attitude,
concerns and expectations regarding the process and outcome of the therapy,
either in terms of a particular session or with regard to the therapeutic encounter
as a whole. These instances of 'journeying' can serve as possible expressions of

the client's initial steps leading to his or her entry into the therapy-world. In like fashion, they might be significant indicators of the client's *way into* the particular worldview that arises within the therapy-world.

For example, one of my clients, Robert, always mentioned to me at the start of our sessions how he valued and enjoyed his journey through Regent's Park to my office. He stated that it was important to him to have a few minutes of relative isolation, walking down paths where he could avoid being seen by, and having to negotiate his way through, the large number of people who might get in his way. One day, some months into our weekly meetings, Robert arrived and immediately announced that he had altered his journey. He had begun his usual route but had suddenly felt angry about his need to escape the presence of others. Now, Robert stated, the lonely path he had been taking no longer filled him with pleasure and peace, and instead served to remind him of his perpetual loneliness. Instead, he had decided to follow the most populous route and, rather than avoid the presence and gaze of others, he had allowed him self to make passing eye contact with several passers-by. Not surprisingly, this shift in his journey to me paralleled a broader shift in Robert's relations with others as a whole.

An Exercise Focused on the Client's Journey to the Therapist

1. Think of a client with whom you are currently in a therapeutic relationship.
2. Detail descriptively what you know of the journey that this client must make to and from your consulting room. What environmental landmarks might the client pass through? How direct is the client's journey? How long is it likely to take?
3. What are the final negotiations that the client must make in order to reach the door to your consulting room? For example, does the client have to speak to a Receptionist or a Personal Assistant? Or talk through an intercom? Does the client come directly to you or do you take preparatory steps to meet the client?
4. Consider what has emerged through your focus on Points 1–3 that might be of relevance both to your client's presenting issues and to your attunement with the client during your sessions. If any aspects of Points 1–3 have altered during the course of your therapeutic relationship do you have any sense of a resonance between these alterations and more general shifts in the client's worldview?
5. Consider the journey that you take (or used to take) to and from your own therapist. In doing the exercise from your own experience of being a client do you note any significant factors or resonances between that journey and the wider issues and concerns explored in your own experience of being in therapy as a client?

The Initial Meeting: Greeting the Client

In my discussions with other therapists, I have always found it somewhat odd how certain some colleagues appear to be concerning the rules of greeting the client either with regard to the first session or for all sessions. Some will remain silent and refuse to reply to the client's everyday questions such as 'How are you?' or to comments concerned with weather or climate or newsworthy events. Others might respond to such queries and comments only until the consulting room door has been shut and both participants are seated. Very few, it seems, just engage with their clients as one might under more ordinary circumstances. When asked about this stance, the majority of existential therapists with whom I have spoken will refer to their unwillingness to engage in 'idle chit-chat' and may even refer to Heidegger as the source for their stance. As discussed in Part One, my own view is that this attitude misinterprets Heidegger's concerns. At the same time, as has also been discussed above, I am ready to concede that this form of initial greeting may be a necessary magic feather for any number of existential therapists.

Nonetheless, the question of the initial meeting captures once again the possible divergences between an existential approach and other approaches in general, especially those primarily influenced by psychoanalysis. In the latter, various directives are urged upon practitioners about such questions as whether to greet the client and, if so, how this might be done in an appropriately professional manner (Smith, 1991). While there is every reason for the therapist to remain appropriately respectful of, and professional toward, the client, nonetheless no formal initial greeting code exists or appears to be necessary within existential therapy. Without wishing to denigrate the views of other approaches, it remains arguable that such rigid codes of conduct may serve no purpose or function in themselves other than to act, once again, as magic feathers for the therapist. Hence, from an existential perspective, there is no reason to suppose that initial greetings in the therapeutic relationship need in any way be different to, or distinct from, initial greetings that might occur in *any* professional setting. In like fashion, how varied these may be in terms of physical movement such as a handshake or verbal utterances would appear to be no more or less than in any other set of similar circumstances.

Whatever is the case, what might be of importance for the existential therapist in such an initial meeting is to monitor and note how he or she responds in terms of greeting style to the client's presence and, in turn, what stance the client adopts in his or her initial encounter with the therapist. Rather than evaluate the relative appropriateness of the way of greeting that has occurred, nor to judge it in relation to other, once-possible, ways of greeting that might have taken place, initial greetings can be seen to be the means by which both the existential therapist and the client *together agree to enter the therapy-world*. Equally, the way in which the client both enacts and responds to greeting may already reveal a stance that is relationally distinct from that of his or her wider-world ways of greeting.

Many of these points are equally applicable to matters related to the *ending* of a session. In general, just as *how* initial greetings and session endings are enacted may raise worthwhile questions for the therapist. Such questions can be extended to include the investigation of the therapist's way of greeting and sessional ending throughout the whole of the therapeutic encounter.

An Exercise Focused Upon the Question of the Initial Greeting

1. Consider your way of greeting your clients at the start of the initial session with them. Is your way of greeting consistent or does it vary from client to client or from session to session?
2. Is this way of greeting typical of your way of greeting someone for the first time in other circumstances?
3. If it is atypical of your way of greeting another, what makes it so?
4. Does this atypical stance seek to express something regarding 'how I am to be with this client and how I am expecting this client to be with me'? If so, what is that?
5. What do you note to your self about your client's way of greeting you? Do you evaluate it in any way? Does it provoke any particular attitude or emotion or behavioural response in you?
6. What was your therapist's initial way of greeting you? How did you experience it? Did it have any impact on the therapeutic relationship as a whole and over time?
7. Repeat the exercise but this time focus your exploration on your way of ending a session.

The Initial Meeting: The Client's Opening Narratives

A significant area of concern to most therapists and closely related to the issue of the initial greeting is the question: Who should initiate any verbal discourse in the encounter?

Once again, for those therapists who are mainly influenced by psychoanalytic tradition, there is a common assumption that, other than the most perfunctory of greeting (such as 'Hello', 'Please sit down'), it is most appropriate for the client to initiate verbal discourse. Something very similar to this stance is adopted by a great many existential therapists, though why they should do so, other than because it serves as another necessary magic feather, remains something of a mystery to me not least because it suggests a shift away from any acknowledgement of the existential therapist's co-active presence. In recognising this, the therapist can neither exclude his or her presence from this process nor is he or she bound to a particular way of being present within the confines of a professional encounter. Therefore, the question of who should be the first to speak cannot be so easily answered. What rules there may be remain uncertain and insecure – just as they are when faced with 'the how' of initiating any spoken encounter. Each participant acts from an uncertain and uneasy space. Perhaps one or the other will speak first. Perhaps both will begin to speak at the same time. Perhaps each will refrain from speaking or have no idea what to say for some indeterminate period of time. Perhaps the client will feel hurt or irritated or unheard if the therapist begins to speak first. Perhaps the therapist may speak up because the client appears to be lost or confused or miserable. Just as, possibly, the therapist may refrain from speaking because the client appears to be lost or confused or miserable. In short: *both therapist and client are faced with the relational uncertainty of their encounter and the existential anxiety it brings forth.*

The argument being presented here is one that neither promotes a set of rules nor, in contrast, celebrates unbridled spontaneity on the part of the existential therapist. Both are potentially valid, just as both create limitations and possibilities in their enactment. Once again, from the existential therapist's standpoint what is being urged is a non-judgemental monitoring of his or her own attitude and behaviour from the context and circumstances of being with a particular client at a specific moment in time. That the therapist may vary his or her attitude and stance toward the question of who speaks first, from client to client or from session to session, seems to be no different than what may happen in any other set of circumstances surrounding the experience of two people meeting and greeting one another either for the first time or on separate occasions under conditions that are bounded by moral and professional codes of conduct. In adopting this stance, existential therapy permits a degree of choice and freedom for the therapist that may not be as available within the dictates of other contemporary approaches.

Whoever it may be who begins the dialogue between therapist and client, what remains of evident importance is *how* what is said is communicated in terms of such factors as the various expressions of emphasis and nuance accompanying them. The ways in which clients' initial statements are expressed often provide an early insight as to how the client has chosen to present him or her self to the existential therapist. Further, they are likely to contain indications of what is wanted of the therapist and what the client's attitude and stance toward self and other being in relation is likely to be. Just as importantly, clients' initial statements can serve to reveal their earliest assumptions about the specific and particular therapy-world that is being co-created, not least in terms of the beliefs and expectations being placed upon it and how its inhabitants are expected to interact and relate with one another within it.

What is critical for the existential therapist is that the client's initial statements are *always* to be treated as valid and appropriate, no matter what they express, or fail to express, as well as what views, attitudes and assumptions they may contain. At first, this may be a difficult stance for the therapist to adopt, especially when the client's statements reveal assumptions or views that directly challenge the therapist's, either in general (e.g.: 'You're the last person left who can help me'), or in terms of a particular factor (e.g.: 'Did you watch *EastEnders* last night?'). This stance can be equally difficult to embrace if the client's statements are excessively self-critical (e.g.: 'I'm always going to be a loser!'), or critical of the therapist (e.g.: 'You weren't my first choice by any stretch of the imagination'), or express views and stances that strike the therapist as being patently incorrect or absurd (e.g.: 'Every Western film being made these days has subliminal anti-Muslim messages in it').

The attempt on the part of the therapist to stay with the client's initial statements is by no means an abdication of challenge. Rather, this stance *permits* a powerful form of challenge which the client is likely to recognise immediately. Here in the therapy-world that is being co-created, the client's first experience of the other (that is to say, the existential therapist) is that of an other who does not immediately set out to transform, reject, dispute, diminish or broadly overwhelm the client's worldview so that it more closely conforms to that other's preferences and expectations. In my view, the inter-relational significance of such a challenge has been insufficiently considered and addressed by existential therapy in general. In brief, this response on the part of the therapist serves to highlight the possible contrast between the client's experience of the other in the therapy-world and that of the wider-world. This is not to suggest that the client may immediately value and prize such possibilities as are being expressed and presented in the therapy-world. On the contrary, the client may well experience disturbance, resentment and anger toward the therapist for not conforming to his or her worldview expectations and assumptions regarding others. Whatever the case, once again, it is vital for the existential therapist to treat clients' responses as being valid and appropriate and thereby maintain the challenge. As a general aid for existential therapists in their attempts to maintain a genuinely receptively challenging stance to their client's statements, the following 'existential mantra' may be of some use: *The client is **always** right.*

An Exercise Focused On The Client's Initial Statements

1. Consider the initial statements made to you by one of your clients that have struck you and remained in your memory.

    o   What was said? How was it expressed?
    o   What, if any, clues to the client's worldview were contained in the client's initial statements?
    o   What, if any, inter-relational elements were contained in the client's initial statements?
    o   Where did the client place him or her self in those relations?
    o   Were they predominantly concerned with the client's relations toward him or her self (e.g.: 'I dislike my self', 'I'm helpless')? Or toward others (e.g., 'They don't appreciate me', 'They dislike me', 'They don't understand or accept me')? Or towards world-constructs (e.g., 'When it's too hot, I lose it', 'Alcohol is a problem', 'The world is just too dangerous')?
    o   Who, if anyone, emerged as the primary focus of the client's concerns?

(Continued)

(Continued)

- o What initial 'story' or narrative was being expressed or suggested through these initial statements?
- o What is the client's role within this suggested narrative? Does the client take centre-stage in the initial narrative? If not, who or what does?
- o What sort of language is being employed to convey the narrative?
- o What sort of narrative is being presented? (Comedy? Tragedy? An extraordinary epic, or a more ordinary 'kitchen-sink' drama?)

2. How did you react to the client? What brought you closer to the client? What distanced you from the client? What changes did you as therapist find your self wanting to achieve for the client?
3. How do you react now to the client-as-recalled? What, if anything, alters your reactions?
4. Now repeat the exercise, but this time focus on a client whom you experience as being particularly problematic or difficult in some way.
5. When you compare and contrast the two examples you chose, does anything of relevance for you emerge?

While an acceptance-focused response to the client's opening statements can be both illuminating and a powerful challenge for client and therapist alike, it should not lead the existential therapist to suppose that through this challenge the inter-related meanings within the client's worldview have been instantly exposed and understood. To assume so, in fact, severely limits whatever value this initial challenge may have, not least as it expresses a more subtle and pernicious means for the therapist to impose his or her biases and preferences onto the client's worldview. Rather, this initial willingness to accept the 'rightness' of the client's worldview statements opens the way for the existential therapist to begin to explore descriptively that which the client has chosen to bring to the encounter.

Descriptively Focused Attunement

Being-with and Being-for the Client

Existential therapy's focus calls upon therapists to respond to the challenges of attuning their encounter with the client who is an unknown presence within the co-created therapy-world. This attunement can be considered from the standpoint of the therapist's attempts at *being-with* and to *being-for* the client.

Being-with the client is a reflection of the existential therapist's intent to respect and accept the currently maintained worldview of their clients as it is revealed through their statements, reactions, their chosen means of dialogue, their non-verbal gestures and movements and their overall way of being present in the therapy-world.

Being-for the client expresses the existential therapist's attempts to engage descriptively with the client who is present in the therapy-world. This way of engagement seeks to avoid judging, dismissing, adjusting, or 'swamping' the client's worldview with alternatives that are deemed to be more appropriate or preferable by the therapist. Being-for the client does not, however, suggest that the therapist seeks to deny his or her otherness in the encounter. Rather, it enjoins the existential therapist to be that other who, in the act of embracing the unknown and alien presenting worldview of the client, co-habits the therapy-world in a way that gives expression to the intent to be-with the client.

Although closely related, the emphasis of being-with the client denotes the intended mode of being or embodied stance that the existential therapist seeks to adopt. Being-for the client is the doing-focused expression of being-with. Together, being-with and being-for the client assist the existential therapist in remaining attuned to *the client who is present*. In addition, being-with and being-for the client subvert the therapist's tendency to be the client's truth-bringer, healer or helper in any purposive or directive manner. Of course, all such may still be experienced by the client in ways that may impact both subtly and dramatically upon the encounter. What is critical here is the therapist's abdication of any directive focused initiatives whose aim is that of shifting the client toward other ways of being and relating.

Although being-with and being-for the client remain aims rather than achievements, nonetheless the undertaking may well reinforce the client's experience of being in the presence of another who, unusually, if not uniquely, attempts to embrace the client's way of being as it presents itself in the immediacy of their encounter. This challenge, in turn, can often initiate the client's own challenges to his or her sedimented stances not only toward how others are but also toward how he or she must or must not be in the presence of others.

The subtle power of this attempted stance can sometimes be experienced by existential therapists as *uncanny* moments of intense embodied resonance with the client such that they feel themselves to be temporarily lost or swallowed up in the client's worldview. Not surprisingly, although this experience can be exhilarating, equally it can be unpleasant, disturbing or even frightening. Nonetheless, however it may be experienced, this encounter with the uncanny, rather than create chaos or diffusion of thought and experience, paradoxically can provoke substantial descriptive clarity for the therapist. The German term *befindlichkeit* – which Hans Cohn translates as a 'dispositional or mood-focused attunement' (Cohn, 2002: 59) – conveys something of this experience. Cohn argues that Heidegger chose this term in order to refer to feeling modes that 'cannot be "split off" from the situation in which they occur' (Cohn, 2002: 61) – which is to say that they 'belong' neither to one participant nor to the other alone, but to both. Conversely, these uncanny resonances can also be experienced by clients if they are led too forcefully or too quickly into the dominant focus of the therapist's worldview. In my opinion, the writings of R.D. Laing remain second to none in their contrasting depiction of what may occur both when a therapist seeks to be-with and be-for a client and when therapists, adopting a more objective model, impose their reality – or a broader consensus reality – upon their clients (Laing, 1960, 1967, 1982).

Readers will recall the allusion to theatre in the earlier discussion of the therapeutic setting. In many ways, the existential therapist's attempts to be-with and be-
for the client resonate with those adopted by actors in their efforts to 'enter into
their character'. Actors attempt to discern and embrace their character's worldview *within the boundaries of dialogue and narrative set by the playwright*. Their craft
lies in the degree to which their attempts to embody the role brings forth unique,
previously unforeseen qualities and characteristics while always respecting and
adhering to its pre-set boundaries. So too, I suggest, does the existential therapist,
like an actor, attempt a similar enterprise of describing and embracing the client's
worldview from within its current dialogical and behavioural boundaries.

An Exercise Exploring the Attempt to Be-with and Be-for the Other

1. Taking turns with a partner, think of a client with whom you have worked as a
    therapist (or trainee) who stands out for you as embodying attitudes, values,
    stances and/or beliefs which are in opposition or are alien to your own.
2. Select a specific instance or example from the therapeutic encounter that
    expresses the above differences and describe it to your partner so that the
    disturbing or unacceptable dispositional elements it contains are sufficiently
    clarified.
3. Imagine taking on for your self the dispositional elements highlighted in Point
    2. What is it like for you to embody these dispositional elements in the pres-
    ence of someone whom you consider to be a close friend or intimate? At your
    work setting with colleagues? At a friend's party? In a public area such as in
    a park or on a bus? When by your self?
4. Consider how, if at all, your attempt to describe and embrace your client's
    alien and undesirable dispositional elements has altered or affected your
    stance toward and understanding of your client.

Other-focused Listening

Within the therapy-world, the existential therapist is the presenting focus for the
client's *other-construct*. As this other, the therapist is both the representative of all
others who contribute to the definition and maintenance of the client's other-
construct and, just as importantly, is also the other who, through the attempt to
be-with and be-for the client, challenges the client's current other-construct and,
hence, the currently maintained worldview as a whole.

Typically, during early Phase One encounters, the client will emphasise the disturbing, inexplicable or problematic conflictual relations taking place in the wider-
world and how these are impacting upon, and challenging, his or her worldview.
These accounts reveal both the *noematic elements* of the client's narrative, which is

to say, the 'story' or, more broadly, the 'what' of the client's narrative, and its *noetic elements,* which is to say, those 'referential' elements of the client's narrative that express the embodied 'how' of the client's experience.

Other-focused listening, as with the attempt to be-with and be-for the client, challenges the existential therapist to remain with the noematic and noetic elements of the client's narrative *in the way that they are being expressed and recounted by the client.* For instance, consider the example in which the client initially elects to enter the narrative being brought to therapy by adopting a verbal focus that speaks in the second ('you') or third ('they') person, and entirely avoids the first ('I'). It would not be atypical for many therapists to intrude upon this narrative and either encourage or insist that the client alter the narrative in favour of first-person ('I') statements. While such a demand might make sense for other models, it is clearly antagonistic to the existential therapist's attempt at other-focused listening. Similarly, consider the example in which much of the client's highly disturbing narrative is presented in a somewhat lifeless, detached fashion. While other approaches may intervene by either inviting or urging the client to repeat parts or the whole of the narrative in an increasingly loud or emotional voice, or suggesting to the client that he or she exaggerate either the dialogue or some physical movement that accompanies that dialogue, such options make no sense as expressions of other-focused listening within the first phase of existential therapy.

These more typical kinds of therapeutic interventions, if enacted, would indicate that the existential therapist has stepped away from an attempted stance of being-with and being-for the client. From an other-focused listening standpoint, however, the therapist has not yet earned the right to be an active co-creator of either a *novel* narrative or novel ways of expressing the narrative which may arise for the client. Other-focused listening reminds existential therapists that before they can consider the client's narrative from their own preferred perspectives, they must first demonstrate their willingness and ability to attempt to place themselves in the narrative as it is being expressed by the client.

Other-focused listening is often understood as an expression of therapist's *empathy* towards the client. There are undoubtedly similarities insofar as other-focused listening concerns itself with attempts at resonance with the client's worldview narratives. However, empathy encompasses much more than partial resonance. As a term, it can express the care for another mingled with the desire to assist them. Equally, empathy may refer to an emotionally focused connection or to the temporary breaking down or experiential separation between self and other (Howe, 2013). Other-focused listening is more participatory, less about the mingling of emotions than about the attempt to clarify the what and the how of the client's experience. Of course, this attempt cannot but expose the therapist to personal thoughts, feelings, memories and experiences that might or might not be resonant with the client's narrative. How these might be offered to, or employed in the service of, the client informs Phase Two of the structural model and will be discussed in detail in the next chapter. For now, other-focused listening can be understood as the attempt to stay with and follow descriptively the client's narrative as it is presented.

An Exercise Exploring the Existential Therapist as 'The Other'

1. Work together with a partner in a structured session, taking turns to be therapist and client. Each session should last 20 minutes.
2. As the client, focus your discussion upon your relation to a specific 'other' in your life who is currently provoking some degree of disturbance or irritation for you.
3. As the therapist, assist the client in focusing upon his or her relationship with that other.
4. As the therapist, whenever it seems appropriate, bring the client's discussion directly into the therapeutic encounter by exploring in what ways, if any, the client's relationship with that other may be impacting upon the client's experience of being with the therapist as 'an other'.

   o How, if at all, is the therapist being experienced as similar to the client's disturbing 'other'?
   o How, if at all, is the therapist being experienced as different from the client's disturbing 'other'?
   o What, if anything, can the client express to the therapist-as-other that cannot be expressed, or is difficult to express, to the disturbing 'other'?

5. As the therapist, whenever it seems appropriate, monitor your experience of being with the client. In particular, consider the following:

   o What are my initial impressions of this client?
   o What are my initial expectations in being with this client?
   o What would I want to know now about this client?
   o What would I want the client to know about me?
   o What would I not want the client to know about me?
   o What is it like for me to be here in the presence of this client?

6. After the exercise has been completed by both partners, discuss with each other:

   o What was it like as a client to focus on a disturbing 'other' while in dialogue with a therapist?
   o Who explicitly acknowledged and utilised his or her presence as 'an other'?
   o What was it like as a therapist to explicitly acknowledge and utilise your presence as 'an other'?
   o What was it like to monitor your own experience of being 'the other' while attending to the client? Was anything useful to the therapeutic process gained from this self-monitoring?
   o What possible value or areas of concern does this focus on the 'therapist-as-other' raise with regard to the effectiveness of a therapeutic encounter?

An Exercise in Other-focused Listening

1. Working together with a partner, take turns in carrying out the whole of the following:

   o Present an event that occurred today which was experienced by you as being in some way disturbing, irritating or problematic.
   o Describe the event solely from its noematic focus (i.e., describe as accurately and comprehensively as you can 'what happened').
   o Describe the event solely from its noetic focus (i.e., describe as accurately and comprehensively as you can what were the significant elements expressive of 'how you experienced the event').
   o Either have your partner re-state the event in the light of the descriptive statements generated from the two points above or re-state your partner's focused-upon event in the light of the descriptive statements he or she generated.

2. Discuss each other's experience of:

   o attempting to describe accurately your partner's focused event;
   o hearing your partner attempt to describe accurately your focused event.

3. Discuss with each other, what, if anything, emerged from the exercise that affected or altered your overall stance toward your own focused event.

Therapeutic Un-knowing

The existential therapist's attempts at being-with, being-for and other-focused listening together express an attitude of *un-knowing*. As was discussed in Part One, un-knowing refers to the existential therapist's acceptance of, and curiosity about, the client's accounts of how it is for him or her to exist both in the wider-world and in the therapy-world *in the way that the client chooses to present them*. An attitude of un-knowing sets the context through which the therapist engages in the descriptive challenging of those statements.

From an un-knowing focus, acceptance is perhaps most directly expressed as:

1. You, the client, have the right to be who you are being as you are being.
2. I, the therapist, have the right to be who I am being as I am being.
3. We, together, have the right to be with each other as we are being.

The existential therapist's *curiosity* informs the questions and statements that make up descriptive challenging and can be expressed as:

1. What is it like to be this client who is present?
2. What is it like to embody the statements and stances being communicated by this client?

3. What is it like for me, the therapist, to be in the presence of this other?
4. What is it like for me, the therapist, to attempt to embrace this other's way of being as it is being expressed?
5. What is it like for both me and the client to experience 'us' engaging with one another?

A stance of therapeutic un-knowing challenges both the therapist's assumptions regarding the centrality of directed change and, instead, urges a focus on 'what is here as it presents itself' as opposed to 'what once might have been there' or 'what may one day be there'.

In addition, a stance of un-knowing raises an implicit challenge to the therapist's excessive expressions of self-criticism and fear of failure, which are usually underpinned by a demand for *perfectionism* (Rasmussen, 2004). Defined by the psychoanalyst Karen Horney as 'the tyranny of the "shoulds"' (Horney, 1991), viewed existentially perfectionism provides a means of eradicating uncertainty. To want or to desire opens us to the unknown: 'I may/may not fulfil my plans', 'I might/might not achieve my desire', 'Taking this step could provoke unhappiness and pain'. Perfectionism insists upon predictability and the intolerance of any uncertainty. For example, some years ago, in a discussion with a friend's daughter who had decided not to sit her A-level exams because of a diagnosed exam phobia, she made the following statement: 'What's the point of sitting an exam if I don't know if I will pass it?'

While a perfectionist attitude is common to many clients, not least those whose narratives are infused with abundant examples of failure (be it their own or the failure of others), its presence and impact upon therapists, and subsequently upon the therapeutic encounter, has not been sufficiently examined. A shared stance of perfectionism would likely severely restrict the extent to which the stance was challenged as well as the degree to which any challenges to it were taken seriously. Finally, un-knowing challenges the existential therapist's demands for a perfectionism focused upon the client such as expressed via complaints about clients 'who just don't do it right', or who are wrong because they don't respond to interventions in ways that the therapist expected or predicted.

An Exercise on Un-knowing

1. Working together with a partner, take turns in discussing and exploring a difficult or problematic therapeutic encounter that each of you has experienced with a client.
2. Take turns in assisting one another to explore in what ways and how adequately you each adopted a stance of un-knowing with regard to the problematic encounter.
3. On the basis of these explorations, consider how, if at all, the difficult or problematic aspects under consideration might be expressions of you and your partner's limitations in adopting an un-knowing stance.

Descriptively Focused Enquiry

Descriptive challenging is *not* the challenging of the client's worldview so that its embodied existential insecurities regarding continuity, dispositional stances and identity are criticised, approved of, rejected or provided with alternatives by the existential therapist. Descriptive challenging *is* the challenging of the client's worldview so that its implicit expressions of insecurity are made more explicit. The more the structural underpinnings and insecurities of the client's worldview are brought to awareness, the clearer will be the inconsistencies, contradictions and areas of tension that are contained within them or which they provoke. Even then, however, the task of the existential therapist during Phase One is not to offer alternatives or attempt their reduction or removal but, rather, to engage with the client in the exploration of their relation to the presenting problematic issues.

The Phenomenological Method of Investigation

Edmund Husserl, the founder of phenomenology, initially developed what has become known as *the phenomenological method* in order that it might be applied to all forms of structured inquiry (Ihde, 1986a, 1986b). Subsequently, variations on the phenomenological method have been developed to provide increasingly adequate descriptive clarifications of any reflective experience. It is principally with this latter focus in mind that existential therapists have adopted the phenomenological method as the foundational stance or attitude for the exploration of the client's worldview as it presents itself in the therapy-world and in relation to the presenting disturbances being brought to therapy. As with previous discussions (Ihde, 1986a; Spinelli, 2005), an initial description of the phenomenological method sub-divides it into three distinguishable, though inter-related, steps.

Step A: The rule of epoché (bracketing)

The first step urges the existential therapist to set aside any initial biases and prejudices and to suspend, or *bracket*, all expectations and assumptions regarding the client's statements and their implicit meaning. In other words, the rule of *epoché* requires the therapist to attempt to set aside any immediate personal predispositions and preferences toward whatever is being expressed about the client's worldview and however the client chooses to express it. Instead, the therapist remains temporarily open to any number of alternatives, neither rejecting any one as being out of hand, nor placing a greater or lesser degree of likelihood on any of the options available. In some instances, this bracketing may be actively practised by the existential therapist via some method of focused attention or meditation that opens him or her to the possibility of a phenomenological attitude. Alternatively, the existential therapist may experience bracketing simply through the descriptively focused monitoring of his or her mental processing as it occurs.

For example, recall the first meeting you had with a particular client. Did you have prior information about this client such as, for instance, the disturbance that had led him or her to decide to see a therapist? If so, how were you influenced by this information with regard to how you met that client, or what expectations or concerns or ideas or doubts presented themselves for you? Had you already formulated some structure or plan or set of achievable goals for the client? And when you first encountered the client face to face, what views and values and attitudes did you hold regarding his or her appearance, age, attractiveness, facility with language, general psychological 'health', and so forth? These are just some of the many biases and prejudices with which the rule of *epoché* is concerned and which it urges therapists to bracket.

Bracketing is often misunderstood to mean 'erasing' or 'removing', as in the therapist's attempts to erase assumptions or remove his or her impacting presence from the investigation. In my view, these interpretations of bracketing are misguided and deviate significantly from Husserl's intent. It might help to consider that, given his initial background as a mathematician, Husserl's notion of bracketing is more akin to placing a part of an equation within parentheses. In doing so, that which is being parenthesised is not being removed but, rather, that its relation to the rest of the equation has been temporarily altered for purposes of clarifying the equation as a whole. I think that this view conforms more closely with the *epoché* in that the investigator is being enjoined not to eradicate bias and prejudice (as if that were even possible!) but, rather, to relate to them in a different way whereby rather than dominate his or her views and assumptions they are 'placed in parentheses', which is to say that an attempt is undertaken both to respond sceptically to their presence once it is noted, and, as well, to approach the whole investigation from a stance that *assumes* conditions of bias and is alert to their disclosure.

Step B: The rule of description

The second step shifts the existential therapist's focus of attention away from theoretical explanations (since, for the moment, no one explanation is more adequate than any other), and, instead, emphasises the task of describing as concretely as possible that which the client presents. The essence of the rule of description is: *Describe, don't explain* – which is to say, rather than step back from the client's statements so that they are explained, transformed or rejected on the basis of the therapist's preconceived theories or hypotheses, assist the client in carrying out a concretely based descriptive investigation of his or her currently lived experience.

For example, imagine that, in an initial meeting, your client expresses her extreme fear of rats. From an explanatory standpoint you might assume that this fear arose from some disturbing earlier experience. Alternatively, you might view the fear as irrational and the fault of some inappropriate set of learning associations. Or you might wonder whether the fear of rats expressed another deeper or wider fear. Or you might even consider the fear from the standpoint of existential death anxiety. All of these responses to the client's presenting statement fail the conditions of the rule of description. Instead, in following the rule you might seek to clarify such issues as:

How is the client's fear being experienced and expressed?

What is it that the client specifically fears?

Is the level of fear the same in all instances of encountering a rat or does it differ?

Do differences in size or fur-colour influence the degree to which the fear is experienced?

Is it the rat as a whole or a particular aspect (such as its scurrying movement or the swish of its tail) or body-part of the rat that provokes the fear?

All of these latter questions – and many more – serve as examples of the descriptively focused investigation expressed in the rule of description.

Step C: The rule of horizontalisation (the equalisation rule)

The third step, the rule of horizontalisation, warns the existential therapist to avoid imposing any immediate hierarchical assumptions of importance with regard to the items of description. Instead, it urges the therapist to attempt a temporary equalisation of their significance or meaning value. For example, a new client comes into your consulting room for an initial session, sits down across from you and says: 'Isn't it a wet and miserable day? I'm so relieved to finally begin therapy. I'd like to take an axe to my husband and watch his brain ooze out of his skull.' Typically, therapists will treat these statements from a hierarchical standpoint, focus on any one of them that strikes them as having the most significance, ask the client to clarify it further and in all likelihood pay no further attention to the remaining statements unless they are raised again by the client.

The rule of horizontalisation challenges the therapist to avoid making such rushed judgements regarding the relative significance of one statement over another and, instead, to attempt to treat each as having equal value or significance so that the disparate statements can begin to be placed within the particular context – or *horizon* – of the client's worldview. On its own, each statement provides a one-sided perspective of the client's overall experiential horizon. In attempting the equalisation rule, both therapist and client are better able to place the statements in relation to one another, thereby considering them from a multi-sided perspective that corresponds more adequately with the client's embodied experience of the statements. However, the extent to which this correspondence is more or less adequate depends upon that initial attempt at experiential equalisation. In not doing so, various possible experiential contexts or horizons will emerge but the degree to which they provide a suitable fit with that of the client may be inadequate or minimal such that the investigation as a whole is skewed in ways from which the client is increasingly detached.

As a way of communicating the attempt to initially apply the rule of horizontalisation, the therapist might offer them back to the client (and thereby demonstrate that he or she has been heard accurately) and ask, for example: 'Do you want to explore any one of these in particular?' Or: 'If you were in my position, which of these would make the best sense to explore further?' Or: 'Do you want to stay with all three statements and explore them together? Or is there anything else that seems more important for us to focus on?'

All descriptively focused enquiry within existential therapy relies upon the phenomenological method. Readers should be able to identify its influence upon the various descriptive strategies discussed below. Nonetheless, it is important to clarify that while the metaphorical 'steps' employed offer a straightforward means with which initially to present the approach, any attempt to adopt a strict and formal 'one-two-three' step approach would be highly artificial. Instead, each step can be viewed as a particular point of focus that highlights the client's worldview.

Likewise, neither the phenomenological method as a whole nor any of the identified steps can ever be truly completed or reach a final all-encompassing conclusion. Nonetheless, while it remains impossible for us to bracket all biases and assumptions, we are certainly capable of bracketing a substantial number of them. In addition, even when bracketing is not likely or feasible, the very assumption of an unknown embedded bias acts as a cautionary reminder to retain some degree of uncertainty in our views and reactions. Similarly, no purely descriptive account is possible, since no description is altogether free of implicit explanatory components. And, in like fashion, the very act of engaging in a descriptive dialogue regarding the various horizons of lived experience will introduce novel horizons in that, as was stated in a previous section, the act of description in and of itself alters that which is being described. In addition, the very enterprise of description requires a focus on that which is being described thereby ensuring the impossibility of achieving an equalisation of presenting statements.

Acknowledging such substantial limitations does not, however, diminish the power of the phenomenological method. At the very least, the method minimises the existential therapist's tendency to rely exclusively upon any self-preferred set of assumptions. Equally, while it cannot claim to lead to correct or complete conclusions, the practice of the phenomenological method serves to establish and maintain an inclusionary form of enquiry wherein the therapist's attempts at clarification are always open to their being *verified* or *amended* by the client. This engagement with his or her own statements, as well as with that other (the therapist) who is attempting to report them accurately, may be gratifying and reassuring to the client, but may also be unnerving and disturbing – not least because in being made explicit they might suggest previously unconsidered connections between the presenting issues and his or her overall embodied existence.

An Exercise on the Practice of the Phenomenological Method

1. Working together with a partner, take turns in being the therapist and client. Each session should last 20 minutes.
2. As the client, select a generally provocative topic that holds some interest and significance to you and discuss its impact from your personal standpoint.
3. As the therapist, assist your client in exploring his or her relationship to the provocative topic while attempting to follow the three 'steps' of the phenomenological method.
4. After you have both completed your sessions, discuss

    o your experience as a client working with a therapist who attempted to explore the topic through the phenomenological method;
    o your evaluation of your therapist's success in attempting to explore the topic through the phenomenological method. (What instances stand out for you as examples of the therapist staying close to the method? What instances stand out for you as examples of the therapist deviating from the method?)
    o your experience as a therapist who attempted to explore the topic through the phenomenological method;
    o your evaluation of your own success in attempting to explore the topic through the phenomenological method. (What instances stand out for you as examples of your relative success in staying close to the method? What instances stand out for you as examples of you having deviated from the method?)

5. Finally, discuss with each other what benefits and limitations you suppose there might be in utilising the phenomenological method as a basis to therapeutic investigation.

Noematically and Noetically Focused Descriptive Challenging

In common with the idea of 'storying' as utilised in some models of narrative theory (Freedman & Combs, 1996), existential therapy's descriptive challenging concerns itself with the clarification of the *noematic* narrative (the story itself) in order to bring to the surface the often implicit *noetic* context that is embedded within it (how the story both reveals and affects the narrator).

Noematically focused descriptive challenges address such issues as:

Who or what persons/objects/events are under focus in the client's narrative?

Who is the most pivotal character in the client's narrative?

What is problematic in this narrative?

What is valued in this narrative?

In what ways does each of the above reveal itself?

What is being emphasised in the narrative?

What is being minimised in the narrative?

What gaps are there in the narrative?

What new narrative emerges if its problematic elements are altered or removed?

What new narrative emerges if its valued elements are altered or removed?

What new narrator emerges if its problematic elements are altered or removed?

What new narrator emerges if its valued elements are altered or removed?

In turn, this noematic focus opens up the means with which to disclose the noetic aspects of the narrative which focus on such issues as:

How does the client's worldview narrative express embodied existential insecurities surrounding continuity? Dispositional stances? Identity?

How are these insecurities being communicated through the narrative?

How do these insecurities impact upon the narrative?

How are these insecurities being maintained?

How does the narrative prevent these insecurities from being altered?

How does the presenting problem impact upon the client's worldview self-construct? The client's worldview other-construct? The client's worldview world-construct?

An Exercise in Noematically Focused Descriptive Challenging

1. Working together with a partner, take turns in being therapist and client. Each session should last 20 minutes.
2. As the client, focus on a recent event that you can communicate as a 'story' (from either a first-person or third-person perspective). Recount the narrative, emphasising its noematic constituents.
3. As the therapist, engage in a process of noematically focused descriptive challenge by helping the client to investigate the various story components in his or her narrative.
4. When you have both completed the exercise, discuss what the experience of doing the exercise was like for each of you when you were being the therapist or the client.
5. What general value, if any, for the therapeutic encounter would you say that noematically focused descriptive challenging might offer?

An Exercise in Noetically Focused Descriptive Challenging

1. Working together with a partner, take turns in being therapist and client. Each session should last 20 minutes.
2. As the client, focus on the same recent event as in the previous exercise.
3. As the therapist, engage in a process of noetically focused descriptive challenge by helping the client to investigate the various referential elements being expressed within his or her narrative.
4. When you have both completed the exercise, discuss what the experience of doing the exercise was like for each of you when you were being the therapist or the client.
5. What general value, if any, for the therapeutic encounter would you say that noetically focused descriptive challenging might offer?

Strategic Questioning

The social activist Fran Peavey developed a manual for what she called *strategic questioning* (Peavey, 1997). This way of questioning creates a sense of opening or movement with regard to a specific concern that is being explored. Paradoxically, however, this same possibility of movement is created through an attitude of questioning that is focused upon a 'staying with' the presented concern rather than directing means to move on from it. In this staying with the concern, the questions posed begin to make increasingly explicit that which has remained implicit or unseen within the concern. In common with Gadamer's distinction of two types of dialogue, as was discussed in Chapter 5, strategic questioning relies upon dialogical uncertainty in that the questions posed cannot be pre-set but, rather, emerge out of the content and direction of the dialogue itself. Many of Peavey's key focus points for strategic questions resonate closely with existential therapy's descriptive enquiry. As I have understood and interpreted them, strategic questions:

*   are questions that have no specified correct answer, but, rather, which expose possibilities and options;
*   avoid yes/no answers;
*   avoid 'why's;
*   provoke ownership and/or empowerment;
*   focus on the clarification of the embodied experience accompanying both the statements that initiated the enquiry as well as the responses given to the strategic question.

As a general principle, strategic questions ask the unaskable. They are the sorts of questions that would normally be deemed to be too obvious or too basic to ask. From an existential therapy standpoint, they reveal the therapist's willingness to ask '*idiotic*' questions. For example:

Client:	These panic attacks that I keep having are just so awful.
Therapist:	I'm sorry, but can you tell me what 'a panic attack' is as far as you experience it?
Client:	What it is? Don't you know what panic attacks are?
Therapist:	I don't know what your panic attacks are. Can you tell me?
Client:	Isn't there a Manual or something that explains what they are and what to do about them?
Therapist:	If there was such a Manual, what do you think it would say?
Client:	You're asking me? I thought you were supposed to be the expert.
Therapist:	What if you were the expert? What would you tell me now about panic attacks?

An Exercise on Strategic Questioning

1. Working together with a partner, take turns in being therapist and client. Each session should last 15 minutes.
2. As the client, focus on a recent experience that irritated you in some way.
3. As the therapist, assist the client in exploring the experience through the use of strategic questioning. Try to provide questions that assume as little immediate understanding as possible of the client's experiential statements. Attempt to remain as uncertainly open, or 'idiotic', as you can be. Avoid preparing or pre-setting questions and instead only ask questions that follow on directly from your client's statements.
4. When you have both completed the exercise, discuss what the experience of doing the exercise was like for each of you when you were being the therapist or the client.

Descriptive Challenging through Body-focus, Metaphorical Attunement and Narrational Scene-setting

In recent years, I have been suggesting that existential therapists adopt a variant of the phenomenological method which can assist them in their attempts at attunement with the client as well as provide a tri–partite focus to descriptive challenges. In general, this approach allows both therapist and client to 'remain still' in the immediacy of the experience under investigation so that what is being described is more adequately accessed experientially as part of the descriptive process. By so doing, therapist and client together focus on an embodied clarification of 'what is there in the way that it is there' by making explicit the thoughts, feelings, emotions and behaviours that provide the overall 'mood' of the client's current experience.

Body-focused descriptive challenging seeks to assist the client in identifying and clarifying how the statements of disturbance and disorder that have been expressed verbally are being communicated in a sensory fashion through the body. In general, body–focused descriptive challenging encourages the exploration and description of feeling located either throughout or in identified parts of the body. It asks questions such as:

- When you say X (a statement of concern or disorder), do you notice any particular feelings in a part or parts of your body? Or your body as a whole?
- Can you identify its/their location in your body?
- Can you describe the body-feeling?
- What makes this body-feeling stand out in relation to your overall body-feeling?
- If your experience is that of having no body-feeling that you notice when you make your statement, what does it feel like for you to feel no body-feeling?

For example:

Client: When I think about what happened, it feels terrible.

Therapist: What makes the feeling terrible?

Client: That I was so stupid! That I gave up the best thing to happen in my life without a second thought!

Therapist: Okay, stay with what you just said. Did you have any feelings in your body when you said that?

Client: What do you mean? I don't understand.

Therapist: Okay. Hear your self say: 'It feels terrible! I was so stupid!' When you say that, do you notice any body sensations? Do your feeling-statements have a location anywhere in your body?

Client: A location? Yeah. It's a tightness in my throat. Like I want to vomit.

Therapist: Anywhere else?

Client: No ... Just that. Oh. And a sort of overall 'tingly' feeling.

Therapist: An overall tingly feeling.

Client: Yeah. Like a charge running through me.

Therapist: Okay. So now when you say: 'It feels terrible! I was so stupid!' what you're experiencing through those words is expressed by your body as: a tightness in your throat, a desire to vomit and an overall tingly feeling that is like a charge running through you. Is that right?

Client: Yeah. That just about captures it.

Therapist: Okay. Stay with those body feelings. See if there's anything else that you notice.

An Exercise on Descriptive Challenging through Body-focus

1. Working together with a partner, take turns in being therapist and client. Each session should last 15 minutes.
2. As the client, select a current issue or dilemma in your life which you have not yet resolved and communicate it to the extent that seems appropriate to you to the therapist.
3. As the therapist, assist the client in exploring the experience through body-focus *alone*.
4. When you have both completed the exercise, discuss what the experience of body-focus descriptive challenging was like for each of you when you were being the therapist or the client.

Metaphorically attuned descriptive challenging seeks to assist the client in identifying and clarifying how statements of disturbance and disorder can be expressed through various analogies or comparisons with objects, conditions or events that initially would be unrelated to what is being expressed. The effectiveness of metaphorical attunement rests very much on the existential therapist's willingness and ability to be *creative* in the descriptive challenges presented to the client. Analogous to the behaviour of a young child interacting with a new and unknown toy, there can exist a playful quality to this mode of investigation. In general, metaphorically attuned descriptive challenging encourages the linking up between the client's often abstract or intangible statements of disorder with specified figures of speech or tangible objects. It asks questions such as:

• If you had to describe your experience as a sound, a gesture, a colour, a shape, a taste, an item of clothing, what would it be?

It is particularly useful to focus on metaphors that are relevant to the client's interests as revealed at various points during the previous and current therapeutic encounter. For instance:

• You've mentioned that you are a great fan of *EastEnders*. If you had to pick a character out of *EastEnders* who best captures your experience, who would it be?
• What song, film, novel, character in a novel best captures your experience?

For example:

Client: When I'm listening to my body, you know what it's like? It's like when I used to read Spider-Man comics and he used to get this 'spider-sense' whenever there was danger. It's like that.

Therapist: So, there's something about 'danger' in it?

Client: I guess so. I don't know what's dangerous, though.

Therapist: You've mentioned Spider-Man comics before. If you took your feeling of 'feeling terrible and stupid' and identified it as one of the characters in Spider-Man comics, who would it be? Anyone?

Client: Oh! Sandman! That's who it'd be. Don't know why, though. I guess I always felt sort of sorry for Sandman. He was always kinda dumb. And he was just all brawn and no brain.

Therapist: Okay. So could we now say that for you 'feeling terrible and stupid' is like being Sandman?

Client: Yeah.

Therapist: And what's it like to be Sandman?

Client: Like I said: kinda dumb. No brain, just brawn. Sort of, I don't know, pointless, really.

Therapist: Kinda dumb. No brain, just brawn. Pointless. When you put those together .... anything?

Client: Eating TV dinners! [*Laughs*]

Therapist: [*Laughs*] TV dinners! Okay. Uh .... So what's the link for you?

Client: It's what they are! Kinda dumb, brainless and pointless! And they make you feel like that!

Therapist: Okay, so now, according to you, 'feeling terrible and stupid' is a tightness in the throat, a desire to vomit, a tingly feeling that's like a charge running all over that you connect with a warning about danger, and Sandman and TV dinners. Is that right?

Client: Yeah. Weird, but right.

Therapist: Is there more?

Client: It's funny ... Just as you said that, I heard a sound.

Therapist: A sound? You mean 'feeling terrible and stupid' has a sound for you?

Client: Yeah. It's weird, but—

Therapist: Can you make the sound?

Client: [*Makes a gargling noise*] It's like trying to speak, but you can't.

An Exercise on Descriptive Challenging through Metaphorical Attunement

1. Working together with a partner, take turns in being therapist and client. Each session should last 15 minutes.
2. As the client, return to the current issue or dilemma in your life which you had explored in the previous exercise on body-focused descriptive challenging and continue your discussion from where you had left off at the end of it.
3. As the therapist, assist the client in exploring the experience through meta-phorical attunement *alone.*
4. When you have both completed the exercise, discuss what the experience of body-focus descriptive challenging was like for each of you when you were being the therapist or the client.

Narrational scene-setting seeks to assist the client to identify and clarify how statements of disturbance and disorder can be explored locationally by focusing upon a single specified instance or example of their being experienced and concentrating upon a detailed description of the narrative scene within which the event took place. For instance:

*   When was the first/most recent/strongest/most vivid/longest-lasting instance that you recall having experienced X? Let's go back to that instance. Where was it? Who was there? If it was in a room, describe the room in as detailed a way as you can. If it was outdoors, describe the setting in as detailed a way as you can. Where were you in that room or setting? What were you doing in the moment that you experienced X? Were you standing or sitting? Holding anything? Were there any sounds? If there were other people or animals present, where were they in the setting? What were they doing? Was anyone saying anything that you recall?

Once any single narrative scene has been sufficiently explored, similarly detailed descriptive enquiry can be carried out on another narrative scene which the client identifies with his or her presenting concerns. This can be done several times so that a number of narrative scenes within which the client's concerns are set can be compared and contrasted with one another.

*   When re-viewing the various narrative scenes that have been described, is there anything that stands out for you that these different scenes might have in common with one another? Are there any recurring events or people or objects, for example? Is there anything about you, what you are doing/thinking/feeling/saying/hearing/wearing that seems to you is being carried over from one set scene to the next?

- When re-viewing the various narrative scenes that have been described, what for you seems to be distinct and different about each one in relation to the others?

For example:

Therapist: When you were making that gargling sound that you've linked with 'feeling terrible and stupid', did you have any picture or image of where you were?

Client: Where I was?

Therapist: If I said to you: think of your self making that gargling sound at some point in your past and just look to see where you are when you're making it. Where are you?

Client: That's odd. I just had a flash of the first house I grew up in.

Therapist: Okay. Stay there. Are you in any particular room?

Client: I'm in the sitting-room. I'm watching telly. I think I'm eating a sandwich or something.

Therapist: Okay. Can you describe the room for me?

Client: It's sort of 'Early Seventies Bland'. Shiny green curtains. An armchair and sofa. A very noisy-coloured green and gold swirl rug on top of buff-coloured wall-to-wall carpeting. A huge telly that's still only black and white. Oh! I can smell left-over cigarette smoke. And orange peel. Yeah! That's what I'm eating.

Therapist: And you're sitting down while you're eating?

Client: Yeah. Oh! My sister's there, too!

Therapist: She's sitting beside you?

Client: No, she's behind— Shit! You know what? That gargling sound. My sister's making it. We used to play together and she'd say things like: 'I've got a really really big secret to tell you. You know what it is?' And I'd go: 'Tell me.' And she'd get right up close to my ear and then make that same damn noise with her throat! That's weird.

Therapist: OKay. So stay with that. 'Feeling terrible' has got you to hearing your sister's 'I've got a secret' noise. You're in the family sitting room and you're watching telly while eating an orange and she's behind you and she's just said: 'I've got a really really big secret to tell you. You know what it is?'

Client: [*Begins to cry*] Yeah …

Therapist: Do you want to say—

Client: [*Yells*] How come I end up feeling so terrible like this? What's so fucking wrong with me?

Therapist: Try to stay with that. Locate a scene where you are saying that. Anything?

Client: I keep going back to the sitting room I mentioned.

Therapist: Okay. Is it same room, same time? Or another time?

Client: It's Christmas when I was 6 years old and I didn't get a fucking thing. Just a stupid gimpy tree with a note saying, 'Sorry …. Father Christmas ran out of presents. He'll bring you some tomorrow.' That's the first time I just went out of control and smashed everything up and then realised how fucking stupid I was because that meant fucking Father Christmas wasn't *ever* going to come back.

Therapist: Okay. Let's look at the scene a bit more closely.

An Exercise on Descriptive Challenging through Narrational Scene-setting

1. Working together with a partner, take turns in being therapist and client. Each session should last 20 minutes.
2. As the client, return to the current issue or dilemma in your life which you had explored in the previous two exercises and continue your discussion from where you had left off at the end of it.
3. As the therapist, assist the client in exploring the experience through narrational scene-setting *alone*. Try to describe at least two different narrational scenes relevant to your client's stated concern.
4. When you have both completed the exercise, discuss what the experience of narrational scene-setting descriptive challenging was like for each of you when you were being the therapist or the client.

Employed together, descriptive challenging through body-focus, metaphorical attunement and narrational scene-setting can provide an often powerfully experienced means to explore the client's presenting concerns. For existential therapists, their primary challenge is that all three require the setting aside of the therapist's own desire to 're–author' the client's narrative.

Immediacy

As should now be clear to the reader, any directive interventions on the part of the therapist to alter or re-interpret the client's statements, or to assist the client in moving on from them would be incongruent with the overall aims of Phase One. Descriptive challenging provides a movement toward *immediacy* in the therapeutic encounter. This immediacy allows the client to examine the concerns being brought to therapy *within the relational setting of the therapy-world itself*. In this way, the concerns being expressed are not only accounts of how it is for the client to be 'out there' (in his or her wider-world). More importantly, these concerns are able to be examined within a much more present-attuned, directly accessed set of conditions. In general, *immediacy re-connects that which is being stated with the being who is making the statement.*

For similar reasons, Phase One as a whole avoids what might broadly be termed analytically focused investigations whose principal concerns lie with explanatory hypotheses about possible past or originating causes of the client's current worldview. This is not to suggest, as some critics have proposed, that the existential therapist cannot or should not ever ask questions focused on 'why?' However, it is clear that just as a why question may serve a descriptively focused enterprise, it may also open the way to abstract explanations that distance the client from the lived immediacy of his or her experience. It is this latter form of why questioning that existential therapists attempt to minimise. Just as why-focused questions and explanations may help clients become more aware of, and connected to, their own implicit meanings and truths, they may also allow them to remain with meanings and truths that, while potentially valid in their general explanatory possibilities, create or maintain barriers to the client's sense of connection with their own currently maintained worldview.

Indications as to the Appropriateness of a Therapeutic Shift from Phase One to Phase Two

As will be discussed below, Phase One and Phase Two of existential therapy reveal significant differences in their focus on, and possibilities of, relational encounter. What then might indicate to the existential therapist that a shift toward Phase Two has become possible? I would suggest the following critical factors:

1. The client is increasingly addressing and investigating his or her presenting concerns as they are experienced in their immediacy within the co-created therapy-world and as contrasted with and compared to that of his or her wider-world experiences of these same concerns.
2. The client's way of being in the presence of the therapist is suggestive of the establishment of a sufficient degree of trust in the therapist as a responsible and valued 'other'.

3. The client shows increasing willingness and ability not only to respond non-defensively to descriptive challenging but also to initiate it at times – whether within or beyond the confines of the therapy-world.
4. There is a noticeably growing ease in the client's engagement with the therapist at a level of immediacy.
5. There is greater willingness on the part of the client to challenge some aspects of his or her own habitual stances and statements regarding any aspect of his or her currently maintained worldview.
6. There is greater willingness on the part of the client to challenge the therapist's statements and challenges.
7. There is an increased willingness to employ and respond to humour in the therapist's and client's discourse, which suggests a greater degree of relational openness and respect.

Factors Preventing a Therapeutic Shift from Phase One to Phase Two

Just as there may be various indications that the therapeutic relationship is at a point that will permit a shift from Phase One to Phase Two, so is it equally the case that this shift may have occurred too soon. In such cases, Phase Two existential therapy is likely to be at best ineffective and, at worst, may have the effect of disabling any further attempts at descriptive challenge. The following are likely to be the most common underlying factors indicative of this possibility:

1. The general setting conditions relevant to therapeutic contract and frame are either insufficiently clear or are not being followed consistently by the existential therapist.
2. The general setting conditions are being consistently challenged or broken by the client.
3. The existential therapist's statements and descriptive challenges are not adequately attuned to the client's embodied experience so that they fail to generate sufficient trust.
4. The existential therapist's statements and descriptive challenges do not follow directly from the client's statements, or the initiatives leading to the statements are not made clear to the client, so that they provoke incredulity, unease, distraction, irritation, suspicion or even fear.
5. The existential therapist's statements and descriptive challenges are too misdirected, too infrequent or too 'parrot-like', so that they are limited in their impact and worth.
6. The existential therapist's inability or unwillingness to accept the client as he or she is being in the therapy-world is expressed through a stance that is anonymous, distant and self-conscious.

7. The existential therapist's inability or unwillingness to accept the client as he or she is being in the therapy-world is expressed through the attempt (however subtle) to change, cure, improve, educate, heal, help or make the client other than as he or she is being.

In the event of the occurrence of any of these factors, it is critical for the existential therapist to acknowledge the tensions in the relationship, to be willing to hear non-defensively whatever critical statements the client might make, consider with the client what options there may be to deal with the situation, if necessary re-formulate the relational frame and, most importantly, re-initiate the attempt to establish a more adequate Phase One encounter.

A Summary of Phase One

From the client's perspective, the principal aim of Phase One is that of providing the necessary conditions that, metaphorically speaking, will permit the client to *hear his or her own voice more accurately and truthfully*. As a challenge, it should not be undervalued or underestimated in its potential impact.

This process of enabling the disclosure of 'what is there in the way it is there' for the client is the primary challenge set for the existential therapist during Phase One. If the existential therapist's presence is experienced by the client as being sufficiently accepting and trustworthy, and if the therapy-world setting is both clear and consistent, the client may well experience – perhaps for the first time – an encounter with another who is neither overtly nor covertly expressing a critique of his or her currently adopted worldview nor demanding that it be altered.

Whatever value the subsequent Phases may have to the whole of the therapeutic process is dependent upon the inter-relational possibilities experienced by the client during Phase One. In my view, Phase One provides the same relationally focused conditions that have been identified by research on non-specific factors and placebo effects (Duncan et al., 2010; Miller & Kaptchuk, 2008; Moerman & Jonas, 2002). As this research indicates, it is arguable that, for many clients, the communication and validation of their issues and concerns in the presence of another who has co-created and co-habits a specified therapy-world setting within which the client's concerns are considered and explored may be all that is required to provoke sufficiently meaningful and lasting therapeutic benefit.

8

Phase Two: Co-habiting the Therapy-world

Introduction

During Phase One the existential therapist's overall task was to be that other whose endeavour was that of attunement to the client's worldview. Now, in Phase Two, the therapist's attempts are to be that other who has earned the right to challenge the client's worldview through those *similarities and differences* that are expressions of his or her otherness. The client's Phase One experience of the therapist as 'that other who challenges through attempts to reflect back to me who and how I am being' shifts to a Phase Two awareness of the therapist as 'that other who challenges through attempts to reflect back how he or she experiences who and how I am being as means to further clarify who and how I am being'. This shift in focus opens the way for the client to begin to engage in a novel dialogue with a distinct other who co-habits the therapy-world in ways that resonate with, diverge from, challenge and conflict with his or her own.

If Phase One provided the means for the client 'to hear his or her own voice more accurately and truthfully', now, in Phase Two the client is challenged 'to continue to hear that voice as it engages with the voice of the other who is the therapist'. Similarly, if the existential therapist's inquiry during Phase One was in various ways akin to that of 'idiotic' descriptively explicit investigation, in Phase Two, the therapist's challenges are more like those that would be posed by a *Fool*. Just as the Medieval Fool was able to challenge the statements, wishes and behaviours of the King or Queen in ways that no other member of the Royal Court would be permitted, or dare, to attempt, so too is the existential therapist now able, like that Fool, to give voice to challenging alternate perspectives for the client to consider.

In this way, during Phase Two, the therapist is experienced more and more acutely as that therapy-world other who is both a representative of all others in the client's wider-world as well as that other whose presence is unlike that of others in the client's wider-world. This combined 'standing-in for' and 'standing apart from' opens the client's worldview as a whole to other-attuned inquiry and by doing so permits the possibility of a novel stance towards the issues and concerns that have been brought to therapy.

As should now be apparent, whatever therapeutic benefit Phase Two may have to offer the client, it is entirely dependent upon the quality of their encounter. From an experiential perspective, Phase Two encounters can be intensely felt by both therapist and client. Equally, in its emphasis upon the immediacy experienced between them, a Phase Two encounter is largely unsharable with others in both the client's and the therapist's wider-world relations. Hence, Phase Two experiences can be beguiling, uncanny, liberating, disturbing, intimate, desirable and undesirable both for and between the therapist and the client.

Listening to and Challenging the Client's Narrative

Phase Two listening and challenging extends the focus of the existential therapist's attunement so that it increasingly encompasses views and possibilities other than those explicitly being presented by the client. This shift in listening can be unpredictably powerful and disturbing for the client and may, in turn, provoke responses that weaken both the trustworthiness of the therapy-world as well as the trust that has been established between client and therapist. As a way of attempting to offset such an eventuality, the existential therapist can always *monitor* the client's experience through straightforward inquiry (e.g., 'Are you okay with this?', 'Is it all right for me to push you a little more here?'). A second option is for the existential therapist to adopt an overtly *invitational* stance to all such investigations so that they proceed only if agreed to by the client (e.g., 'I'd like to offer an alternative here – is that okay with you?', 'Can I suggest something? If you don't like it or want it, that's fine'). Three useful and straightforward, yet surprisingly powerful, means for existential therapists to express Phase Two listening and challenging are addressed below.

Shifts Between the Particular and the General

This first aspect of Phase Two listening and challenging invites the client to reconsider those narratives focused upon a particular experience from a perspective that opens the experience to its more general experiential possibilities. Conversely, this mode also invites the client to re-consider those narratives that are focused upon general experiential stances from a perspective that opens these to focus on a particular instance. For example:

(From the General to the Particular)

Client: I just can't stand it when people are so phoney!

Therapist: Can you give me an example?

Client: An example?

Therapist: Yeah … Tell me about the most recent time that this happened.

Client: Uhm … The waitress at the restaurant last night. It was that pho- ney 'I'm having an orgasm just because I'm so pleased to serve you' look.

Therapist: And what is it that you couldn't stand about that?

Client: Well, it's such an obvious lie, isn't it? She didn't give a fuck about me. She was just after a big tip.

Therapist: And what was it about her wanting a big tip that got to you?

Client: It wasn't that she wanted a big tip! I could understand that. It's the way she did it. Like she was saying: 'You are such a worthless waste of space and I am *so* going to fool you into thinking that you're something when you clearly are not.'

(From the Particular to the General)

Therapist: So if you took the waitress and lined her up with all the people that you say that you can't stand, what would they all be saying?

Client: They'd be saying: 'We think you're such an idiot that we're going to take as much advantage of you as we can just' cuz you're so dumb and you don't mean anything at all to us.'

Therapist: That's it?

Client: Yeah. And also the way they look at me. That's a big part of it, too.

(From the General to the Particular)

Therapist: Think of that look that they give you. Anyone come straight to mind?

Client: Oh yeah … When my son looked at me like that, like I'd let him down. I felt like I was totally worthless as a human being.

Therapist: That was the same look?

Client: Yeah.

Therapist: So you're saying that your son is another phoney?

Client: Uhm … No. No, I was the phoney that time.

Therapist: You were the phoney.

Client: Yeah …

(From the Particular to the General)

Therapist: Okay. Stay with the 'I was a phoney'. Can you make any other con- nections to it? Has anyone else ever given you a look that makes you the phoney?

Client: Yeah … My grandmother when she caught me taking money out of her purse.

Therapist: Okay. Anyone else come to mind?

Client: I don't know. Maybe an old friend of mine, Jimmy, when he saw me act like a real jerk with my then girlfriend.

Therapist: So ... Your son, your grandmother and your friend Jimmy all gave you a similar look to that of the waitress. And did that look make you feel like a phoney in all instances?

Client: Oh, yeah. And just worthless.

Therapist: Worthless. Just like the look that the phoney waitress gave you last night.

Shifts from the Explicit to the Implicit

Throughout Phase One, the existential therapist's focus centred upon the clarification and challenge of the client's *explicit* statements. During Phase Two, this focus shifts upon that which *implicitly* underpins the client's explicit statements in an attempt to disclose that which remains unstated. As an example of this, let us continue with the previous client/therapist dialogue:

Therapist: Can we look at this sense of 'being worthless' a bit more?

Client: Yeah, whatever.

Therapist: This may sound stupid, but what's so bad about being worthless?

Client: You're right. It does sound stupid! It's obvious what's bad about it.

Therapist: Okay. It's obvious and maybe I'm just thick, but what makes it so bad? I mean, hear your self say: 'I'm worthless.' What's being said in that?

Client: That ... that I don't live up to expectations. That I'm a failure.

Therapist: Okay. So 'being worthless' for you is not fulfilling expectations, being a failure. Let me try out something here: 'I tried and I failed. So, I'm worthless. Even if I gave it my best shot, I'm still worthless because I didn't succeed.' Does that fit with your experience at all?

Client: Yes. A lot.

Therapist: So anything other than being perfect, in that I always succeed, is to be condemned as worthless.

Client: Yeah.

Therapist: So when your son and your grandmother and Jimmy all gave you that look that made you feel like a phoney, would it be right to conclude that their 'look' was basically saying: 'We've found you out! You're not perfect! And therefore you're worthless.'

Client: That's right.

Therapist: Okay. Can I try out something else here?

Client: Yeah, go ahead.

Therapist: Tell me whether this fits or not: What made the waitress a phoney
                was that you found her out. She was faking perfection and you saw
                through it.

Client: You know ... that feels right. It's about perfection. And not getting
                there. You have to be perfect, otherwise you can only be a worth-
                less phoney.

The Existential Therapist's Use of 'Self-as-Other'

As in Phase One, the exploration of the contrast between the client experience of
co-habiting the therapy-world and that of being part of the wider-world beyond
its boundaries can offer a valuable means to the clarification and challenging of the
client's worldview. Readers will recall that such shifts toward experiential *immediacy*
have the effect of locating the client's wider-world issues and concerns within the
boundaries of the therapy-world. In Phase Two, immediacy can be extended to
include directly the client's experience of engaging with the existential therapist as
the other in the therapy-world who both stands in for, or represents, all others as
experienced by the client, yet who also challenges the client's typical responses to,
and assumptions about, others. For example:

Client: I guess that somewhere along the way, the world taught me that
                you can only be either perfect or a phoney.

Therapist: So, what about here, between us? Does that rule still hold true?

Client: You mean me here with you?

Therapist: Yeah. Imagine asking your self: 'Can I only be either perfect or a
                phoney when I'm here with Ernesto?'

Client: Uhm ... I don't know. Probably. I don't know. It's difficult—

Therapist: Can I ask you this: Is this your experience? 'Ernesto's demanding
                that I be perfect because otherwise he'll judge me to be a phoney?'

Client: No.

Therapist: So what's different about Ernesto, or about this experience of being
                with Ernesto, that this world-rule gets broken?

Client: [*Laughs*] What's different? Well, I pay you for one thing ...

Therapist: You paid the waitress as well, but that didn't break the rule.

Client: Yeah, but you're not a waitress, are you? You can't compare her to you.

Therapist: Okay, aside from the obvious physical differences, what's different between the waitress and Ernesto?

Client: Well, for one thing, she's a phoney.

Therapist: So does that mean: 'Ernesto's perfect'?

Client: [*Laughs*] No!

Therapist: So 'Ernesto's not perfect and Ernesto's not a phoney.' How can that be? Within the scheme of things that's been laid out, there's only one or the other.

Client: Yeah, but this is different. We're doing therapy here.

Therapist: Oh ... So, does that mean that 'Ernesto doesn't have to see me as either only perfect or only a phoney'?

Client: No, I guess not.

Therapist: So, let me ask you this as though it was you asking it and see what comes up for you: 'How is Ernesto experiencing me right now?'

Client: You know what? It's like you couldn't care less as to whether I was perfect or a phoney. It wouldn't make any difference to how you relate to me.

Therapist: And when I hear my self say that, what's that feel like?

Client: It's great. It's freeing ... Liberating. I want to take a deep breath [*breathes deeply*]. I don't feel worthless. But I also don't feel perfect.

Therapist: And you're not insisting that I also have to be perfect or else be judged by you as worthless?

Client: Nope.

Therapist: So what's different here – about me, about you, about us – that we can be other than perfect or worthless?

An Exercise in Phase Two Listening and Challenging

1. Working together with a partner, take turns in being the therapist and client. Each session should last 20 minutes.
2. As the client, select a recent encounter that has shaken or stayed with you in some way. Begin the session by describing the encounter and discussing its impact from your personal standpoint.

(Continued)

(Continued)

3. As the therapist, listen and challenge the client from a Phase Two level by making use of (a) shifts between the general and particular, (b) shifts from the explicit to the implicit, and (c) bringing into the discussion your presence as 'the other'.
4. After you have completed the exercise, discuss how you each experienced the encounter from these perspectives and what it was like for you to listen and challenge or to be heard and challenged at the Phase Two level.

Working with Tensions in Existence Polarities

The term *existence tensions* was first proposed by Bill Wahl, a counselling psychologist who aligns his views and approach to practice with those of existential therapy. Drawing on his analysis of several key texts on existential therapy, Wahl developed a preliminary list of *existential polarities* which he argued are 'intrinsic to human experience' (Wahl, 2003: 267). Below, I have included some of the more pertinent and common existential polarities derived from Wahl's initial list:

ACCEPTANCE————REJECTION	HEALTH——————DISEASE/ILLNESS
ACTION——————STASIS	HEDONISM—————ASCETICISM
APATHY——————CONCERN	IDEALISM—————STATUS QUO
ATTACHMENT————SEPARATION	INTELLECT—————EMOTION
AVOIDANCE————CONFRONTATION	POWER——————IMPOTENCE
BALANCE—————EXTREMES	REASON—————INTUITION
BODY——————MIND	RITUAL——————SPONTANEITY
CONTROL—————LETTING GO	SECURITY————RISK
CONVENTIONALITY—UNIQUENESS	SELF-CENTREDNESS—OTHER-FOCUS
EFFORT——————EASE	SOLITUDE————SOCIABILITY
FINITUDE—————INFINITY	TRUST——————SUSPICION
FUTURE—————PAST	UNION——————SEPARATENESS
HARMONY————CHAOS	WORK——————LEISURE/PLAY

Obviously, the list is far from all-inclusive of both the range of possible existential polarities that are humanly experienced as well as the diverse options in identifying and labelling them in their relation to one another. Nonetheless, it serves as a working template upon which the exploration of *existential polarity tensions* can be initiated.

As was discussed in Part One, the most basic existence tensions arise from the dissonances and consonances between worlding and the worldview in that there will always be an inevitable incompleteness or inadequacy of any essence-based reflection (the worldview) upon process-like existence (worlding). As such, any particular experience of existence can be located somewhere along the polarity continuum whose extremes are worlding——worldview. However, simply in locating itself somewhere along that continuum, the experience will generate some degree of existence tension simply *because it is located somewhere rather than everywhere along the continuum*. Only if an experience could, in some way, encompass *simultaneously* all locations along the polarity continuum, then existence tension would be eliminated. But because no experience can achieve this, existence tensions are inevitable. For example, consider the existential polarity that is hedonism——asceticism. Any experience that is identified within this polarity must locate itself somewhere along its continuum. It may be approaching one extreme of the polarity or the other, or may be located somewhere around the mid-point of the two. But wherever it is located it will be tension provoking. The only possibility of no existence tension would be if the experience somehow were able to express *all* points along the polarity continuum all at once.

It can be of immediate investigative value to identify and explore the client's problematic issues from the focus of polarity tensions. For example, Gary has just had a serious dispute with Nigel, his business partner. As a result, Gary feels terrified about the future of their company and, in turn, feels guilty, can't sleep and is plagued by the idea that he is 'a bad person who deserves everything that he is getting'. As he speaks, Gary's words highlight a number of existential polarities, usually through his naming of one extreme of the polarity continuum (e.g. future or uncertainty). The polarities that recur in his statements are:

```
ACCEPTANCE————REJECTION        SECURITY————RISK
CONTROL————LETTING GO          UNION————SEPARATENESS
FUTURE————PAST
```

When asked to locate his current embodied stance along each of the polarities as a consequence of his difficulties with Nigel, Gary produces the following:

```
ACCEPTANCE————X–REJECTION      SECURITY————X–RISK
CONTROL–X————LETTING GO        UNION————X–SEPARATENESS
FUTURE–X————PAST
```

When asked to locate his embodied stance along each of the polarities prior to his difficulties with Nigel, Gary produces the following:

```
ACCEPTANCE–X————REJECTION      SECURITY————X-RISK
CONTROL–X————LETTING GO        UNION————X————SEPARATENESS
FUTURE————X—PAST
```

Simply through the act of 'mapping' his location in each polarity, Gary notes the significant shifts that have occurred but also those locations that have either not shifted or have only shifted marginally. This awareness allows Gary to address and consider his presenting issues from novel perspectives. For example, he is intrigued by the shift in the FUTURE——PAST polarity and considers whether something of his current experience might be understandable simply on the basis that he is not used to focusing on issues from a FUTURE-dominant polarity perspective.

Existential polarity tensions can also serve as useful challenges when the identified polarities are considered from the focus of any of the remaining primary constructs of the worldview. For example, when asked to locate where he imagines Nigel's embodied stance along each of the polarities to be as a consequence of their dispute, Gary produces the following:

```
ACCEPTANCE———X–REJECTION        SECURITY-X————RISK
CONTROL-X————LETTING GO         UNION-X—————SEPARATENESS
FUTURE————X——PAST
```

In general, the investigation of existential polarity tensions provides a means with which to *map* or to get a more concrete reading of those structures and insecurities maintaining the client's worldview that have been most locationally disturbed or which have not shifted location but have nonetheless stood out in relation to the client's presenting issues. The aim of such investigations is *not* one which seeks to re-locate or de-emphasise any of the identified polarities. Its value is entirely descriptive, not prescriptive. As the example above has also suggested, the exploration of existential polarity tensions may also be useful for the concrete investigation of the other-construct and the world-construct components of the client's worldview. This is particularly so when the client's issues centre upon his or her relations with that other who is deemed to be difficult, different or disturbing.

The descriptive exploration of existential polarity tensions is most typically carried out in a semi-structured fashion that is reliant upon the client's own statements as the primary means through which to identify the most pertinent polarities. Nonetheless, although it would be unusual, there is no inherent reason against the existential therapist and client engaging in a more formal and structured investigation that begins with the client being presented with a list of existential polarity tensions (as above) and asked to locate his or her current stance toward each tension either verbally or by placing a mark somewhere along each continuum. While some existential therapists might be disturbed by, or antagonistic to, an enterprise that could be construed as some sort of manualised procedure, others might find it both an appropriate and worthwhile means to encourage descriptive inquiry and, more importantly, to address directly the inter-relational aspects of the client's worldview. Indeed, it is possible that presenting such an exercise at various times throughout the therapy (or even only at its start and completion), could highlight significant shifts which the client identifies as being beneficial in themselves or which serve as catalysts for beneficial change.

Having carried out the latter exercise with various groups of participants in a number of Masterclasses that I have facilitated, I must admit to some degree of surprise as to how fruitful an exercise it was and how valuable the participants found the discussions arising from their explorations to be. Many noted how powerful it felt for them to be involved in co-creating an inter-related overview of (usually) implicit tensions in various structures maintaining their worldview. Others noted that while the location at which they had placed themselves along the continuum of each separate existential polarity was accurate *when considered in isolation*, viewing the various polarities together and in relation to one another provoked their awareness of significant contradictions and unforeseen disparities. For example, one participant who greatly valued 'union' but who had consistently found difficulty in initiating and maintaining lasting intimate relationships noted that he had also highlighted overwhelming tendencies toward 'suspicion', 'rejection (of others)' and 'control'. While none of these points was necessarily novel in itself, the effect of considering each inter-relationally was startling for him.

Of course, carrying out a structured exercise in the context of a Masterclass is a significantly different enterprise from that of engaging in a therapeutic encounter. Acknowledging this, and also that, personally, I tend to recoil from anything in therapy that hints at rigidified procedures, I am, nonetheless, prepared to accept that a structured investigation focused upon existential polarity tensions, which remains exclusively descriptively focused, and which is offered to the client in a fashion that permits and accepts its rejection, is not intrinsically inconsistent with the aims and practices of existential therapy. Indeed, in the *realpolitik* of contemporary publicly funded, evidence-based provision of therapy, it might make sense to explore its possibilities.

An Exercise Exploring Existential Polarity Tensions

1. Utilising the list of existential polarities presented above, mark where you currently place your self along each polarity continuum.

   o Note any existence tensions that tend toward either polar extreme.
   o Note any existence tensions that tend toward the centre.

2. What is your reaction to the emergent 'map' as a whole, or inter-relationally? Is it as you would have predicted? If not, what is different?
3. Consider a current concern or bothersome issue in your life from the locational focus of the existential polarity tensions which seem most pertinent to you. In what ways, if any, does this means of considering the problematic issue provide novel and useful perspectives?

(Continued)

(Continued)

4. Focus upon a current client whom you would describe as being difficult or irritating in some way. Now repeat Points 1 and 2 as a mapping exercise for that client's existence tensions.
5. Compare the two maps that have emerged. What, if anything, stands out for you when you examine your own and the client's points of continuum that have been located at either extremity of the polarity and which are closest to a polarity's mid-point?
6. Select one example of what disturbs you about the client and consider it in relation to the two existential polarity tensions maps that you have created. What, if anything, emerges that strikes you as worth further consideration?

Exploring the Client's Worldview

Sigmund Freud, the founder of psychoanalysis, employed the analogy of archaeological 'digs' in order to express the psychoanalytic aim of bringing to the surface of consciousness the deeply buried artefacts of the unconscious (Ellenberger, 1970; Gay, 1988). For Ludwig Binswanger, one of the first psychiatrists to employ a form of existential analysis, a more appropriate analogy was that of anthropology. The expertise of the anthropologist lies in the exploration and elucidation of differing, often novel, cultures in terms of their beliefs, aspirations, interactions, societal structures, artistic expressions, public and private behavioural codes of conduct, as well as many other socio-cultural features. For Binswanger, the task of the existential therapist held close parallels. Each of his patients could be understood as an initially unknown and novel culture. The therapist who enters and explores this novel culture must remain open both to its particulars and to the universal concerns that these particulars express. In brief, Binswanger sought to carry out an 'anthropological analysis' of his psychiatric patients' various relations through a world-dimensional investigation focused upon the patient's engagement with (a) the natural world with its physical, environmental and biological dimension (the *umwelt*, or *with-world*); (b) the world of everyday, public social relations with others (the *mitwelt* or *around world*); and (c) the world of private and intimate relations both with themselves and with the significant others or significant meanings in their lives (the *eigenwelt* or *own world*). Further, Binswanger argued that the exploration of these world-dimensions, the relative value ascribed to each by the patient, and the possible tensions arising between them provided a useful means with which to expose the implicit, and often unconsidered values, attitudes and beliefs that underpinned and maintained each of these world-dimensions on its own and in relation to the others (Binswanger, 1963; Stadlen & Stadlen, 2005).

In many ways, Binswanger's focus corresponds closely with the exploration of the client's worldview as discussed in Phase One. Unlike Binswanger, however, who concluded that an alignment of, and balance between, the various world-dimensions was the key to mental health, the structural approach being outlined in this text makes no such claims. This is not to say that Binswanger's hypothesis is either incorrect or inappropriate, only that, as Heidegger noted (Valle & King, 1978), it deviates somewhat from a number of the implications of the foundational Principles of existential phenomenology that were discussed in Part One.

Even so, there is a great deal that remains from Binswanger's ideas that is of value to the investigation of the client's worldview. Some existential therapists such as Emmy van Deurzen, for example, continue to use a variation of Ludwig Binswanger's world-dimensions in highly creative ways (van Deurzen and Arnold-Baker, 2005). Indeed, van Deurzen has added a fourth world-dimension – the *uber-welt* (or *over-world*) – which seeks to make explicit those factors concerned with the person's relations to the ideals and aspirational aspects of living which were implicitly presented in Binswanger's discussion of the *eigenwelt* (Binswanger, 1963; van Deurzen-Smith, 1988; van Deurzen & Adams, 2011; van Deurzen & Arnold-Baker, 2005). Other existential therapists, such as Naomi Stadlen and Anthony Stadlen, however, take issue with this perspective, arguing that Heidegger's original use of the term *mitwelt* was not intended to imply

> ... just one 'world', or 'dimension', among others. Mitwelt needs no supplementing with [the other world dimensions] for the simple reason that it includes them .... Being-in-the-world with others is not one 'dimension' of being human. It is what being human *is*. (Stadlen & Stadlen, 2005: 135)

My own approach to the debate about the world-dimensions is to offer an alternative to what they seek to express through the analysis of the worldview. I take this stance for the following reasons: first, the focus on existential insecurities (i.e., continuity, dispositional stances and identity) and primary structures (i.e., the self-, other- and world-constructs) maintaining the worldview is more immediately accessible to clients. Second, the focus demarcations are less obviously artificial. And third, the embedded sedimentations and dissociations that both maintain and define the worldview are more immediately discernible. For example, consider the following case vignette: Dora sees her self as being a warm, caring, bright and attractive person. However, all of her relations with men, whether intimate or at a social or public level, are judged by her to be 'total failures'. How can she find a way to success with men in general and with a male life-partner? Her inability to form a lasting relationship with a man is making her feel empty, desperate and suicidal. One of the focus points to which Dora constantly returns is her body. She is able to speak of it in a fairly detached and distanced fashion, relating what 'it' wants, how 'it' does or does not function properly, how 'it' is one of the main sources of her troubles and difficulties.

From the self-construct perspective, Dora's statements regarding her body include: 'I keep myself in good shape through exercise', 'I have most of the features that would define me as physically attractive and I believe my self to be so', 'I enjoy sex', 'I can't see a problem with my body, but I must be avoiding that.'

From the other-construct perspective, Dora's statements regarding men's (as representative 'others') stance towards her from a body-focused standpoint include: 'Men demand perfection: perfect bodies, perfect sex, perfect everything', 'When men get to see me as a body, they like what they see but they don't "handle with care"', 'When I think of how I'm letting a man invade my body when we have sex, I feel pretty disgusted.'

From the world-construct perspective, Dora's statements regarding her body as a physical, material 'thing' or 'object' inhabiting the world include: 'It's like a cat. It only relates to you on its own terms', 'It's very jealous and wants all of my attention', 'It's entirely unpredictable as to what will please or satisfy it.'

A schematic representation of Dora's worldview from the standpoint of its primary structures is shown in Table 8.1.

TABLE 8.1

SELF-CONSTRUCT	OTHER-CONSTRUCT	WORLD-CONSTRUCT
I am warm, caring, bright and attractive. I am empty, desperate and suicidal. I keep myself in good shape through exercise. I have more of the features that would define me as physically attractive and I believe myself to be so. I enjoy sex. I can't see a problem with my body, but I must be avoiding that.	Men demand perfection: perfect bodies, perfect everything. When men get to see me as a body, they like what they see but they don't 'handle with care'. When I think of how I'm letting a man invade my body when we have sex, I feel pretty disgusted.	My body is like cat. It only relates to you on its own terms. My body is very jealous and wants all my attention. My body is entirely unpredictable as to what will please or satisfy it.

When we take a statement that arose from her self-construct and reconsider it in relation to the remaining constructs, what might emerge? For example, from a self-construct perspective, Dora states 'I enjoy sex'. What emerges when this statement is placed within the other-construct? Immediately we are presented with a possible contradiction: Dora enjoys sex *and* feels repulsion at the thought of a man invading her body. Together, these statements require further clarification on Dora's part. It is not necessarily that the two don't 'fit' with each other, only that it is not yet understandable what that fitness is for Dora. Equally, if we consider any of Dora's world-construct statements and place them within the framework of her other-construct, what emerges? Is Dora suggesting, for example, that 'bodies-as-things' are more 'man-like' or more allied to men than they are to Dora? And, if so, does this help to clarify Dora's self-construct view that the unknown problem with regard to her body is that it is 'man-like'? What might be the implications of this with regard to Dora's presenting problems?

On further investigation, the significance given to bodies in all three primary structures becomes apparent. Nonetheless, Dora's statements suggest that she must pay a price for this importance, in that the ultimate cost to her of being recognised as physically attractive is to be with a man who, as a man, can only repulse her. In a related fashion, Dora claims that she can't see a problem with her body (even if this is just avoidance on her part) and at the same time presents her body as being cat-like, jealous, wanting all of her attention and entirely unpredictable as to what will please it. The possibility emerges that Dora's competing claims might have a pay-off for her. Can Dora's presenting problems now be re-considered in the light of this? Is it not possible that the problems she presents (to her self, as much as to her therapist) actually serve, and express, the divided demands of her worldview? Would not the solving of the problem actually destabilise that worldview?

When these statements are explored further in order to disclose more of the implied existential insecurities which infuse them, what emerges is a strong critical, if not punitive, stance: Dora *must be* physically attractive and the only evidence that matters for her to prove that she is has to be the establishment of a lasting relationship with a man. At the same time, her anger is also directed towards men: 'I love men's bodies; it's the creeps inside them that I can't stand!' With further probing of these statements, Dora is very specific in her felt sense that her body is too much like the men in her life: it is always threatening to do something awful to her, it constantly betrays her and yet she can't live without it and what it provides.

A schematic representation of Dora's worldview from the standpoint of its existential insecurities is shown in Table 8.2.

TABLE 8.2

INSECURITIES CONCERNED WITH CONTINUITY	Dora's sense of her own continuity rests upon her establishing a lasting relationship with a man. And if she can't?
	Perfection is a male demand. Can she be perfect and continue to be in demand?
	To exist as a body Dora's body must be cat-like. How can she continue to be cat-like?
	Dora can't live without her body and what it provides. What must Dora do to ensure that she lives?
	Dora's body is a constant threat to her. How can that threat be controlled or removed?
INSECURITIES CONCERNED WITH DISPOSTIONAL STANCES	Dora is a total failure in her relationships with men.
	Dora's body is one of the main sources of her problems and difficulties.
	Dora keeps in good shape through exercise.
	Dora has most of the features that would define her as physically attractive.
	Dora believes that she is attractive.
	Dora enjoys sex.
	Dora believes that she must be avoiding seeing whatever is problematic with her body.
	Men demand perfection
	Men don't handle with care.
	The thought of men's sexual invasion of her body is disgusting for Dora.
	Dora's body only relates to her on its own terms.
	Dora must be attractive.
	The only worthwhile evidence that Dora is attractive is that she is in a lasting relationship with a man.
	Dora loves men's bodies.
	Dora can't stand the creeps who inhabit men's bodies.

(Continued)

TABLE 8.2   (Continued)

INSECURITIES CONCERNED WITH IDENTITY	Dora is warm, caring, bright, attractive.
	Dora is not her body.
	Dora is sometimes defined as a desirable body by men.
	Dora's body is defined as cat-like, jealous, wants all of her attention and is unpredictable as to what will please or satisfy it.
	Dora's body is her betrayer.

Considering Dora's presenting problem from the descriptive standpoint of her existential insecurities, we can clarify a number of dilemmas centred upon her relationship with her body. For example, at the Identity level, Dora is clear that she is not her body. However, she states that men define her as a desirable body. Equally, at the level of her Continuity, Dora claims that she cannot live without her body and what it provides, even though this same body remains a constant threat to her. At the level of her Dispositional Stances, there is once again a confusion of statements regarding bodies: Dora keeps fit and enjoys sex, she loves men's bodies (though not the men who inhabit them and invade her body) and her body relates to her only on its own terms, is the source of her problems and difficulties even though she must be avoiding seeing what these are. From this, we can begin to consider whether Dora's presenting concerns regarding her establishing and maintaining a lasting relationship with a man might express her desire for an existence that is free of bodies in general and of the jealous, cat-like attention-seeking and unpredictable demands of her own body in particular. At the same time, Dora's desire cannot be fulfilled because men relate to, and know, only her body, not Dora her self. What kind of man would it have to be for Dora to be in a relationship with him? What kind of relationship would it be? Could it be a sexual yet non-body focused relationship? These and many more questions might further clarify Dora's problem and the impact that her desired solution might have upon her worldview.

We can now attempt to construct a schematic representation of Dora's worldview which considers her statements from the combined perspective of her primary constructs and existential concerns (see Table 8.3).

From this wider perspective, we can see that although Dora initially considered her presenting problem as being directly focused on her relations with men, this partial clarification of her worldview reveals that the main tensions exist between Dora and her body. Dora's body-focused world-construct emerges as the main determinant, and threat, to Dora's sense of her self-construct's insecurities regarding Continuity. Equally, when considering this relationship from the focus of her insecurities regarding Identity, Dora's self-construct and body-focused world-construct stand in stark opposition to one another, as though each were the negation of the other. In terms of Dora's men-focused other-construct, what presents itself is a consistently negative view of men, with the exception of men's bodies, which

TABLE 8.3

	SELF-CONSTRUCT	OTHER-CONSTRUCT	WORLD-CONSTRUCT
INSECURITIES CONCERNED WITH CONTINUITY	A lasting relationship with a man is essential. Dora must be cat-like. Dora can't live without her body.	Men sexually invade Dora's body.	Dora's body is a constant threat. Dora's body betrays her. Dora's body is a main source of her problems and difficulties. Dora's body only relates to her on its own terms. Dora's body is unpredictable with regard to what pleases or satisfies it.
INSECURITIES CONCERNED WITH DISPOSTIONAL STANCES	Dora is a failure in her relations with men. Dora keeps in good shape. Dora must be attractive. Being in a relationship with a man is the only worthwhile evidence of being attractive. Dora believes that she must be avoiding seeing whatever is problematic with her body. Dora is disgusted by the thought of men's sexual invasion of her body.	Men demand perfection. Men don't handle with care.	Dora's body must have all her attention.
INSECURITIES CONCERNED WITH IDENTITY	Dora is warm. Dora is caring. Dora is bright. Dora is attractive. Dora enjoys sex. Dora is not her body.	Men's bodies are loveable. Men are creeps, inhabiting bodies. Men sometimes define Dora as desirable.	Dora's body is cat-like. Dora's body is jealous.

are lovable. Here again a potential contrast between Dora's body and men's bodies would be worth further clarification, as would men's relationship with Dora's body, as opposed to Dora as she construes her self.

Obviously, there is far more that is open to a detailed investigation regarding the descriptive exploration of the worldview through its primary constructs and existential concerns. What must be stressed is that, just as in Phase One, the clarification of these various inter-relations and their implications emerged *entirely* from descriptively focused inquiry. No analytic interpretations were required, no statement was treated initially as being any less – or more – significant than any other, nor were any assumptions made regarding the greater or lesser truthfulness of any statement even when apparent contradictions arose.

An Exercise on the Exploration of the Client's Worldview

(Although you may do this exercise on your own, it is recommended that you work together with a partner and take turns in facilitating the exploration of each other's client's worldview.)

1. Identify a client whom you have worked with as his or her therapist.
2. Identify a specific focus topic related to that client's presenting problem or issue.
3. What statements regarding the primary structures as expressed through that presenting problem were made by your client?
4. What statements regarding existential insecurities as expressed through that presenting problem were made by your client?
5. As with the example of Dora discussed above, explore the various inter-relations between the three constructs.
6. How might this exploration add to and clarify with greater adequacy the relatedness between the client's presenting problem and his or her worldview?

Exploring Sedimentations and Dissociations in the Client's Worldview

As was discussed in Chapter 3, while some structures of the worldview remain relatively flexible and open to reconstitution and redefinition in response to experiential challenge, it is also the case that many – perhaps the great majority – of structures, in response to challenge, resist redefinition and remain fixed or inflexible *sedimentations*. Via their clarification, various emergent disowned or *dissociated* experiences that would otherwise threaten the maintenance and stability of the worldview can begin to be identified. Although dissociations, like sedimentations, also serve to maintain the stability of the worldview, their impact imposes experiential limitations that can provoke problematic, undesirable or even seriously debilitating disturbances and disorders. Nonetheless, sedimentations and dissociations should not be seen to be inherently problematic. No coherent, definable or meaningful worldview would be possible without them. For example, if at the self-construct level the statement 'I am Ernesto, the author of this book' is to have any meaning whatsoever, then this self-construct derived Ernesto must be distinguishable from the plethora of potential non-Ernestos. Sedimentations and dissociations validate the claim to 'be Ernesto' who can be distinguished from his non-Ernesto alternatives.

Given the option of either de-sedimenting inadequate sedimentations so that more of the previously dissociated experiences can be re-owned, or of maintaining the inflexible sedimentation even if it requires ever-increasing dissociations of experience, our most common response is the latter. The adoption of the first strategy of de-sedimentation provokes an increasing inability to sufficiently maintain a stable and definable worldview. The more open and flexible the worldview is in its attempts to reflect the experience of worlding, the less fixed become its sedimentations and, as a consequence, the less structurally stable and definable it becomes.

The descriptive investigation of the client's worldview throughout Phase Two permits both the existential therapist and client to identify the sedimentations and dissociations that present themselves through the descriptive investigation and challenge being undertaken. In addition, as well as identifying these, Phase Two challenges to the worldview allow the clarification of the depth or rigidity of the sedimentations (and the parallel strength of their concomitant dissociations). Together, these investigations can more adequately place the client's presenting problem *in relation to the worldview* rather than consider it as separate and alien to it. In this way, the presenting problem can be better understood as expressive of several distinct dilemmas of which four in particular are the most recurring.

a. *The presenting problem is an attempt to maintain the worldview's sedimentations and dissociations.* As an example of this, let us return to the earlier example of Dora's body-focused dilemma and consider this in the light of sedimentation and dissociation. Dora's presenting problem is that it is an essential need for her to be in a lasting relationship with a man. However, she constantly fails to achieve this. One possibility that emerged from the previous descriptively focused investigation was that as well as Dora wanting and recognising how essential it was to her to be in a lasting relationship with a man, it was *equally* essential to the maintenance of her current worldview that she failed to achieve this. Thus it can be seen that the sedimented stances presented by Dora (such as 'there must be a problem with my body if even I cannot identify what it is') serve to maintain the current worldview in that it permits for the continuing desire to be in a lasting relationship while also creating obstacles to its achievement. In the same way, Dora's various statements reveal significant dissociations (e.g., Dora is not her body. Men's bodies are lovable. Men are the creeps inside bodies) that also permit both the desire and its obstacles to be maintained. Were it the case that Dora began to challenge any of her sedimentations, the continuing maintenance of her worldview would be threatened in ways that cannot be predicted. Miserable and distraught as she is, Dora can at least stabilise her experience of any one or all of her core existential concerns regarding embodied continuity, dispositional stances and identity. Her sedimentations and dissociations are her means to do so.

b. *The presenting problem suggests an inability in the worldview to maintain stability through its sedimentations and dissociations.* As an example of this, consider my client Philip's presenting problem: 'I don't know who I am anymore.' Philip holds a self-construct focused dispositional sedimentation that 'I must always be 100% honest in all of my relations with others.' At the same time, Philip is in a difficult work situation that has convinced him that he will soon be fired from a position he has maintained all his working life. In reaction, he has begun to steal various items of office stationery and has recently also been 'raiding the office kitty'. However, when Philip steals the items, he insists that he is unaware that he is doing so. As a result Philip can temporarily maintain his worldview, but at a heavy price: how can he explain these moments of not knowing what he is doing other than by committing him self to a view of serious mental disturbance or imbalance? In any case, Philip has discerned a dishonesty that cannot be maintained by his sedimented worldview. Hence, the presenting problem partly permits the maintenance of that sedimentation for the time being, but also expresses his growing awareness that the current sedimentation cannot be maintained for long and is becoming increasingly unstable.

c. *The presenting problem arises as a result of the unwanted and unplanned consequence of rigid, yet positively valued, sedimentations and dissociations in the worldview.* As an example of this, consider the dilemma posed for Geraldine, whose presenting problem is 'My colleagues are jealous of me and are trying to ruin my career when I'm only trying to do my job.' Geraldine, who has worked as a teacher in a Further Education College for 15 years, was, until recently, well-liked by her colleagues, and was strongly supported by them when the opportunity arose for the appointment of a new Head of Department. Geraldine applied for the post and was offered it. Unfortunately, Geraldine holds extremely rigid views about 'being an authority' and has begun to behave in ways that are excessively demanding of her colleagues. Increasingly, the 'free and easy' relations that she had previously maintained with them and which she values as a desirable aspect of her self-construct have begun to be overwhelmed by the strict sedimented stance regarding 'being an authority'. Geraldine's presenting problem, although focused on her other-construct (i.e. her colleagues), expresses the increasingly restrictive impact of a rigid sedimentation which, as a result of the new role with which she identifies her self (i.e. Head of Department), has extended so that it replaces previously more flexible aspects of her worldview that could be maintained when Geraldine previously identified her self and her colleagues as 'equals'. In this instance, Geraldine has no desire to de-sediment her self-construct focused disposition on 'being an authority' since she continues to value it. However, the presenting problem reveals the unexpected and less desirable 'consonant conflict' issues that can arise when the context around which a sedimented dispositional stance is being expressed undergoes alteration.

d. *The presenting problem arises as a result of the unwanted and unplanned consequences of de-sedimenting a previously fixed sedimentation.* As an example of this, consider my client Armand's dilemma. Armand has had great difficulties throughout his life in trusting other men and developing close friendships with them. Increasingly unhappy with what he saw as a 'gap' in his life, he had attended an intensive group process restricted to men and which was intended to 'celebrate manhood'. The group experience had been dramatic and highly significant to Armand and, as a consequence, he felt that he had broken through his uneasiness in being around and close to other men. Thus, Armand has successfully challenged a rigid sedimentation. When Armand comes to see me, his presenting issue is 'I feel lost. I think I may be gay and need to explore this. But if I am, my marriage and family fall apart and I don't want this to happen.' Through our discussions, it becomes more evident that Armand's life-altering experience in the men's group has allowed the de-sedimentation of his previous reluctance to be close to men. In doing so, however, his experience of the possibilities of being close and developing friendships with men has also stirred previously dissociated stances regarding his possible sexual attraction to, and desire for, other men. Prior to this, Armand had seen him self as a heterosexual male and had developed a close and harmonious life with his wife, Julie, with whom he continues to have enjoyable and active sexual relations. The recent de-sedimenting of Armand's self-construct-focused dispositional stance toward men in general has had the undesired effect of also de-sedimenting Armand's ability to identify him self with regard to his sexual orientation, which he did not actually want to de-sediment and whose possible de-sedimentation he deems to be problematic.

As the above examples attempt to demonstrate, while it is of great value to consider the sedimentations and dissociations in the light of the client's presenting concerns, it is also vital that the therapist carries out these explorations with great care since their relatedness to, and impact upon, other – possibly problematic, possibly desirable – client-held sedimentations and dissociations cannot be known in advance. Once again, the existential therapist's focus on descriptive clarification and challenge is likely to decrease the probability of unexpected and overwhelming upheavals in the client's worldview.

Two Exercises Exploring Sedimentation and Dissociation

Exercise 1

1. Working with a partner, take turns in being the therapist and client. Each session should last 20 minutes.
2. As the client, focus on your self-construct and select an example of 'someone I could never possibly be' (for example: 'I could never possibly be someone who lies to her friends' or 'I could never be a committed member of X political party') that you feel sufficiently at ease to explore with your partner. Focus your exploration on the following: 'Who would I be if I became the person I could never possibly be?'
3. As the therapist, help your client to explore his or her presenting situation by challenging its impact upon the client's wider-worldview. In doing so, pay particular attention to the examples of sedimentation and dissociation that might become apparent.

Exercise 2

Working with a partner, take turns in exploring the presenting problem of one of your clients (or a client from a published case study) from the focus point of how, and in what ways, the presenting problem might be expressing issues of sedimentation and dissociation in the client's worldview.

The Inter-relational Realms of Encounter

In various earlier papers and texts, I have proposed a particular descriptive approach whose primary advantage lies in its utilisation of the relational immediacy in the therapeutic encounter (Spinelli, 1994, 1997, 2001, 2005). This approach focuses upon four distinct *inter-relational realms* – the *I-focused*, *You-focused*, *We-focused* and *They-focused* realms of encounter. The first three of these realms are of particular significance to the aims of Phase Two (the fourth, the They-focus, will be considered as part of the discussion on Phase Three). Each of the first three realms can be briefly distinguished in the following way:

The I-focused realm of encounter attempts to describe and clarify the embodied existential insecurities (i.e., insecurities surrounding continuity, dispositional stances and identity) that arise through 'my experience of being "my self" in any given relationship'. It asks, in effect, 'What do I tell my self about my current experience of being me in this encounter?' The following are dialogical examples of an I-focused realm of encounter: 'I'm scared', 'I wish I was more interesting', 'I am being reminded that I was not good to my parents.'

The You-focused realm of encounter attempts to describe and clarify the embodied existential insecurities that arise from the locational focus of the other-construct. The You-focus expresses the self-construct's view of the other-construct (i.e., 'my experience of the other in any given relationship' as in 'You are ...', 'I see you as being ...') *as well as* the self-construct's assumptions regarding the other-construct's views of the self-construct (i.e., 'my experience of the other's experience of me in any given relationship' as in 'I think that you see me as ...'). The following are dialogical examples of a You-focused realm of encounter: 'You aren't trustworthy', 'I don't like the way you dress', 'You don't seem terribly interested in what's being said', 'You're trying to hide your sadness', 'You find me boring', 'You like me', 'You laugh at my jokes as though I need to be humoured.'

The We-focused realm of encounter attempts to describe and clarify the embodied existential insecurities that arise through each participant's experience of 'us being in relation with one another'. It asks, 'What do I tell my self about the experience of being *us* in the immediacy of this encounter?' The following are dialogical examples of a We-focused realm of encounter: 'My sense is that we really seem to be connecting right now', 'As I see it, even though neither one of us is saying anything at the moment, it feels like we're communicating in important ways', 'It feels like we keep missing each other and this makes us over-cautious in what we end up expressing.'

While existential therapy attempts a descriptive exploration of all three realms of encounter, throughout Phase Two an explicit emphasis is placed upon the third (We-focused) realm of encounter (Spinelli, 1994, 1997, 2005). The existential therapist's willingness to examine and consider what emerges experientially through this realm as being real and valid (rather than substitutive, symbolic or transferential) serves to place his or her active presence within the immediacy of the interactive relationship with the client. Further, this focus serves to expose and clarify in that immediacy the self-same inter-relational issues that clients express as being deeply problematic within their wider-world relations.

As an clarification of how these realms can be identified and their potential value to the therapeutic process, let us return to a previous dialogical example regarding the existential therapist's and client's exploration of 'the phoney-ness of others' and consider their dialogue from the perspective of these three realms:

Therapist: Look, I wonder if I can interrupt you here for a moment. I'm trying to hear what you're saying and getting some sort of fix on it [**I-focus**].

Client: Sure. Why? Do you have any thoughts or feelings about what I said [**You-focus**]?

Therapist: What I think or feel about what you're saying [**You-focus**]?

Client: Yeah. Because I'm not sure I know how I feel about what I'm saying [**I-focus**].

Therapist: You don't?

Client: Nope. I'm sorta confused.

Therapist: Maybe we both are [**We-focus**]. Could I ask you something that might clarify things for both of us [**We-focus**]?

Client: Go ahead. We could both use a break [**We-focus**].

Therapist: Okay. So, for instance, I'm wondering if you are hearing your self make any private statements about your self while you're speaking [**You-focus**]?

Client: You mean like judgements or criticisms?

Therapist: Are there judgements or criticisms?

Client: Sure. Plenty. All of the time.

Therapist: Okay. So … 'When I'm talking about something I said or did to someone, I am also privately judging and criticising my self' [**I-focus**]. Is that right?

Client: Yeah. And I bet you want to know what they are, right [**You-focus**]?

Therapist: Sure. Of course. But before you tell me, can I ask you if any of those judgements and criticisms are directed toward the people you're talking to? Or are they just focused on your self?

Client: What a weird question. [*Pauses to consider it*] They're mainly toward me. But they're also directed outward. It's like I criticise them for the words they're using, or how they've dressed that day, or any old thing. I never thought about that [**I-focus**]. Weird.

Therapist: So, in the private judging and criticising that you're doing *here* are there any statements you're making privately about me?

Client: You? [*Pauses*] Well … Yeah. Sometimes you say things in a complicated way [**You-focus**]. Like now, when you asked the question. It made me feel like I had to talk 'posh' [**I-focus**]. Don't get me wrong, I appreciate what we're doing here [**We-focus**].

Therapist: Thank you. I really value it, too [**We-focus**].

Client: [*Touched by the therapist's statement and also angered*] See? There it is again! As soon as you said that, I thought: 'What a phoney!' [**You-focus**]. But I don't believe that! You're not! [**You-focus**].

Therapist: Was it what I said that triggered that private judgement? Or the way I said it [**I-focus**]?

Client: No! No! It was the look you had on your face when you said it [**You-focus**].

Therapist: And the look said: 'Ernesto's a phoney' [**You-focus**].

Client: Yeah … But … No. It did say that. But mainly it said that *I'm* the phoney [**I-focus**].

Therapist: So we're both phoneys? [**We-focus**].

Client: [*Laughs*] Yeah! We're both phoneys! [**We-focus**]. But I'm the 'phonier' phoney! [**I-focus**].

Therapist: Okay. So ... 'I'm a phoney' [**I-focus**]. Can you make any other connections to it?

Client: Yeah. That phoney waitress from last night. It was like she could just see through me [**You-focus**].

Therapist: Okay. Let's stay with that for a minute. Am I another person who can 'just see through you [**I-focus**]?'

Client: You? Well ... You see through me at times, that's for sure. But it's different [**You-focus**].

Therapist: How's it different?

Client: I don't feel like you're seeing me as a phoney [**You-focus**].

Therapist: What if neither one of us is ever being a phoney [**We-focus**]?

Client: Yeah, good point. I feel the same, even though we're such different people [**We-focus**]. But, you know I just realised that although I believe in what I just said, and I'm not ever being phoney here, I can still hear this voice inside saying, 'But I *am* a phoney!' [**I-focus**].

Therapist: Okay. Stay with that. Hear that voice inside saying: 'But I *am* a phoney!' [**I-focus**]. What's your reaction?

Client: When I hear you say it, I get suspicious about you [**You-focus**]. I'm wondering whether you're playing some sort of therapeutic game with me and that, in spite of what you say, you really do believe I'm a phoney [**You-focus**]. I don't trust you [**You-focus**].

Therapist: Thank you. You sounded really honest to me [**You-focus**]. Does what you said sound at all like something a phoney would say [**You-focus**]?

Client: [*Shows facial signs of being affected by the therapist's question. Becoming tearful*] I didn't mean it when I said I didn't trust you. I do [**You-focus**]. I just felt threatened in a weird sort of way by what you said [**You-focus**].

Therapist: What was that sense of your feeling threatened [**You-focus**]? Do you feel it now between us [**We-focus**]?

Client: No. But you know what I wanted to say before? I wanted to say: 'How dare you? How dare you just sit there and pontificate about whether I am or am not a phoney? [**You-focus**]. Who do you think you are? [**You-focus**].

Therapist: What's it like to say that, what you just said?

Client: I feel shit-scared! [**I-focus**].

Therapist: Because ...

Client: Because I realised that it's what I wanted to say to that waitress. And to my grandmother, and Jimmy. [*Turns to face away from the therapist. Shakes his fist. Grimaces.*] How dare you! [*Faces the therapist again.*] But I couldn't. I was terrified it would destroy our relationship [**We-focus**]. And now I've said it here and I'm just as terrified about what it'll do to *this* relationship [**We-focus**].

Therapist: So, okay. Now I'm wondering this: If I were you right now, I'd be asking my self, 'What has saying it done to me? [**client's I-focus**]. To Ernesto? [**client's You-focus**]. To us? [**We-focus**].

Two Exercises on the Exploration of Three Inter-relational Realms

Exercise 1

Throughout the whole exercise try to avoid pauses or preparations in advance of completing your statements.

The I-focus

1. Together with a partner take turns in completing the following statement: *'What I am telling my self about me right now is that I ...'*
2. After you have both completed the statement, repeat the exercise and continue to do so for 3 minutes.

The You-focus

1. Together with a partner take turns in completing the following statement: *'What I am telling my self about you right now is that you ...'*
2. After you have both completed the statement, repeat the exercise and continue to do so for 3 minutes.
3. Now, together with a partner, take turns in completing the following statement: *'What I am telling my self right now is that you are experiencing me as ...'*
4. After you have both completed the statement, repeat the exercise and continue to do so for 3 minutes.

The We-focus

1. Together with a partner take turns in completing the following statement: *'What I am telling my self about us right now is that we ...'*
2. After you have both completed the statement, repeat the exercise and continue to do so for 3 minutes.

Discussion

1. Discuss with your partner what the experience of doing all three parts of this exercise was like for you.
2. What general value, if any, for the therapeutic encounter would you say that any aspects of this exercise might offer?

Exercise 2

The I-focus

1. Working together with a partner, take turns in being therapist and client. Each session should last 10 minutes.
2. As the client, focus on a recent encounter that has provoked you in some way. Begin the session by describing the encounter and discussing its impact from your personal standpoint.
3. As the therapist, assist the client in exploring his or her experience of the encounter and its impact *by restricting all your statements and interventions so that they are attempts to disclose the client's I-focused realm.*

The You-focus

1. As the client, continue to focus on the encounter discussed above for a further 10 minutes.
2. As the therapist, assist the client in exploring his or her experience of the encounter and its impact *by restricting all your statements and interventions so that they are attempts to disclose the client's You-focused realm.*

The We-Focus

1. As the client, continue to focus on the encounter discussed above for a further 10 minutes.
2. As the therapist, assist the client in exploring his or her experience of the encounter and its impact *by restricting all your statements and interventions so that they remain at the We-focus realm of encounter.*

Discussion

1. Discuss with your partner what the experience of doing all three parts of this exercise was like for each of you.
2. What value, if any, for the therapeutic encounter would you say that any aspects of this exercise might offer?

Working with Intimacy

Therapist Disclosures

Although many of the more strident theory–derived objections toward therapist disclosures have eased somewhat over time, and, consequently, have been the subject of critique and reformulation (Rowan and Jacobs, 2002), many of these attitudes and regulations remain fixed areas of concern, in some form or other, for the majority of therapists, regardless of the model they espouse. To my knowledge, existential therapists have, on the whole, written little about therapist disclosures and, thereby, have implicitly suggested that their stance is no different to that of therapists from other approaches. As I have argued elsewhere, the most recurrent arguments both for and against disclosure fail to take into account the inter-relational factors that are so central to an existential approach to therapy (Spinelli, 2001).

The issue of *therapist disclosure*, considered from the perspective of existential therapy, touches upon issues relevant to the *immediacy* of the therapeutic relationship in general, and in particular to the three inter-relational realms discussed above. Most pertinently, I believe, it is the We-focused realm that is critical with regard to the question of disclosure. At the We-focused realm of relation, I, as existential therapist, experience and reflect upon what emerges, or is disclosed, through the interaction between us. This could include my reflections upon what it is like for us to be with one another in this currently reflected moment, my sense of what we might be sharing at an experiential level, and what may be being expressed by us in an indirect, or metaphorical manner that is resonant with our current way of being together. It is here, I would argue, that the possibility of therapist disclosure becomes most pertinent.

However, the question arises: what is the existential therapist attempting to promote or achieve through disclosure? My view is that *therapist disclosures are valid when they serve to further clarify the inter-relation between the client's presenting issues and his or her worldview.* I would suggest that two forms of disclosure are available to the existential therapist: covert and overt disclosures.

Covert disclosures are those disclosures whereby the existential therapist makes use of his or her own lived experiences in order to clarify and challenge the client's worldview statements, but does so in a way that does not directly reveal the source of the challenges as being the therapist's personal material. For example:

Client: When he finally told me that he didn't want to stay in the marriage and that he'd found a new life-partner, I just felt so sick and angry. I hated my self more than I hated him.

Therapist: Can you say a bit more about what it was like for you to hear him say these things? How was that sense of feeling sick and angry, for instance?

Client: I can just feel it, you know? It's hard to put words to it.

Therapist: [*Accessing his own experiences of being rejected and the feelings that arise in him regarding this*] Would it be okay for me to try to find the words and say them?

Client: Yes ...

Therapist: Now, I'm just guessing here. So anything I say that feels wrong to you, that's fine. You let me know. Okay, so what I'm imagining when I put myself in your experience is: I get an overwhelming dizziness; a tightness in my gut; a restriction in my throat so that I can't even reply to him; I see flashes of all sorts of earlier moments in our life together – happy moments, sad ones, silly ones, private ones; and as I see them I hear his voice saying over and over, 'It's finished. This is the end.' I feel a rage that is directed toward him, but oddly it's also directed toward my self. How's that so far? Is it at all close to your experience?

Client: Yes, a lot of it is. But as you were talking, what mainly came up for me was a sense of failure. That was the main thing. 'I've failed and I'm not worthy.'

Therapist: Okay. So let's stay with that. 'A lot of those statements Ernesto made are correct and they've provoked my overwhelming sense of failure.' Are you feeling it now?

Client: Yes, really strongly.

Therapist: So what's it like to feel it right here with me present?

Client: It's like I felt with Harry when he told me he was leaving me.

Overt disclosures also make use of the existential therapist's own personal material in order to clarify and challenge the client's worldview. However, they are explicit in acknowledging their source as the therapist's own lived experience. For example:

Client: I felt like such a complete fool! I thought that she'd been attracted to me because we'd got on so well together. But I was completely wrong! She started laughing at me! Can you believe that? Do you have any idea how something like that could feel?

Therapist: Tell me.

Client: I can't! It's just so painful. [*Begins to cry*]

Therapist: Okay. I want to offer something here. As you were speaking, I was reminded of an incident from my own life that maybe had some similar feelings to your own. I wonder whether it would be okay for you if I gave you a sense of it and focused on what it evoked for me so that we can see whether your experience and mine share anything in common. But if you think it's pointless, just say so. Or stop me at any point.

Client: No, go ahead. I'd appreciate that.

[*Therapist recounts his experience of being rejected, focusing on the challenges to his existential uncertainties that accompany it.*]

Therapist: Was any of that at all like what went on for you?

Client: Yeah. It brought a lot of my feelings back up.

[*Client discusses the points of connection between his narrative and the therapist's disclosure.*]

Therapist: What was it like to know that it was my story and not yours?

Client: Well, I knew it was your story. But it also felt like mine. I don't feel so alone in my stupidity.

Therapist: So ... 'The fact that my therapist also got rejected and feels stupid about it, stops making me feel alone?'

Client: [*Laughs*] Now you're reading my thoughts.

Therapist: [*Laughs*] Maybe you're reading mine.

Covert and overt disclosures during Phase Two acknowledge the existential therapist's presence in the therapy-world as genuine and immediate. While the primary aim of the therapist does not deviate from that of assisting to explore, clarify and challenge the client's presenting worldview, these disclosures rely upon the therapist's own experience as an additional means with which to pursue this aim.

As the above examples indicate, disclosure, from the perspective of existential therapy, has little to do with permitting the therapist to express him or her self in order to be 'congruent' or 'real' (as in 'I am feeling really bored right now'). Rather, the existential therapist's use of disclosure provides another way into the clarification and challenge of the client's worldview and permits a dialogue that in its immediacy opens up the therapeutic possibilities of discourse at the We-focused realm of encounter. These disclosures focus predominantly upon the description of the existential uncertainties in the therapist's personal narrative and, in turn, are followed by the therapist's explicit invitation to the client to examine his or her (the client's) experiential response to the therapist's disclosure in the immediacy of their dialogue. It is in this latter part of the disclosure process that most of its potential worth as a form of descriptive clarification and challenge can emerge.

At the same time, as can also, I hope, be seen from the examples above, the existential therapist's use of disclosure always seeks to remain both *tentative* and *invitational*. The genuine opportunity for the client to reject such an invitation must be part of the process. Equally, whatever the client takes from such disclosures, including that they bear no relation at all to the client's experience (or, indeed, as may sometimes occur, that they provoke the client's anger in that the disclosure is seen to misunderstand, demean or minimise his or her experience) cannot be disputed by the therapist nor be responded to in a possessive and defensive manner which rejects the client's reactive stance.

There is always a genuine risk involved in the existential therapist's use of disclosure. Disclosures may miss their mark, and confuse or burden the client. Equally, they may enfold the therapist in the feelings and memories they contain and, in doing so, deflect inquiry from its focus upon the client's worldview. It is also the case that in making such disclosures, the therapist cannot know whether the alternate option of having remained silent and allowed the client to 'sit' with the issues may have been more therapeutically beneficial. At the same time, disclosures can provide a powerful means for the client to access elements of his or her own experience that might otherwise have been minimised or missed.

Covert and overt disclosures are best offered during Phase Two, during which the existential therapist's presence and 'voice' within the therapy-world are more explicitly focused on his or her otherness. If employed during Phase One, covert disclosures are more likely to be experienced by the client as uncanny ('How on earth could the therapist have known *that*?') and in turn may add unnecessary imbalances to the power aspects in the relationship. Equally, overt disclosures offered during Phase One may seem to the client to be implicit directives to change, or may swamp the client's own explorations. Both covert and overt disclosures made during Phase One may unintentionally counteract their intent by provoking unease as well as suspicion and distrust of both the existential therapist and the therapy-world. As is generally the case with all Phase Two challenges by the therapist, it may be best to offer them only once the 'mood' of the encounter suggests a sense of the therapist having earned the right to do so.

Two Exercises on Therapist Disclosure

Exercise 1

1. Working together with a partner, take turns in being therapist and client. Each session should last 15 minutes.
2. As the client, focus initially on a recent event that has provoked a strong reactive response from you.
3. As the therapist, assist the client in exploring his or her relationship to the focus topic *but only in such a way that all your interventions are at the covert level of disclosure.*
4. When you have both completed the exercise explore the experience of utilising covert disclosures and what value, if any, they have to the therapeutic enterprise as a whole.

Exercise 2

1. Working together with a partner, take turns in being therapist and client. Each session should last 15 minutes.
2. As the client, focus initially on a recent event that has provoked a strong reactive response from you.

(Continued)

(Continued)

3. As the therapist, assist the client in exploring his or her relationship to the focus topic *but only in such a way that all your interventions are at the overt level of disclosure.*
4. When you have both completed the exercise explore the experience of utilising overt disclosures and what value, if any, they have to the therapeutic enterprise as a whole.

Daniel Stern's *Present Moments in Therapy*

An invaluable text by Daniel Stern, entitled *The Present Moment in Therapy and Everyday Life* (Stern, 2004), focuses upon 'present' or 'now' moments of meeting 'in which therapist and client know and feel what the other knows and feels' (Mearns & Cooper, 2005: 46). For Stern, this is a 'shared meaning voyage' (Stern, 2004: 172) which also encapsulates a significant shift from a one-person to a two-person psychology (ibid.) – which is to say that its focus is upon inter-relatedness rather than upon an isolationist subjectivity. Exploring various research data, Stern maintains that sufficient evidence exists for a foundational species-based system for inter-subjective (or inter-relational) knowing whose aim is achieved in those instances of *present moments* (ibid.).

Stern's understanding of present moments rests upon his phenomenologically derived understanding that 'we are psychologically and consciously alive only now' (Stern, 2004: xiv). In taking this view, Stern acknowledges his indebtedness to the ideas on temporality advocated by existential phenomenology in that the present moment is infused with, and structured by, both retentive (immediate past) and protentive (anticipated future) horizons (ibid.). The spontaneity of the present moment – a shared laugh, a touch of the shoulder, a glance that connects – cannot be initiated in some directive fashion and thus runs counter to any emphases given to technique.

From a therapeutic perspective, present moments often occur at crisis points in the therapeutic encounter when the client and therapist are disconnected or 'missing' one another or, alternatively, when they are together in the intensity of their meeting. Such instances can often express themselves as direct challenges to the therapist by the client, which require the former to respond to the immediacy of the inter-relational encounter in a way that reveals his or her willingness to meet the other in a spontaneous self-revealing response, rather than falling back on a 'formulaic role-based one' (Mearns & Cooper, 2005: 134). For Stern, therapist responses that remain at the immediacy of the present moment are far more valuable and beneficial both to the ongoing process and to the outcome of the therapeutic encounter than are the theory-laden interpretations with which therapists might feel more at ease (Stern, 2004).

Staying with this immediacy does not, however, *oblige* the therapist to disclose. Present moments can be equally powerful when the therapist rejects the client's entreaties to express something of his or her personal experience. What is critical is that the client hears the therapist's statements or responses as personally owned, expressive of who the therapist is being in the presence of the client, rather than technique or theory-based manoeuvres. For example:

Client:	I really, really, need to know what you think about what I did last night.
Therapist:	Yeah. I hear that. But I really, really don't want to say.
Client:	Why not? It would make me feel an awful lot better. No matter what you think.
Therapist:	I wish I had a better answer for you, but I don't. I just have this sense that it wouldn't help at this point for me to tell you what I think. Can you trust me on this?
Client:	I guess. [*Sighs*] What else can I do?
Therapist:	Can you stay with that sigh a bit?

During Phase Two, instances akin to those highlighted by Stern as the present moment can indicate to the therapist the degree to which the focus taken on the exploration of the client's worldview is attuned to the immediacy of encounter. The existential therapist's openness to disclosure and to We-focused discourse is likely to promote psychological and relational conditions sympathetic to the experience of the present moment. In my view, one relatively common phenomenon associated with the present moment is that of the therapist's spontaneous completion of the client's statement as it is being uttered. Such moments require the therapist to be-with and be-for the client in a highly connected or intimate manner. While they can generate a sense of closeness and trust, they can also be jarring and disturbing in their 'quasi-telepathic' appearance.

As readers are likely to have noticed through the various dialogue examples provided, therapist statements and reflections are often voiced in the first person (I) rather than in the second person (you) when reflecting back the client's self-construct narratives. As well as providing the client with a more direct confrontation with his or her statements in a fashion that makes plain their ownership at the first-person level, this way of reflecting can also facilitate the experience of present moments. For example:

Client:	I don't know whether you've understood me or not and I'm feeling anxious about that.
Therapist:	Let me see if I got what you said: 'I can't be sure as to whether or not Ernesto's understanding me and that makes me feel anxious.'
Client:	Yes! That's exactly how I feel. And now I'm feeling that maybe you know me too well and I don't know *you* at all!

An Exercise on the Present Moment

1. Together with a partner, discuss those instances of the present moment that you have experienced both within the therapeutic relationship and in other non-therapeutic encounters. Explore the felt sense of these experiences. What was their impact upon your relationship with the other with whom the experience occurred?
2. As a therapist, how have you responded to those present-moment challenges presented by the client? What were the consequences to the therapeutic relationship of your response?
3. As a client, how has your therapist responded to those present-moment challenges that occurred in the course of your therapy? What were the consequences to the therapeutic relationship of these responses?
4. What value, if any, do you place on present moments in therapy?

General and Erotic Attraction

Because of the sometimes intense focus on the immediacy of the encounter taken throughout Phase Two, it is not overly surprising for the possibility of a deeply felt sense of closeness and connection to develop between the existential therapist and his or her client. This movement toward intimacy might be expressed in terms of a growing sense of care and affection toward the client by the therapist, or *vice versa,* which also, at times, may be mutual. Often, this sense is associated with notions of friendship; less often, as erotic attraction. Equally, such intimacy may provide the means for clients to experience and express explosive, highly charged feeling-focused reactions that may be centred upon anger and aggression or combinations of love and hatred directed toward the therapist. Such experiences are usually understood as instances of *transference* and *counter-transference* (Gay, 1988). I have explored these terms critically elsewhere (Spinelli, 1994, 1995), but for present purposes let me simply state that, in my view, these hypotheses deviate the investigation away from the immediacy of the current encounter. In addition, whatever their explanatory value, they obscure and deflect attention away from the clarification of the currently felt attraction in and of itself and its possible relation to the client's worldview. Most significantly, they impose an element of unreality and inappropriateness upon such experiences that hampers the existential therapist's attempt to stay with that which presents itself, as it presents itself, in the therapeutic encounter.

   That the great majority of therapists *do* experience attraction of one sort or another towards their clients is beyond doubt (Pope, 1990). Nonetheless, the experience of attraction – be it specifically erotic or more diffuse in its focus – can surprise, disturb and confuse. Therapists may experience guilt, fear of discovery by other professionals or of losing control of their desires, and, in turn, may experience or express anger and blame toward the client for somehow having provoked these feelings (Pope, Sonne & Holroyd, 1993). Most commonly, the response given by therapists to these experiences is either one that interprets such as counter-transferential or which seeks to somehow eradicate it by means of some form of determined 'willpower' (Spinelli, 1994). These strategies attempt to defend the therapist from directly felt ownership of attraction. The first, through dissociation, the latter through denial. Both, in my view, provoke reactions all too similar to those generated when we tell our selves, or are told, 'Whatever you do, don't think of the colour red.'

Instead, as I have suggested elsewhere,

> rather than seek to deny or suppress such feelings, or, alternatively, to 'transform' them or minimise their impact by invoking such terms as 'counter-transference', therapists might do better to *acknowledge* them as being present in their experience of, and relationship with, their client. (Spinelli, 1994: 114)

This acknowledgement of 'what is there for me' enables existential therapists to place this particular aspect of their encounter alongside whatever other experiential factors may be present, just as would be the case in attempting the Rule of Equalisation. Rather than be oppressed by such experiences, the therapist might then include them in his or her ongoing clarification and challenge of the client's worldview. Through this accepting stance, that which was previously experienced as being problematic might well be transformed into something both appropriate and advantageous to the therapeutic process.

Thus, in dealing with attraction by first acknowledging it, existential therapists can remain *within* the lived conditions of the therapy-world. This stance requires the shift from considering something that is initially experienced as being in some way problematic – and, hence, unwanted or not permitted to be present – to that of being open to its actuality and, through that, avoiding the experience of being overwhelmed by this one dispositional focus of experience. In this way, the experience of attraction, while by no means denied, is nevertheless prevented from distracting the focus of attention away from the client. Equally, in the choice of acknowledging 'what is there' for them, existential therapists might discern relevant aspects of the client's worldview that had been previously set aside or left unconsidered. Further, in their acceptance of attraction within the therapy-world, existential therapists (and clients as well) may find that, in many instances, such intense feelings often simply reside within the confines of that world and either do not extend beyond it, or dissipate once they have stepped out into the wider-world. Perhaps most significantly, in their attempt to adopt this open and receptive stance toward that which would otherwise be avoided or shunned, existential therapists can *embody* their theory and, by so doing, become living expressions of a way of being that the client, in turn, may experience and consider.

In line with what has been suggested above, a 2001 study investigating UK counselling psychologists' experiences of sexual attraction toward their clients not only confirmed that sexual attraction toward clients was a common experience, it also argued that such feelings were not necessarily detrimental to the therapeutic process. Indeed, approximately 50 per cent of those who disclosed these feelings of attraction to their clients reported a positive impact on the therapeutic relationship (Giovazolias & Davis, 2001). These findings suggest that there is nothing intrinsic to the question of attraction that demands significantly different responses on the part of the therapist.

An Exercise on Attraction

1. Working together with a partner, take turns in exploring an example of how you have experienced and worked with general attraction in the therapeutic relationship, both as a client and as a therapist.
2. Working together with a partner, take turns in exploring an example of how you have experienced and worked with erotic attraction in the therapeutic relationship, both as a client and as a therapist.
3. On the basis of your discussion, take turns in examining how you would work as a supervisor with a supervisee who came to you concerned that mutual erotic attraction had developed between him or her self and a client.

Differences in Gender and Sexual Orientation

In his text, *An Inquiry into Sexual Difference in Ernesto Spinelli's Psychology: An Irigarayan Critique and Response to Ernesto Spinelli's Psychology*, Aloysius Joseph argues that 'the sexually specific differences of the two subjects – both sensory and morphological' (Joseph, 2009: 13) cannot be avoided in therapy. Much of Joseph's thesis follows a number of themes developed by the philosopher and psychoanalyst Luce Irigaray, who argues that all discourse – not only between men and women, but also between men and men and women and women – is currently always and only one of male subjectivity (Irigaray, 1985; Irigaray, Hirsch & Olson, 1995). This argument provides the basis for Joseph's critique of both my own 'psychology' and of existential therapy in general. As therapists engaged in discourse with our clients, we cannot avoid talking, hearing, thinking and experiencing in ways that are not in some way biased with regard to differences in gender and, implicitly, in sexual orientation. For Joseph, some corrective focus in the encounter that addresses these matters is essential.

Joseph's argument highlights an existential wariness in over-generalising differences into various forms of divisive categorisation. As Meg Barker has pointed out, this concern has its basis in the view that 'gendered roles vary across dimensions such as culture, class, generation, sexuality ... it is worth approaching each client with curiosity about the way such messages may play out in their world'

(Barker, 2011: 213–214). The issue, then, is not that gender difference and variations in being sexual are experienced in a variety of ways which generate differences in meaning and experience. Obviously, they are. Rather, what is being debated is whether it makes sense to categorise those differences into fixed and generalised category givens such as gender and sexual orientation. For example, current Western cultural perspectives perceive gender from the standpoint of binaries – male and female. But such binaries are open to reconsideration. In her book, *Gender Trouble*, Judith Butler argues that rather than be considered as a fixed binary given, gender can be more appropriately viewed from the perspective of variable fluidity whose shifts express its response to, and relation with, differing contexts. 'There is no gender identity behind the expressions of gender; ... identity is performatively constituted by the very "expressions" that are said to be its results' (Butler, 2006: 25). In line with this view, meta-analyses of research studies focused on the question of the essentialist basis to gender differences and sexual orientation are consistent in their conclusions that, in spite of polemical claims, essentialist assertions lack any evidential basis (Fine, 2010; Jordan-Young, 2011; Wilson & Rahman, 2005).

Interestingly, Butler's hypothesis provides a novel perspective for an attraction-based phenomenon that many therapists and clients experience. In such instances, individuals who have previously identified themselves as oriented exclusively towards heterosexual or homosexual attraction discover, to their surprise, confusion, and even dismay, that this exclusivity is being challenged through the erotic attraction they experience toward the other in the therapy-world. One way of considering how these experiences might arise is, as Butler proposes, to view them as instances of shifts in context and relation. As has been discussed in the previous chapter, the co-creation of and co-habitation within a therapy-world distinguishable from both the client's and therapist's wider-world experiences can in itself impact significantly upon the worldview being maintained. This therapy-world worldview may be very similar to each participant's wider-world worldview in numerous ways but may also reveal experientially noted differences among which might well be those related to gender-oriented attraction. The more distinguishable is the therapy-world from the wider-world, the more likely will be the felt experience of a partially novel worldview and the key distinctions that set the two worlds apart rely upon differences in context and relation. However fleeting or specific to the confines of the therapy-world worldview shifts – including those related to sexual orientation and attraction – may be, they provide the lived experience of fluidity that challenges essentialist predispositions regarding issues of difference.

Nonetheless, this fluidity should not be confused with any attempt to dismiss or invalidate the various concerns raised surrounding the issue of differences. Regardless of their fluid potential, differences may be so rigidly fixed along socio-cultural divides that, as Butler highlights, they appear to all within that culture as 'natural' and, hence, shared by all in a roughly similar fashion. Again, the argument is not whether differences of any sort, including those that generate attraction, exist.

Rather, it is how such differences are to be understood. Of course, it is vital to acknowledge difference and in particular to be open to the exploration of difference when working therapeutically. But such an attunement, it seems to me, ought to be ever-present in *all* encounters with clients, and others in general. Equally, this alternative acknowledgement of differences as interpretative variations arising out of a shared grounding of relatedness in no way diminishes the significance of dominant modes of thought and language that restrict, inhibit and proscribe. Nor does it encourage the denial of the 'otherness of the other' – however that other self-defines or is defined.

As existential therapists, we seek to clarify with clients their particular embodiment of any differentiating term or label. Such explorations are undertaken between beings who encompass vast differences that cannot be reduced only to variations of gender or identity. That these differences are all too likely links to issues of dominance and subjugation should not predispose us to conclude that *only* difference and power exist. Instead, with the acknowledgement of that which *unites* persons in their diverse experiences of difference and power, a view of far greater complexity and uncertainty regarding these very same issues emerges. From this perpetual interplay, matters of difference and power are seen to be fluid, revealing shifting patterns of conditions and relations between beings as well as within the boundaries of any particular being's sense of self and other.

An Exercise on Differences of Gender and Sexual Orientation

1. Working together with a partner, take turns in exploring how each of you defines and feels defined by gender. What, if any, are the major gender-defining differences that you uphold? What gives them their significance for you? What would be the impact upon your worldview if you could no longer rely upon, or accepted, these differences?
2. Working together with a partner, take turns in exploring how each of you defines and feels defined by sexual orientation. What, if any, are the major sexual orientation defining differences that you uphold? What gives them their significance for you? What would be the impact upon your worldview if you could no longer rely upon, or accepted, these differences?
3. Note what differences, if any, exist between the significant gender and sexual orientation differences upheld by you and your partner. How do these differing experiences affect the way that each of you views the other? Views him/her self?

Rollo May's Hypothesis of the Daimonic

The American existential therapist Rollo May suggested that the expression of creative and destructive thoughts, feelings and behaviours is a universal aspect of human existence (Hoeller, 1996; May, 1969). May adopted the term *daimonic* as a descriptive means with which to express experiences associated with uncontrollable, at times self-assertive, at times self-transcending, demands that appear to spring from a source that is not directly identified with the person's worldview. Rather than view the creative and destructive as separate and distinct 'either/or' tendencies, the daimonic expresses them as inter-related 'both/and' polarities expressive of a single urge either to assert or to enfold one's being in, and upon, the world.

In cultures where the daimonic is suppressed or identified only with the undesirable, the proscribed or evil, it finds various 'underground' means through which to express itself. May argued that often the daimonic 'comes to the fore in times of transition in a society' (May, 1969: 129) and, in such instances, is revealed both in movements of novel and challenging expressions of creativity – whether artistically or scientifically focused – and in reactive and assertive aggression, hostility and other forms of destructiveness. So, too, from an individual perspective, the daimonic urges of creativity and destruction can be directed toward self, others or the world. In all such instances, the daimonic reveals an accompanying ambiguity in meaning and identity. In that transitional moment when the daimonic erupts, all is uncertain.

One cultural example of what May is suggesting can be seen in the explosion of the underground 'rave' culture of the 1990s. Through their use of dance, music and drugs, raves offered a communal experience of connectedness, trust and affection among participants which served as counter-example to the 'overground' culture's elevation of unbridled egoism and the elevation of the individual. In this way, the underground culture of raves challenged in a daimonic fashion that which the overground culture had dismissed as irrelevant or non-existent. Following May's argument, such expressions of the daimonic emphasise the inter-connectedness and co-existence of the creative and the destructive, not only in the underground rave behaviour, but also in the attitudes and biases of overground culture. May argued that the daimonic must be channelled, structured and integrated so that the potential for creating anew is not overwhelmed by the potential for only destroying that which is present. In order for such to occur, society must be brave enough to welcome the daimonic and recognise the necessity of its presence and expression.

From a more individual perspective, May viewed therapy as one of the few remaining sanctioned means in Western culture for the individual to experience daimonic eruptions under structured conditions so that these would be sufficiently harnessed and thereby increase the likelihood of a reconstructive rather than a merely destructive set of circumstances. For May, the provision of therapy had little to do with the attempt to make people happy; rather, therapy was in the service of their potential for freedom (May, 1981). Paradoxically, May suggested that the personal confrontation with the possessive forces of the daimonic provides a pivotal means for individuals to experience the freedom inherent in their existence (May, 1969).

May's hypothesis remains controversial for many existential therapists, not least because of his tendency to present the daimonic both as an entity and as a somewhat vague biologically in-built force which serves as the existential equivalent to psychoanalytic drive theory. Nonetheless, even if the notion of the daimonic were to be considered solely as a metaphorical expression of the human potential for creation and destruction, much of the import of May's proposal remains. For example, the daimonic can be seen as a way of expressing the foundational tension between worlding and the worldview. When the worldview reveals its sedimented and dissociative limitations, the ensuing struggle between the attempt to maintain the existing worldview and the push to reconstitute it parallels the depersonalised (or dissociated) possessive force of the daimonic. In such instances, the consequences of this struggle remain unpredictable. They may destabilise the worldview, thereby provoking extreme forms of unease that are subsequently expressed in various aggressive or destructive tendencies focused upon self, others or the world. Alternatively, they may generate a creative reconstitution of the worldview or they may elicit temporary creative dissociations which generate the experience of possession, diminution or transcendental expansion of one's self-construct. If the person's experience of worldview ambiguity is contained within a suitably adequate structure that allows it to be embraced, explored and worked through, then it is more likely that both the process and its outcome are primarily creative and re-constitutive rather than destructive. Prayer or meditation, artistic expression, dance, running or exercise, are all examples of activities that can all raise possessive experiences of the daimonic while harnessing it within an adequate structure intended toward meaningful, life-enhancing and creative outcomes. So, too, can therapy.

The co-created therapy-world provides the baseline conditions within which the emergence of the daimonic can be both embraced and contained. Indeed, it is likely to be the case that the client has turned to therapy *because* he or she experiences some disturbing ambiguity in the currently maintained worldview. Existential therapy's explicit focus upon the investigation of the client's worldview under circumstances of its being in at least partial transition can also encourage the expression of the daimonic. In this sense, existential therapy can both assist the expression of the daimonic and offer inter-relational possibilities that may help the client to direct the encounter with the daimonic in such a way that its consequences are more likely to be predominantly creative rather than destructive.

Considered from the perspective of Phase Two, the daimonic is likely to occur as a direct consequence, and expression, of the exploratory focus being undertaken and the inter-relational intimacy within which such exploration is channelled and contextualised. Therefore, at any point throughout Phase Two, the existential therapist should be prepared for those indications of the client's movement toward, or immersion in, the daimonic. Such are likely to be expressed via intense feelings that spring up for the client in ways that may surprise, shock, disturb, excite, repel or dismay him or her. These may be directed toward the client him or her self, toward others in the client's wider-world core existence concerns associated with the client's challenged worldview, and, just as likely, toward the therapist who, in turn, may experience some equivalent to any and all of these as challenges to his or her own worldview.

Rather than seek to dissolve, reduce, intensify or explain these daimonic explosions, it remains the task of the existential therapist to attempt to 'stand beside' the client throughout their appearance and to pursue their investigation through descriptive clarification and challenge. The sharing of these moments can be intensely intimate and may involve a minimal exchange of verbal discourse. It is during such confrontations that existential therapy's emphasis upon the embracing presence of the therapist within the co-created confines of the therapy-world, and the possibilities of this particular stance toward truthful and trusting relatedness, truly come to the fore.

An Exercise Exploring the Daimonic

1. Together with a partner, take turns in exploring a personal instance of a confrontation with the daimonic.
2. Examine what were the circumstances that provoked this from the standpoint of the worldview that was then currently maintained. What were the effects of this encounter with the daimonic upon the then current worldview?
3. Discuss how the notion of the daimonic might impact upon your practice as a therapist.

Working with Dreams

Working with clients' dreams has been a major area of interest to numerous approaches within contemporary therapy, in particular those approaches that have been most influenced by psychoanalysis. The dreams recounted by clients often involve events and images that might appear to be highly unusual, absurd, symbolic and/or disturbing, suggesting the need for an interpretation that will transform these so that they can be made meaningful. Existential therapy proposes that '[t]hey are not puzzles to be solved but openings to be attended to' (Cohn, 1997: 84). Medard Boss, who was originally a psychoanalyst and a Jungian analytical psychologist, was one of the first existential analysts to argue against what he saw as the unnecessary emphasis being placed upon the interpretation of the unconscious as a means to the understanding of dreams (Boss, 1957, 1977). Greatly influenced by Heidegger, Boss proposed that dreams expressed a form of lived reality that deserved a descriptively focused investigation. Rather than concentrate on symbols and analytically derived forms of dream interpretation which assumed that the manifest material of the remembered dream had been disguised in various ways which now required un-disguising, Boss argued that the dream-world was to be treated as equally valid and straightforward as the waking-world. Instead of demanding interpretation, dreams addressed the issues and concerns of embodied experience as expressed through the dreamer's own private language, which, presented in stark fashion and in ways that did not focus on its relatedness to the dreamer, could appear to be absurd or obscure. In acknowledging the common thread between the 'dream-world' and the 'waking-world', Boss argued that each could shed light on the other. In this way, the dream content, rather than disguising meaning, could be treated as the bridge that interconnected the two worlds.

The analysis of dreams addresses an important aspect that has tended to be overlooked by therapists: the exploration of dreams can be a deeply *intimate* enterprise in that dreams have the potential of revealing us in very direct, often raw, ways that may disclose more than do our more guarded waking-world discourses. Being aware of this, existential therapists working with their clients' remembered dreams would do well to balance the opportunity that they provide to explore experiential possibilities that might not otherwise be noted nor given sufficient significance with a recognition of, and respect for, the intimacy that the dream-focused discussion can bring to the encounter.

Like Boss, my own way of working with clients' dreams is to avoid treating them as some sort of substitutive stand-in for hidden concerns or revelations. Instead, I encourage the client/dreamer to place him or her self 'in' the 'dream-world' and initiate a process of descriptively focused clarification and challenge. In general, I view working with dreams in existential therapy as a co-operative inquiry which parallels the therapeutic encounter as a whole. *In my view, dreams allow the dreamer to challenge the currently maintained worldview, particularly in terms of its currently problematic sedimentations and dissociations, by providing dream-world alternatives to that worldview for the dreamer to experience, explore and play with.*

The following example of a recounted dream by one of my clients, Tom, provides an overview of my approach to working with dreams:

1. Allow the client to recount the remembered dream in his or her own initially preferred way.

Tom first presents his dream in the following way: 'I was at my desk, attempting to write my report when I suddenly had the urge to suck the ink out of my pen. It tasted surprisingly sweet. I looked in the mirror and saw I had ink all over my mouth and shirt. I suddenly thought: "Mom's going to kill me!"'

2. Invite the client to offer any additional information that seems immediately relevant to the remembered dream.

Tom states: 'The night I had the dream, I had avoided writing the report because I was bored with it and just wanted to relax and watch some television. When I went to bed, I was glad to have done that but also felt a bit guilty and was dreading what I'd have to do the next day to make up for it. I think I did suck ink out of a pen once when I was a kid, and it didn't taste sweet at all! When I woke up, I felt sad and sort of weepy because mom's been dead for three years now and I don't really have anyone in my life, other than my self, to sort of "kill me" when I do something stupid.'

3. Invite the client to explore the dream from a narrational scene-setting focus. For instance:

    i.   *Spatial contextualising:* Was the dream-world room Tom was in the same as that of his waking-world? Or was it a room and a desk from another time in Tom's waking-world life? Or was it a room belonging to someone else? Or an imaginary room?

    ii. *Temporal contextualising:* Did the dream occur in Tom's waking-world present time? Or was it set in the future? Or the past?

    iii. *Contextualising dream-world objects:* What did the pen look like? Is it a pen Tom uses today? Or another pen that he recalls? And the desk? What was the report? Was it the same as the one he didn't write in his waking-world or another report of some kind?

    iv. *Contextualising the dreamer in the dream-world:* Is Tom the same age in the dream-world as he is in his waking-world? Are the clothes he was wearing the same or different to those he'd worn during the day prior to the dream? If not, what was different about them?

    v.   *Contextualising key behaviour:* When Tom, following the suggestion of his therapist, mimics the act of putting a pen in his mouth and sucking out its ink, as in the dream-world, what does this look like? Does the act provoke any thoughts or feelings connected to the remembered dream? Equally, when Tom repeats aloud the dream-world statement 'Mom's going to kill me!', how does he do it? How does he sound? Does the act provoke any thoughts or feelings connected to the remembered dream?

Anything that arises from this descriptive scene–setting of the dream can then be further clarified and added to or amended by the client.

4. Following these initial steps, invite the client to repeat the remembered dream, but this time expressing it verbally and, whenever feasible behaviourally, in the present tense. In addition, if it is helpful to the client, the therapist can offer to repeat the dream in the present tense, using the first person ('I') throughout, keeping as exactly as possible to the same words as those employed by the client and imitating key behaviour as has been previously demonstrated by the client.

Tom says: 'I'm at my desk, trying to write my report [*Tom imitates writing at his desk*]. I pick up my pen. I am sucking the ink out of it [*Tom places imaginary pen in his mouth and sucks*]. It's sweet! I'm looking into the mirror. I see ink all over my mouth and shirt. "Mom's going to kill me!"'

5.   Explore whether the mutual repetition of the dream in the present tense has provoked any further thoughts or remembrances about it for the client.

Tom states: 'When I look at it again in this way, it feels very kid-like, even though I'm an adult in the dream. Sucking out the ink is very enjoyable. Maybe even erotic. My mother keeps coming back to me. I wish she was still alive. I miss her. We had such great times together and she was as much a friend as she was a mother.'

6.   Identify the various key relational constituents that are linked to the dreamer in the recounted dream.
     The different constituents linked to Tom in his dream are:

   i. The room.
   ii. Tom's desk.
   iii. Tom's unwritten report.
   iv. Tom's pen.
   v. The act of sucking ink.
   vi. The statement 'It's sweet.'
   vii. The mirror.
   viii. Tom's inky mouth.
   ix. Tom's ink-stained shirt.
   x. Tom's mother.
   xi. Tom's statement 'Mom's going to kill me!'

7.   Explore descriptively with the client the associated meaning relationship between each of the above relational constituents and the dreamer. Or, if there are too many, ask the dreamer to select those that provoke the greatest interest or curiosity.

In Tom's case, his relationship to the unwritten report (constituent iii) provides the realisation that in the dream-world he was enjoying the act of writing the report – something that was an entirely alien experience to his attempts to write reports in the waking-world. This led Tom to wonder what the topic or content of his dream-world report might be and various challenging possibilities arose for him to consider. Similarly, the exploration of Tom's relation to the statement 'Mom's going to kill me!' (constituent xi) generated a very powerful and painful, yet much appreciated, emotional reaction. This phrase brought forth all manner of significant memories for Tom that, while tinged with some degree of fear, were also expressions of his deep love and respect for his mother. At the same time, Tom realised that within the dream-world, it was fear alone that he associated with the statement. This awareness challenged Tom to look again at his relationship with his mother so that the fearful aspects of this relationship could be more truthfully acknowledged. Through this, Tom began to see his mother as 'more human' than he had previously allowed her to be.

8. Explore what meaningful connections, if any, emerge when considering the potential inter-relations between any one constituent and any other.

For instance, when Tom places together 'Mother' and 'sucking ink', does any meaningful connection occur? Or when he connects together the statement 'It's sweet' with the statement 'Mom's going to kill me!' does any novel meaning come to mind? If so, how might these relate back to the dream as a whole? For example, following the points discussed above, when Tom considered the possible relation between the unwritten report and his statement 'Mom's going to kill me!', he connected the feeling of pleasure to that of overwhelming fear. Staying with the content elements but now adding the noetic constituents of fear and pleasure, Tom was further enabled to investigate his relationship with his mother, as well as his own failed attempts at both 'mothering' him self and finding a 'substitute mum' in the relations he had formed with various women.

9. Explore what has emerged from the above points in relation to the presenting problem or issues that have concerned the client during the most recent therapy sessions or throughout the therapy as a whole. Does anything emerge through this exploration which sheds light on both the dream and the problem?

Tom had initially come to therapy because of an overall sense of disinterest in, and detachment from, living. He was not suicidal; he 'just didn't feel alive'. What interests he conjured up in his work, his social and romantic relationships 'just seemed to fizzle out' after a while. At the same time, he was dissatisfied with having permitted him self to have become, as he termed it, 'a bystander on life's highway'. The dream proved to be significant for Tom in that it demonstrated to him that he could still experience intense feelings – pleasure and fear – even if only in his dream-world. Although there was a great deal of material relevant to his often-troubled relationship with his deceased mother, it was primarily this rich, felt sense that he could still experience something that he'd felt had been forever lost to him which he most valued about this dream.

10. Explore what has emerged from the above points in relation to whatever sedimentations and dissociations in the client's worldview had been previously discerned and/or have been mentioned in the course of the investigation of the dream. Does anything emerge that suggests a relation between the dream and these sedimentations and dissociations?

Tom's most clearly identified sedimentations, in relation to his presenting problems, rested upon existential insecurities related to (a) his disinterest in everything and (b) his inability to complete that which he initiated, simply out of boredom (but, also, implicitly, because he feared the judgement of anything he'd completed far more than he feared the complaints that arose as a result of his unfinished work). Although Tom's report was also unfinished in the dream world, what was of significant difference was his acknowledged sense of enjoying its writing. This dream-world experience directly challenged Tom's sedimentation of disinterest. Similarly, the enjoyment of sucking ink from his pen, even if the act led to significant fears, nonetheless also challenged this sedimentation. Moreover, Tom also saw that the act of sucking ink out of the pen was a completed act, and although it generated fear (as his sedimentation had 'predicted'), nonetheless his pleasure could not be denied or dismissed. Thus, the dream also challenged Tom's insecurities regarding completion not by challenging its validity, but by revealing to Tom that this validity was only part of his narrative.

As the above example should indicate, working with dreams from an existential perspective follows the same descriptive focus as applied throughout the whole of the therapeutic encounter. The client is challenged through clarification and descriptive challenging alone. At no time is there an attempt on the therapist's part to add to, distort, transform or assume any symbolic aspects to the dream material.

Although it may consume a good deal of time and attention, working with dreams can be highly rewarding and challenging for the client. My personal view is that dreams permit clients to address difficult concerns and issues from the initially more secure and distanced third-person perspective of 'the dreamer in the dream'. In this partially dissociated manner, views, values, fears, beliefs that would otherwise be difficult, if not impossible, to own in the client's waking-world worldview are permitted their expression and exploration. In the course of working on the dream with the existential therapist, it may become more possible for the dream's de-sedimenting challenges to the waking-world worldview to be explored and considered.

In many cases, the therapeutic session focused on a dream may simply initiate an investigative process that the client can be encouraged to continue outside the therapy-world. At least as importantly, working together on the client's dream often permits an intimacy between client and therapist that expresses the client's experience of both the trustworthiness of the therapy-world and his or her trust of, and ease in being with, the therapist. These, in turn, allow the therapist to further clarify and challenge the client's worldview and its relatedness to the client's concerns.

An Exercise on Working with Dreams

1. Working together with a partner, take turns in exploring a remembered dream, or, if it is too long, a section of it that most intrigues, surprises or disturbs. Each session should last 30 minutes.
2. As the client, initially recount the dream, or the section of the dream, in your own preferred way.

(Continued)

(Continued)

3. As the therapist, follow the investigative sequence outlined above to help you and your client explore the dream.
4. When you have both completed the exercise, discuss what personal value, and what value, if any, for the therapeutic process, you have found in working with dreams from this perspective.

Reconfiguring the Setting, Frame and Contractual Conditions of the Therapeutic Relationship

Below are various instances wherein either the client or the therapist might ask that the existing setting, frame and contractual conditions that have been agreed to may be opened to renegotiation:

1. The intensity of the Phase Two relationship is such that the client requests, or the therapist offers, the possibility of either an increase in the frequency of meetings or an extension of their duration.
2. The intensity of the Phase Two relationship is such that the client requests a decrease either in the frequency of meetings or in the duration of the existing meetings.
3. The intensity of the Phase Two relationship is such that the client requests the possibility of being able to contact the therapist by telephone, email or text messaging during times beyond those set in the agreed contract.
4. For reasons of convenience or owing to changes in life conditions, either the client or the therapist requests a change in the times or location of meetings or of the fee-structure that had been agreed.
5. The client requests that the therapist suggests some other sources, such as books or films that might serve to further challenge issues and concerns that have been discussed in the therapy-world.
6. The client offers the therapist the opportunity to read a book, listen to music or watch a film that means a great deal to the client and which might help the therapist to better understand some aspects of the concerns and issues raised by the client in the therapy-world.
7. The client proposes that either one or a set number of sessions are focused upon a meaningful item in the client's life, such as a particular piece of music, or an extract from a novel, or a painting or photographs relevant to a particular topic of therapeutic discussion that, the client, believes, will assist its exploration. For example, one client, who had been examining the effects of the sudden and unexpected death of her younger brother upon her life, requested that she be permitted to bring in photographs taken of their relationship from its earliest period, when they had both been children, right up to the photograph she had taken of his corpse.
8. The client puts forward the idea of an extension of the therapy-world such that it can now exist within a different space as well as the current one. For

instance, one of my clients proposed that I see him for several meetings in his office space since he felt that this would allow him to tap into his 'way of being a manager', and the concerns we'd discussed about this, in a much more immediate way that would assist him. Another client expressed the desire to have a session with me outdoors, in the public space of the park surrounding my office since, for her, the sense that being in a space unrestricted by walls and permitting physical movement seemed a matter of some significance, even though she could not state why.

9. The client suggests the possibility that someone else be temporarily admitted into the therapy-world. For example, one client requested that he be allowed to introduce his boyfriend to me at the start of the subsequent session because so much had been said about me by my client to his boyfriend that it would resolve a great deal of curiosity (and possible jealousy) if I could just meet him. Another client requested that she be allowed to bring her dog to one session because she felt that it was only in her dog's presence that she could begin to broach a particularly painful topic.

All of the above examples, and many others similar to them, might occur at various points throughout an existential therapist's professional career. In different ways, they all express the intent to alter the existing agreed-upon relational and contextual conditions that have, thus far, distinguished and maintained a discrete therapy-world. Rather than focus upon questions regarding the relative appropriateness, or lack of it, in either acceding to or rejecting any of the amendments proposed above, I simply want to suggest that there is nothing within existential therapy during Phase Two that would automatically demand the rejection of any of these requests or others like them. Nor is there anything in existential therapy that would automatically require their agreement. What is critical is that, in each case, unless previously specified as potential options within the agreed-upon contract, it is important to approach the potential change in conditions as *a request that either party is entitled to refuse*. At the same time, any amendment proposed by the client deserves consideration and descriptively focused exploration, even if the therapist is in no position, or has no desire, to agree to its being implemented.

As was discussed in the previous chapter, unlike other contemporary approaches, so long as they exist within the givens of codes of professional practice and ethics, existential therapy's 'rules' can contain and express any number and variety of possible, and appropriate, conditions. Their one proviso is that both existential therapist and client own whatever conditions arise as appropriate and sufficient to maintain their 'magical beliefs' about when and whether a structured relationship is or is not a therapeutic relationship.

Even so, it remains to be asked: what value might there be in re-appraising a frame that has demonstrated its reliability in fulfilling these inter-relational requirements and possibilities? One possibly worthwhile answer would be that the various setting, frame and contractual conditions which so adequately provided a structure for the therapy-world during Phase One may have begun to impose unnecessary and undesirable limits to the encounter possibilities as they exist in Phase Two. The reconfiguration of Phase One conditions (whether permanently or temporarily) may well parallel the client's own awareness of shifts in the worldview that have already occurred and which are either better suited to the proposed re-negotiated conditions or whose change-focused implications are better explored through the new conditions.

Unexpected Encounters Between Client and Therapist Beyond the Confines of the Therapy-World

The above discussion acts as a reminder of a fear commonly expressed by train-ees and practising therapists alike: the unexpected meeting of a client outside the therapy-world, such as in a supermarket or at a party. In these circumstances, it is not unusual for therapists to seek to avoid all contact or to deny any acknowledge-ment of their own, or their client's, presence on the grounds that to do so could endanger the established frame in ways that range from a minor infraction to a cataclysmic deviation.

If we consider the issue from the perspective of existential therapy, it becomes clear that the therapist's avoidance response in such circumstances parallels the dis-sociative strategy of the worldview. In this instance, avoidance and denial permit the various currently existing relational and contextual conditions that maintain the therapist's therapy-world worldview to remain secure. Alternatively, were the therapist to accept the event and engage with the client in a wider-world relational context, this novel encounter would impact in some de-sedimenting way upon the therapy-world worldview. Either option has its desirable features as well as its limi-tations and risks. Equally, the consequences arising from either strategy cannot be entirely predicted in terms of their subsequent impact upon the therapeutic relation-ship. Once again, both the therapist and the client are confronted with uncertainty.

My own most common stance with regard to these instances is to permit the challenge to the therapy-world worldview and seek to remain open to its unforeseen consequences and possibilities. In the event of an unexpected contact with a client (whether current or past) I initially acknowledge his or her pres-ence in some non-verbal fashion, such as a slight nod or a smile, and then leave it to the client to determine whether he or she wishes to approach me or, alter-natively, prefers to keep our relationship unacknowledged within a public arena. This strikes me as a way of remaining professionally respectful of the client's right to anonymity as well as being open to the possibility that the client might want to acknowledge publicly in some fashion the existence of a professional relationship between us. Should the client decide to engage in a conversation, I have found it to be always possible to ensure that its content remains at a level that retains the privacy of our professional relationship. In fact, my experience has been that clients are usually as concerned and responsible about this as I attempt to be. What does seem to me to be of importance – particularly with current clients – is that our meeting, as well as our separate reactions to it, are addressed in some way during the subsequent therapy session.

An Exercise on Reconfiguring the Frame

1. Together with a partner, discuss what you believe to be the pros and cons of reconfiguring Phase One structural conditions of setting, frame and contract during Phase Two. What would be the circumstances, if any, that you would deem to be appropriate for such reconfiguration? As therapist, how would you go about addressing this reconfiguration to the client?
2. Together with a partner, focus on the specific examples of potential therapy-world reconfiguration summarised above. How do you each personally respond to these possible instances of reconfiguration? How would you respond to your client's request that the structural conditions be reconfigured on the basis of any one of the stated possibilities?
3. If it has happened to you during your practice, describe an incident of meeting a client outside the therapeutic environment. How did you react? How did the client react? Following the discussion presented on this issue, how do you now evaluate your reaction? If such an incident were to occur again, what would be the differences, if any, in your way of responding to it?

Indications as to the Appropriateness of a Therapeutic Shift from Phase Two to Phase Three

What indications might there be for the existential therapist that a shift toward Phase Three has become possible? I would suggest that at least the following should be reasonably apparent:

1. The client has begun doing most of the therapeutic work. That is to say, a challenging focus on the worldview is increasingly being adopted by the client such that, in many ways, the client has begun to be his or her own therapist.
2. There are clear-cut indications of an experiential and dispositional shift in the client's stance toward the sedimentations and dissociations that have been investigated throughout Phase One and Phase Two.
3. In line with point 2, there are strong indications that disturbing ambiguities in the client's worldview are either no longer so disturbing and can be better owned by the client, or that some aspects of those ambiguities have been challenged and the client's worldview has shifted in some discernible ways.
4. The client's narrative is increasingly concerned with the consideration of novel possibilities. Often, this is expressed by the client as reaching a point where decisions can be made as to various novel ways of being outside of the therapy-world.

5. The client's narrative is more focused on the explication and investiga-tion of his or her experience of 'testing out' ways of being outside of the therapy-world.
6. The client's narrative is increasingly future-directed.
7. There are frequent indications of the evident ease with which the client engages with the therapist at a level of intimacy.

Factors that Prevent a Therapeutic Shift from Phase Two to Phase Three

Just as there may be various indications that the therapeutic relationship is at a point that will permit a shift from Phase Two to Phase Three, there may also be indications that the intimacy established during Phase Two is, itself, provoking previously unforeseen issues and concerns for the client. Once again, the uncertainty that accompanies a growing sense of intimacy may well impact upon the client's worldview in any number of unpredicted and surprising ways so that, although the client's initial presenting concerns have found some sort of acceptance or resolution, nevertheless the stability of the worldview has been threatened or novel ambiguities have arisen such that the client experiences disturbing or intolerable levels of tension in the worldview that had not previously been apparent. If so, the following are likely to be indicators of the client's unease with, and lack of preparedness for, a shift to Phase Three:

1. The client expresses a reluctance in contemplating possibilities that might extend the experience of relatedness within the therapy-world beyond its boundaries and into the client's wider-world relations.
2. The client is able to contemplate ways of enacting novel experiential possibili-ties beyond the therapy-world but makes little or no attempt to do so.
3. The client characterises the experience of co-habiting the therapy-world as being so interesting or so noticeably real in comparison to its wider-world alternatives that an explicit or implicit desire to maintain their distinctiveness is expressed.
4. The client's wider experience of intimacy remains substantially dependent upon the presence of the therapist or upon the therapist's initiatives in inves-tigating it.
5. In the course of discussion with the client, new concerns arise, or unforeseen aspects of previously discussed concerns emerge.
6. The client returns regularly to the expression of, and confrontation with, vari-ous intense and explosive feelings directed toward self, others beyond the therapy-world, or the therapist, but appears unable to consider and use these as exploratory challenges to the currently maintained worldview.

All of the above suggest that significant constituents of the client's worldview as a whole, or of the inter-relations between its primary constructs, have either been

missed or have not been sufficiently investigated. If so, these require further exploration within Phase Two. Equally, however, such instances may also reflect insufficiently
explored client tensions or unease with aspects of the therapy-world – including the
client's relationship with the existential therapist – that would suggest that the move
to Phase Two had been premature and what is now required is the re-establishment
of the conditions of the therapy-world at the Phase One level.

Summary

Throughout Phase Two, the otherness of the existential therapist, while still
seeking to 'stand beside' the client, nonetheless stands out as a distinct presence
which can speak on its own behalf and thereby challenge the client through its
experiential differences and similarities. Considered from this standpoint, Phase
Two demands of the existential therapist a willingness to embrace the uncertainties
that arise in the therapy-world as both an expression and a consequence of the
often intense intimacy that can only be generated between persons who engage
with one another from a grounding that acknowledges both their experiences
of similarity and difference as sources of connection rather than disconnection.
Perhaps the following quote by Vaclav Havel begins to capture something of the
uncertainty that exists throughout Phase Two:

> There are no exact guidelines. There are probably no guidelines at all. The
> only thing I can recommend … is a sense of humour, an ability to see things
> in their ridiculous and absurd dimensions, to laugh at others and at ourselves,
> a sense of irony regarding everything that calls for parody in this world ….
> Those who have retained the capacity to recognise their own ridiculousness
> or even meaninglessness cannot be proud. (Havel, 2000: 20)

9

Phase Three: Closing Down the Therapy-world

Introduction

Most obviously, Phase Three seeks to ensure the completion of all contracted arrangements between existential therapist and client so that the therapy-world that has been co-created by them and which has served as the principal structure within which to disclose and challenge the client's worldview can be formally closed down. Just as significantly, however, Phase Three also explores the extent to which the client's experiences of co-habiting in the therapy-world can – *and cannot* – be extended beyond its boundaries and into the client's wider-world relations. In this sense, Phase Three is concerned with the exploration of whatever potential 'bridging' is possible between the client's therapy-world and wider-world worldviews.

The stance adopted by the existential therapist during Phase Three is the equivalent to that of *executioner* (Yalom, 1989). First, as executioner, the existential therapist assists in the investigation of which of the client's therapy-world experiences can be translated and maintained, in whole or in part, in the client's wider-world. Second, as executioner, the existential therapist makes explicit the link between this partial bridging process and the conclusion of therapeutic relationship. And third, as executioner, the existential therapist engages with the client in ways that bring into focus the presence of those wider-world 'others' who, unlike the therapist, adopt relational strategies which may be inimical to the client's attempts to implement newly discerned worldview possibilities.

In its widest sense, Phase Three encourages the client to *hear the voice of those wider-world others* within the investigatory-focused boundaries of the therapy-world so that some partial success in the client's efforts to bridge both worlds is more likely to be achieved. A pertinent quote by the psychoanalyst Hans Trüb captures much of Phase Three's primary concern: 'The analyst must change at some point from the consoler who takes the part of the patient against the world to the person who puts before the patient the claim of the world' (Trüb, 1947, as quoted in Friedman, 1964:

520). In taking this stance, existential therapy offers a novel means through which to address and respond to the persistent critique regarding contemporary Western therapy's tendency to both isolate and elevate the individual. Because so little has been stated explicitly regarding this latter point, I will focus my initial discussion upon it and then return to the question of therapeutic endings.

The They-focus

As was argued in Part One, notions of freedom, choice and responsibility tend to be addressed as aspects of an internalised and isolated subjectivity that can be divided and categorised as belonging to, and be about, a discrete individual. In this way, a divide is created between those matters or experiences of freedom, choice and responsibility that are identified as 'mine' as opposed to those that are assumed to belong to another or others in general. In contrast to this stance, I have proposed that the more complex and disquieting implications arising from existential phenomenology's foundational Principles explicitly locate the source of all individual experience, including those centred upon questions of choice, freedom and responsibility, in an unavoidable foundational grounding of relatedness. In doing so, all that was previously understood and presented as being either mine or yours becomes, inseparably, *ours*.

To my mind, the person who most eloquently addressed these issues within the arena of therapy was the iconoclastic relational therapist, Leslie Farber (1967, 2000; Gordon, 2000). Farber's work as a therapist subverted the exclusivity of the therapeutic relationship and highlighted its possibilities as a unique meeting point between the client's engagement with the therapist and those that he or she undertook in the wider-world. Unlike most other therapists, Farber did not exclude the wider-world either from his consulting room or from the therapeutic enterprise as a whole. For Farber, whatever value could be claimed of therapy could not be sequestered within the confines of the therapy-world but should rather find its place within the client's ongoing wider-world relations where the consequences of therapy could find their expression. Farber's attempts sought to highlight that even if, from within the boundaries of the therapy-world, an individual manages to adopt a novel stance toward previously debilitating distress and disorders there is no guarantee that this novel stance can exist, much less thrive, in the wider-world. Similarly, although that individual may have found the means with which to improve his or her life, that means cannot be removed from its unknown and unpredictable impact upon others in the world. Farber's perspective complicates any notions of therapeutic success, since, within his framework, success can no longer be considered solely within conditions of individualistic value and benefit. Further, this focus may irritate the client in so far as it imposes the recognition that no act can be truthfully considered in isolation and instead must be placed within its inter-relational context. By so doing, its impact and consequences are rarely straightforward or easily evaluated in terms of therapeutic success or failure.

In my opinion, existential therapists have not paid sufficient attention to these issues. I find this somewhat surprising and, more to the point, disturbing. To not do so seems, to me at least, to conveniently forget, if not violate, the very foundations upon which existential therapy rests. Readers will recall that in the previous chapter's discussion of Phase Two, the topic of the inter-relational realms of encounter was first raised. In that section, the first three realms – the *I-focus,* the *You-focus* and the *We-focus* – were introduced and examples of possible ways of working with them within the therapy-world were provided. I now want to address the fourth realm, the *They-focus,* whose relevance to the present discussion should become apparent.

They-focused inquiry challenges the client to explore imaginatively how wider-world others might respond to his or her novel therapy-world worldview. Further, They-focused inquiry challenges the client to consider the impact of his or her worldview upon those others' inter-relations with one another. As such, the They-focused realm is concerned with:

1. The descriptively focused exploration of the imagined impact that a client's worldview may have upon another's – or various others' – existential insecurities (i.e., insecurities concerned with continuity, dispositional stances and identity) as focused upon the other's self-construct. For example: 'If I finally tell my mother that I will always be there for her, she'll stop worrying so much about her future', 'I've realised that every time my daughter sees me when I am so depressed, she feels she must blame her self in some way', 'Because I've been so distant for so long, he finds it difficult to define him self as my partner.'

2. The descriptively focused exploration of the imagined impact that a client's worldview may have upon another's – or various others' – existential insecurities as focused upon the other's other-construct. For example: 'If I finally tell my mother that I will always be there for her, she'll get on better with her neighbours', 'I've realised that every time my daughter sees me when I am so depressed, she always ends up having an argument with her brother', 'Because I've been so distant for so long, he's become over-dependent on the rest of the family.'

3. The descriptively focused exploration of the imagined impact that a client's worldview may have upon another's – or various others' – existential insecurities as focused upon the other's world-construct. For example: 'If I finally tell my mother that I will always be there for her, she'll pay a lot more attention to the state of her flat', 'I've realised that every time my daughter sees me when I am so depressed, she loses all of her appetite and is terrified by any unexpected noises', 'Because I've been so distant for so long, he's going off on more and more countryside walks and says that he feels more in touch with nature than with people.'

As I see it, in their overt acknowledgment of this They-focus, existential therapists have an important means of remaining consonant with their assumptions regarding the inter-relational dimensions of existence, and, by so doing, they counter the more common therapeutic tendency to consider the client in isolation. The exploration of this fourth relational realm is particularly significant during Phase Three when, as a consequence of therapy, the client has reached a point of considering changes and making choices from the standpoint of a newly discerned worldview. The existential therapist who is attuned to They-focused realm of inquiry can assist the client in considering the various relational effects of his or her proposed or initially enacted experiences of change from the standpoint of those others in the client's wider-world relations who have been singled out as being significant. The following example should provide a straightforward means to clarify the potential impact of the They-focus within the therapeutic relationship:

> *Client:* I've finally decided what to do.
>
> *Therapist:* Oh, yeah? What's that?
>
> *Client:* I'm going to take the deal on early retirement and invest the bonus on a house in Bavaria.
>
> *Therapist:* Uhm ... Sounds like that's what you've been hesitating over for quite some time.
>
> *Client:* Yeah. But I'm sure about it now.
>
> *Therapist:* And everyone's happy with the decision [**They-focus**]?
>
> *Client:* What do you mean 'everyone'?
>
> *Therapist:* Well ... I'm thinking of Dorrie [client's wife], and Karl and Olivia [client's son and daughter], and your mum, and your friends. And, I suppose I'm also thinking of Brutus [client's dog] [**They-focus**].
>
> *Client:* Oh, Brutus is going to love it! All that space and countryside for long walks. He'll be like a puppy again, he will! [**They-focus**].
>
> *Therapist:* Okay. Great. And the others? [**They-focus**]
>
> *Client:* Uhm.
>
> *Therapist:* What's 'uhm' mean?
>
> *Client:* It means that we're not all on the same page.
>
> *Therapist:* Okay.
>
> *Client:* Dorrie's fretting about what it's going to be like for her and the kids to have to learn German [**They-focus**]. And Karl's saying he's definitely not going to give up his mates [**They-focus**]. Olivia, I don't know. She hasn't said much [**They focus**]. And mum's – well, you can imagine [**They-focus**].

Therapist:	So not a great deal of cheering going on with regard to your decision [**They-focus**].
Client:	You got it. It's just so incredibly dispiriting. They've been going on and on at me for months to do something and get myself out of my depression [**They-focus**]. And I listened to them, came here week after week to see you, get myself sorted. And now that I know what I want and feel really happy and excited about the new possibilities, they go and ruin it [**They-focus**]!
Therapist:	How do they ruin it [**They-focus**]?
Client:	They're just being bloody selfish [**They-focus**]! They keep saying that it's for my good that we all really think things over [**They-focus**]. But I know it's about them and what they want [**They-focus**]!
Therapist:	Okay. Let's look at some of that. So, when Dorrie says to you that it makes sense to look at the decision more carefully, what's that about as far as you're concerned?
Client:	It's about Dorrie needing total security and being scared to try new things, that's what it's about [**They-focus**].
Therapist:	Okay, so your decision makes Dorrie insecure and brings out her fear of trying new things [**They-focus**]. How do you feel about that?
Client:	I feel bad – I don't want her to feel those things. But she's got to take a risk sometime [**They-focus**]. Life's too short and—
Therapist:	Let me ask you something. Imagine that Dorrie agrees to your plan and she still keeps feeling like she does. So you're all living in Bavaria, and Dorrie's feeling insecure and fearful of all the new things going on— [**They-focus**]
Client:	Oh god … Then the kids and I are going to be eating a lot of meals in the local beer hall!
Therapist:	Why do you say that?
Client:	Because when Dorrie gets like that, she doesn't want to cook [**They-focus**]. And when Dorrie doesn't want to cook, you don't want to eat what she does cook!
Therapist:	And what impact does that have, say, between Dorrie and the kids? [**They-focus query**].
Client:	Oh, Karl just sulks and starts to be a pain with everyone [**They-focus**]. And Olivia gets really angry and says to her mum that she's taking over the cooking just so we don't all have to starve to death and that starts a real battle royale between her and Dorrie [**They-focus**]. And then Karl pipes in that he isn't going to eat anything

prepared by his sister and then they start rowing to the point where
they'll argue over who has the right to take the damn dog for a walk
[**They-focus**] – which usually you have to beg one of them to see
to, and ... Oh, it's just awful.

Therapist: And all this relates back to the decision you want to make.

Client: Yeah! But ... It's not fair! I've dreamed of this for years. And they
know that! Why did they let me keep dreaming about it if they knew
that they didn't want to be part of it [**They-focus**]?

Therapist: And if you can't fulfil your dream without them being part of it?

Client: You know what? Fuck them! I want to fulfil it anyway! I've got a
right to have what I want! I slaved for years at that damn job.
They should have more concern for me rather than worry about
themselves so much [**client reaction to They-focus**]!

Therapist: Is that what it seems like? Dorrie and the kids and your mum and
your friends are more concerned with what they want rather than
respect what you want [**They-focus**]?

Client: Well ... I wouldn't say that about mum.

Therapist: Okay. So what's your mum's view on this?

Client: Well, on the surface she's being encouraging and telling me to
follow my heart [**They-focus**].

Therapist: You said, 'on the surface'.

Client: Yeah ... I think that deep down – or maybe not so deep down – she
thinks that she's being punished by God or something for having
had that affair and going ahead and divorcing dad and then things
not working out as she'd planned and ending up on her own and
now she's going to be even more on her own [**They-focus**]. And it'll
be like if she walks down the street or something she'll have the
equivalent of the 'Mark of Cain' that the whole bloody world can
see and she'll be shunned for the rest of her life [**They-focus**].

Therapist: And ... she wants you to follow your heart.

Client: Yeah. Good ol' mum [**They-focus**].

Therapist: And does this have any impact on your decision?

Client: What do you think? But it's still so unfair! And I wish I could just tell
them all to let me be so that I can fulfil my dream.

Therapist: And can you tell them all that?

Client: I want to.

Therapist:	And *can* you?
Client:	But it's a good dream!
Therapist:	Yeah. It's a good dream. And can you tell them: 'Let me be so I can fulfil my dream'?
Client:	I don't know. I think it's right for me to go to Bavaria. I thought they'd think so too, but they don't [**They-focus**]. But does that mean they're right? And even if they are, that doesn't mean it's not right for me. Oh, God! This is so complicated! Why can't things be simple for once?

Considered from a therapeutic standpoint that adopts a non-relational, isolationist subjective perspective, in the above vignette the client's initial statement that he had decided what he wanted to do and that it felt like the appropriate decision for him to take would be seen as having been beneficial. Indeed, from this perspective one could argue that the client is being 'more honest and congruent', more focused upon his 'real self', or more integrated. Equally, even if the subsequent discussion had developed, this non-relational view would adopt a position that assumed that each person was responsible solely for his or her particular experience, that the appropriateness of the choices being considered could be accurately evaluated if considered solely from within the embodied worldview of each separate person, and that each person's sense of freedom could be understood in terms of their personal congruence with, and allegiance to, their own specific wants and desires.

From the inter-relational perspective that I have argued existential therapy adopts as an expression of its foundational Principles, however, the client's decision opens up a great deal to be examined. Via inquiry centred upon the They-focused realm, the challenge to the client is to also speculate on his decision from the standpoint of his wife, his children, his mother, the dog, his friends, and so forth. Secondly, the They-focused perspective challenges the client to consider the meaning and impact of his decision upon, for instance, his wife's relations with each of the children, or each child's relations to his or her sibling, or the client's mother's relations to her world-derived beliefs and values.

What the exploration of the They-focused relational realm makes plain is that there exist so many wider-world relations upon which the client's decision impacts that it would be inter-relationally irresponsible not to attend to at least those that the client has highlighted as being significant or meaningful in some way. The acknowledgement of a They-focus *embeds* the client's decision within an indissoluble matrix of relations, all of which are affected by, and impact upon, one another in ways both subtle and obvious. *Together, they evoke the possibility of a world that does not share an individual's desired experience but which nonetheless exists.*

At the same time, it is important to make clear that the existential therapist's intent behind They-focused inquiry is neither to prevent the client's decision, nor to propose more 'they-friendly' alternative options, nor to impose either the thera-pist's or the others' own moral stance upon the client's perspective. Nor is it the purpose of They-focused exploration to expose the *actual* views of all of these others in the client's world (although this, of course, could be something for the client to attempt to discern if he or she deemed it to be a possible, and desired, option). Instead, a They-focus is taken during Phase Three simply to acknowledge the wider-world context within which the client's novel worldview stance is being experienced.

My insistence upon this point may appear to some readers to be something of an imposition upon the client. Why should the client be forced to accept what is, after all, the existential therapist's stance regarding relatedness and which may not be his own? Once again, it is important to make clear that I am not proposing that it is necessary for the client to make only relationally attuned choices. The client has every right to respond to the existential thera-pist in ways that reject the significance of relatedness. The client could simply state: 'I don't care what others think. I'm still going ahead with my deci-sion.' From an existential phenomenological perspective, this decision is *still* grounded in relatedness (even if it is that expression of relatedness that seeks to minimise or deny relatedness) and is as inter-relationally valid as any other. In such an instance, the existential therapist would, I hope, acknowledge the client's stance and continue to pursue its clarification in relation to the client's existing worldview. *All that is being argued is that the existential therapist cannot avoid raising these inter-relational issues since the whole of the therapeutic process has been, and continues to be, grounded upon their assumption.* To avoid their implications just at the point when the client is reaching, or has reached, change-focused decisions makes no sense and is inconsistent with the existential therapist's claims to embody this stance.

Two Exercises on the They-focus

Exercise 1

1. Working together with a partner, take turns in being therapist and client. Each session should last 20 minutes.
2. As the client, focus on a decision that you have made, or are considering mak-ing, about some change in your life that is impacting upon another or others.
3. As the therapist, assist the client in exploring this decision from a They-focused perspective.
4. When you have both completed the exercise, consider how a They-focused exploration may be of value to the therapeutic process during Phase Three.
5. Discuss your own views on the They-focus and what its place, if any, should be in therapy.

Exercise 2

1. Working together with a partner, take turns in exploring your work as a therapist with a client who arrived at a point of making a change-focused decision that had a direct impact upon another or others in the client's wider-world relations.
2. Together, explore the impact of the decision from a They-focused perspective.
3. Consider how the They-focused exploration may have assisted your client, if at all.
4. Consider how the They-focused exploration may have assisted you as a therapist, if at all.

Attempts at Bridging the Client's Therapy-world and Wider-world

Possibilities and Limitations in Bridging Attempts

To what extent can the client's temporary therapy-world worldview be maintained in the wider-world?

For some therapists, the appropriate outcome of therapy would be that in which the divergences and distinctions between the client's therapy-world and wider-world worldviews are broken down so that the ability to discern one from the other becomes effectively non-existent. However desirable this aim might be in an ideal sense, its fulfilment seems altogether too ambitious. For one thing, important differences between the client's therapy-world and the wider-world worldviews are bound to remain and, as such, require their acknowledgement. First, although the therapy-world need not be seen to be artificial or unreal in relation to the client's wider-world, nonetheless their differences should not be minimised. A therapy-world consisting of (usually) only two directly present participants is inter-relationally less complex than the wider-world made up of a multitude of participants whose differing views, expectations, demands and behaviours impact upon and bombard the client's worldview in ways that no therapy-world relationship could ever fully replicate. Similarly, the clarity of the rule-setting that occurs within the therapy-world as well as the attempt to respect and follow what has been agreed are conditions that cannot easily, if at all, be maintained in the client's wider-world relations simply because the numerous others who exist will not, for various reasons, conform to the client's relational preferences and expectations.

A potentially more satisfactory enterprise to undertake is that of exploring whether and to what extent *some* novel shifts in the client's therapy-world worldview might continue to be embodied in the wider-world. Because neither the client nor the existential therapist can accurately predict *which* shifts in the therapy-world worldview will lend themselves to extrapolation beyond its confines, Phase Three can be a period for the client to test out various inter-relational possibilities in the wider-world and then bring back to the therapy-world that which he or she has discovered and concluded about each of these attempts. In this way, Phase Three can be considered as that Phase in existential therapy during which the client becomes the primary investigator of the worldview as he or she embodies it beyond the confines of the therapy-world.

This investigative focus can be both empowering and dispiriting for the client. He or she may be pleasantly surprised, if not overjoyed, by the degree to which the therapy-world worldview can be established, expressed and owned in the wider-world. Equally, the client may be forced to confront its limitations and, in turn, face the very real anguish of knowing something of the liberating possibilities of a temporary worldview of which he or she has had direct experience within the confines of the therapy-world but which is not able to withstand the relational and contextual challenges it experiences in the wider-world. Phase Three, therefore, is also a period of discovery for the client: To what extent will he or she be able to establish and maintain a novel wider-world worldview that is only partially resonant with that which has been experienced within the therapy-world? And how will the client confront the painful awareness of his or her inability to establish or maintain a wider-world worldview that is entirely resonant with that which was experienced in the therapy-world?

Assignments Focused on the Exploration of Bridging Possibilities and Limitations

How might investigations focused upon the above concerns be initiated? Many existential therapists, the present author included, remain uneasy with the thought of providing clients with homework or specified tasks to undertake between sessions. On reflection, however, it can be clarified that this sense of unease centres more upon the way such tasks might be assigned and, therefore, suggest that they are being passed on to the client by someone who maintains a position of higher authority. On further reflection, it can be recognised that, in many cases, clients themselves either ask for practical guidance, or announce their intention to 'test out' their novel worldview possibilities, or just simply go ahead and initiate explorations without discussing their intent to do so with the therapist. Although client-initiated investigatory tasks and assignments may be preferable, at least as far as existential therapists are concerned, the potential value of therapist-initiated homework suggestions cannot be entirely dismissed. As such, therapist-led offerings of assignments need not be alien to existential therapy so long as it is made clear to the client that:

- the task or assignment being proposed is nothing more than a suggestion;
- the client is free to refuse to enact the assignment;
- the client is free to amend the assignment as seems appropriate;
- the client is free to cease the assignment at any point;
- the client's experience of the assignment will be discussed in the next therapy session.

As well as inter-sessional assignments, Phase Three explorations regarding the potential bridging of the client's therapy-world and wider-world worldviews can include
structured role-play (with the therapist and client taking turns in representing the
imagined wider-world response to the client's novel worldview), and *guided imaginary narratives* designed to help the client access and describe his or her expectations,
concerns, hopes and fears surrounding the attempt to initiate these with various
others or under differing circumstances. Perhaps more controversially (for at least
some existential therapists), these explorations might also include the therapist and
client together 'testing out' these possibilities beyond the established confines of the
therapy-world and in the *actuality* of the wider-world. In general, all of these Phase
Three explorations serve to reveal the extent to which the boundaries between the
client's therapy-world and wider-world worldviews are open to being blurred or
even broken down in ways that the client judges as being beneficial and desirable.

Just as the therapy-world worldview begins to make its impact upon the client's
wider-world worldview, so, too, do the client's attempts to establish and maintain a
novel worldview in the wider-world begin to resonate within the therapy-world.
Some consequences of these attempts may be to make the therapy-world seem
less special, distinctive and important to the client. Equally, however, some consequences may highlight for the client just how special, distinct and important
the therapy-world has been, and to some degree still is. Phase Three of existential
therapy can therefore be exciting and adventurous for the client, but equally may
be tinged with sadness and regret, not merely because of the approach of its being
closed down, but also because of the realisation that not all inter-relational possibilities discerned and explored within the temporary therapy-world worldview can
be expressed in the same way, if at all, in the client's wider-world relations. This last
point once again highlights the often unstated, execution-like aspects of therapeutic
outcomes. No matter how successful therapy may be experienced to be, indeed,
the more successful it is deemed to be, the likelihood remains that the client will
have to face the undesirable realisation that genuine inter-relational experiences of
connection with another have been experienced within the therapy-world and that
these are unlikely to be entirely transferable to wider-world encounters. Indeed,
how the client responds to this latter awareness may be a critical indicator of his or
her readiness to bring the therapeutic encounter to its ending.

An Exercise on the Possibilities and Limitations in Bridging the Therapy-world and the Wider-world Worldviews

1. Together with a partner take turns in discussing your attempts as a client to
    introduce what you had taken and valued from your therapeutic relationship
    into other wider-world relationships. What success, if any, did you have? What
    failures, if any, did you encounter? How did you experience these instances

(Continued)

(Continued)

of success and failure? How did the successes and failures influence your evaluation of the therapy you had undertaken?

2. Together with a partner take turns in focusing upon one of your clients who has either ended or is about to end therapy. Discuss the client's attempts to introduce what he or she had taken and valued from the therapeutic encounter into other wider-world relationships. What success, if any, did this client have? What failures, if any, did he or she encounter? How did your client experience these instances of success and failure? How did the successes and failures influence your client's evaluation of the therapy?

3. Discuss your views on structured between-session assignments. As a client, were you ever asked to undertake such? If so, how did you respond? What was it like to attempt them? To complete the assignment or to be unable to complete it? To report back to the therapist? As a therapist, or trainee, do you make use of structured assignments and homework? If yes, how do you introduce them to your clients? If no, how do you respond to your clients' requests for such?

Endings

When we consider the diversity of endings in our own various non-therapeutic, wider-world relationships we realise that they can, and do, occur in any number of ways and under just about any conceivable set of circumstances. Sometimes endings are planned and acknowledged through some sort of shared ritual or ceremony. Sometimes they occur at the instigation of one party without the prior knowledge or agreement of the other party or parties. And sometimes endings occur unexpectedly without prior consideration by any party, but simply as a result of unforeseen circumstances or events. Why should any of these endings necessarily be seen as being more or less of an ending than any other? That the ending which presents itself may not be what either party, or all concerned, would have preferred does not make that ending inappropriate, nor lead to claims that no ending has occurred. So, too, is it the case with endings in therapy. Every model, and every practitioner and client, may have ideas as to what the preferred ending should be like or how it should occur. Sometimes, possibly more often than not, the preferred ending *is* the ending that occurs. Sometimes, it is not. And it is still an ending. Readers who have diligently followed and considered the arguments relating to the structural model under consideration are likely, by now, to register little surprise in reading that, in my view, existential therapy does not recognise one form of ending as being intrinsically better than, or superior to, any other.

Like many other therapists from other models and systems, the majority of existential therapists tend to prefer those endings that have been discussed between participants and which follow a shared plan of action. Most frequently, such plans involve the agreement that the therapist and client will continue to engage in therapy for a specified period of time in order to allow a winding down of the therapeutic relationship. While such a plan of action related to endings may make sense to existential therapist and client alike, and in this sense is desirable, it must still be asked: What is it about the therapeutic relationship, from the perspective of existential therapy, that requires its being wound down? After many years of asking this question to my self and my colleagues, I have come to the conclusion that the only sensible answer I can offer reflects, once again, the significance of the Dumbo Effect, certainly for the therapist and possibly for therapist and client alike.

Thus, from the standpoint of existential therapy, the issue of endings is not so much centred upon endings *per se* but rather has more to do with the degree of openness that exists to whatever form of ending actually occurs. The critical question for existential therapists to ask is: What is it about a particular ending that permits or prevents me from embracing it as appropriate to this particular relationship?

In my own 30-odd years' experience of practice as an existential therapist, I have worked with endings that followed a pre-arranged plan or which have resulted from a spontaneous decision by the client to end therapy with that session. In one instance of the latter, my willingness to go along with this decision seemed, for the client, to be *the* critical moment of the whole of our therapy together as it brought to life for her the reality that another could actually accept that she was capable of making sound and appropriate life decisions – and that, as a consequence, *she* could accept her own authority and ability to make appropriate decisions.

Some endings in existential therapy are already included in the contract agreed to at the very start of the therapeutic process. The client and existential therapist have set a specific number of sessions, or may be limited to a certain number of sessions because of the conditions imposed by the agency (such as an insurance provider or a National Health Trust) through which the therapist is employed and to whose services the client is entitled. Alternatively, the existential therapist may be meeting the client in a private capacity but for various reasons is prepared to see the client only for a limited number of sessions. Equally, the existential therapist may be flexible with regard to the duration of therapy but the client has restricted him or her self to a specified number of sessions. In such circumstances, barring the constant possibility of the unexpected event that alters everything, the approach toward an ending is reasonably clear-cut. Indeed, in their text on *Existential Time-Limited Therapy*, Freddie and Alison Strasser make a strong case for the value of explicitly reminding clients of the remaining number of sessions and utilise this as a parallel to the 'time-limited' conditions of human existence (Strasser & Strasser, 1997).

The majority of existential therapists who work in a private capacity, however, tend to adopt an open-ended approach to the number of sessions made available to the client. In such instances, the ending of therapy often remains ambiguous and the question of ending only arises when something like the idea of ending is 'in the air' and requires addressing. What factors should alert existential therapists to the possibility of an ending?

In my view, it would be appropriate to address the issue of an ending when:

- The client's narratives are increasingly concerned with the impact and effects of testing out the novel therapy-world worldview in the wider-world.
- The client's therapy-world discussions increasingly are focused on his or her experiences, and encounters, in the wider-world. Often the client's *ways of speaking* about these, revealing an ownership of, and connection to, the novel wider-world worldview being adopted, serve as useful indicators regarding the introduction of a discussion on endings.
- The client's statements about, and engagement with, the presenting issues and problems that had initiated the therapy suggest that these are no longer considered as being major areas of discourse or, indeed, have lost (or diminished) their problematic features.
- The topics and concerns that the client brings to therapy express the client's increasing focus on future options or activities beyond therapy.
- The client's way of relating directly to the therapist shifts in ways that suggest the lessening of the client's reliance upon the therapist as primary ally, confidante or 'special other'.

Nonetheless, while such instances often do turn out to be the precursors to an ending, sometimes they are not, and, if anything, act to initiate new investigations that may considerably prolong the therapeutic alliance. Such instances are most likely to occur when the client raises the issue of ending, or expresses the desire to end therapy and the therapist responds to them without sufficient investigative clarification as to what might be being stated at a covert or implicit level and thereby misses a significant aspect of the client's communication. For example, clients might raise the possibility of ending when they are experiencing a growing unease or fear that the therapist may be irritated or bored with them, which, for some reason or other, they find themselves unable to address directly with their therapist. Equally, the existential therapist's raising of the question of ending may provoke strong client reactions of unease, anger, hurt or betrayal.

However uncertain and anxiety-provoking the broaching of ending may be for therapist and client alike, the therapist who adopts a stance of *un-knowing* is likely to be more accepting of whatever way the client responds to such challenges as valid and genuine. In those instances when the suggestion of an ending provokes a disturbed reaction from the client, an un-knowing attitude assists the therapist in engaging non-defensively with the reaction in order to clarify what worldview insecurities may have prompted it. In doing so, both therapist and client might discover important structures in the client's worldview that previously had been insufficiently addressed or may have been missed.

Occasionally, as well, the client might express the desire to end therapy, is willing to discuss it non-defensively and consider it in relation to his or her worldview, while at the same time the therapist, acknowledging all of the above, still remains genuinely convinced that there is a great deal more for the client to explore. Such events can serve as useful examples as to when an *overt disclosure* on the part of the therapist can be helpful, and, if so, the therapist could offer the client the opportunity to hear and consider an alternative perspective. Often, the client will respond openly to invitations of this sort, but if the client rejects the offer then I would suggest that the most appropriate response is for the therapist to accept the client's decision in spite of his or her silent misgivings.

In some extreme instances, clients elect to end therapy simply by no longer attending their scheduled sessions. In some cases, they may inform the therapist before or after the missed meeting. More often, they simply cease all communication. Such forms of endings are likely to reflect a prior and unacknowledged critical breakdown in some aspect or aspects of the therapeutic encounter. Perhaps the therapist has shifted the dominant mode of encounter too rapidly from one Phase to the next and, by so doing, has provoked an unbearable degree of unease for the client. Just as likely, the therapist may not have challenged the client's worldview sufficiently, or challenged it in ways that generate distrust or a felt sense all too consonant with the client's wider-world worldview of others' oppressive tendencies. But it may also be the case that this way of ending has been adopted by the client because the therapist has been highly diligent and effective in challenging and that, in response, the client has decided that it is not what is desired or what he or she is currently able to tolerate. These forms of endings, still valid as they are, are also likely to be the most disturbing primarily because the client's decision may have come as a genuine surprise to the therapist and, as well, may be provoking the therapist's own professional and/or personal insecurities. Even in such circumstances, it still makes sense for the existential therapist to embrace all of these possibilities as another form of ending. In doing so, he or she is more likely to access that which is being experienced as disturbing about the client's chosen way of ending and be better able to challenge the assumptions that may be embedded within that sense of disturbance. This attitude is particularly worthwhile for the therapist to adopt as a precautionary step should the client subsequently change his or her mind and ask to return to therapy at a later point in time. Equally, the existential therapist may, for various reasons, decide to contact the client by post, email or text message in order to ascertain the client's intention to return. In such cases, the explicit acknowledgement that this desire to know is primarily for the therapist and is not intended as a covert demand that the client return to therapy seems vital. While these attempts may provoke no response from the client, they can also provide a means for the client either to assert that he or she stands by the decision or to raise the possibility of initiating therapy once again.

Gift-giving and receiving is closely associated with the issue of endings in that it can be clients' chosen way to mark the end of their therapy. It is less common, but by no means unusual, that therapists may offer a gift to their client on completion of their last session together. In either case, the gift may be in the form of a physical present (which has often been carefully considered), an act expressive of affection such as a hug, or both. While some approaches include in their contractual agreement with the client that no gifts can or will be accepted, for existential therapists such decisions rest with each therapist. Usually, but not always, gift-giving and receiving occurs between clients and therapists who have been meeting over a lengthy period of time. While one can always find good reason to be suspicious of the client's (or, indeed, one's own) intent, my own view is that while the recognition that hidden motives may exist should not be dismissed, neither should it deny the acknowledgement of the explicit motives that there may be to express an appreciation of the therapy and the wish to commemorate such through the ritual of gift-giving.

The above discussion once again makes clear that every acted-upon possibility has its implications and, of necessity, eliminates those possibilities that once were but which, in not having been enacted, are no longer. This awareness, of course, extends beyond the issue of endings and can be seen to be the underlying *motif* throughout the whole of the existential therapeutic encounter. Considered within the specific issues raised by therapeutic endings, my own conclusion, following Gadamer, is that if the dialogue is permitted to find and pursue its own direction, it will, equally, address its own way of ending (Gadamer, 2004).

An Exercise on Endings

Working together with a partner, take turns in discussing the following ending-related issues:

○ How have you ended therapy as a client?
○ How do you ordinarily work with endings as a therapist or a trainee?
○ What is an example of an ending from your own practice that surprised or disturbed you?
○ What kinds of therapeutic endings do you find to be desirable?
○ What kinds of therapeutic endings do you find to be acceptable?
○ What kinds of therapeutic endings do you find to be unacceptable?
○ Consider your responses to the last three questions from the focus of your wider-world experiences of endings? Are your responses similar to those you gave to the three above? In what ways, if any, are they different?

Life after Therapy

What is possible, relationally speaking, for the client and existential therapist after therapy has ended? Can they, for example, remain in contact with one another? And, if so, what are appropriate and inappropriate forms of contact? Such questions bedevil existential therapy at least as much as they might other models – and, perhaps because of the approach's openness to the uncertain, even more so. Further, such questions cannot and should not deny the facticity of Professional

Codes of Conduct that may themselves specify what post-therapeutic relations are permissible and which cannot be allowed to occur without their professional consequences.

Existential therapy usually leaves open the possibility that a new therapeutic relationship between client and therapist may be established at some future point in time. What is important to understand here, however, is that any eventual therapeutic relationship cannot be seen to be a continuation of the one that has just ended. Instead, the existential therapist who is willing to initiate a new therapeutic relationship with a past client should attempt as far as possible to treat the relationship as he or she would any other that was occurring for the first time. The bracketing difficulties of this enterprise are as plentiful as they are obvious and are further aggravated if either the therapist or the client persists in imposing the past relationship upon the present one. Nonetheless, the possibility of a new therapeutic relationship with a previous client remains an option. My own limitations in such attempts at bracketing have led me to make it explicit to clients that should they wish to commence therapy with me at some future point, they are welcome to contact me but that they might find it advantageous to leave a substantial gap of time – usually not less than six months – before initiating such contact.

A different, if equally challenging post-therapeutic contact option is that of the client's request to meet up again informally in order to see whether a friendship or some less formal relationship can be established. On this topic, there are often specific guidelines drawn up by Professional Bodies and I urge readers to ascertain what these may be according to the Body that accredits, licenses or charters their professional practice. My own experience, which may or may not be typical, is that very few clients either want or request post-therapeutic meetings. This may say something about the way I present my self or my style of working as a therapist. Equally, however, it may also express the genuine desire to treat the therapeutic encounter, and the often painful honesty exposed therein, as something special and different from other meaningful relationships.

Nonetheless, on occasion, the possibility of post-therapeutic meetings that might lead to the development of a friendship does present itself, and while one can remind the client of the rules set by Professional Bodies as a means to offset this challenge, it is also appropriate to consider this dilemma in other, *present moment* influenced ways. My experience as an existential therapist (but I suspect this to be the case with any model of therapy) is that the odds in favour of developing a close friendship with a past client are exceedingly low. My own, admittedly rare, experiences of meeting a former client in a social setting, once an appropriate time since our last professional meeting has elapsed, have tended to be somewhat disastrous in that (a) we found very little to talk about and (b) what we did talk about, and how we talked with one another, more resembled our previous therapy sessions than they did any other sort of dialogue.

Having wondered about this phenomenon over the years, and having heard equivalent accounts from other therapists who attempted something similar, I suspect that what both I and my former clients sufficiently did not take into account was how significant in themselves were the *structural context conditions* that defined the therapy-world. Increasingly, it seems to me that these were pivotal in permitting a mutual accessing and experience of inter-connection and intimacy. Just as, in the same, if opposite, way, their non- (or inadequate) existence was pivotal in its impact upon our somewhat disastrous social encounter. The deep levels of connectedness and intimacy that we had experienced in the therapy-world were simply not available within the insufficiently negotiated social structure we were now co-habiting. Indeed, we could only regain something of that closeness when we sought to re-establish the previous therapy-world structure, even if that was antagonistic to our purpose in meeting. Perhaps, if we had persevered ... But, again, this has not been the case.

In addition to the above, over the years it has also become clearer to me that while the establishment of a friendship with a past client might be possible and desirable to both parties, the price that the client in particular pays for this is the loss of any possibility of a future therapeutic relationship. Thus, when requests to explore the possibility of friendship are put to me by clients toward the end of our therapeutic relationship, I present the options. The most common choice by far made by clients when this stark, if truthful, choice is put to them is best summarised by the remark made by one of them. 'Okay. I'll stick with the possibility that you might be my therapist again at some point in the future. Real friends are tough to find, but finding a good therapist is even tougher.'

Notwithstanding the above, I would be dishonest if I were to claim that the establishment of a close and lasting friendship with an ex-client is simply not possible. As rare as it is, and acknowledging the sacrifice it entails for the former client, it *can* happen and I do have personal experience of it. Interestingly, though we rarely discuss our first relationship as therapist and client, I suspect that this avoidance says as much about what we have lost as it might be a desire to 'let the past lie'. And because I think this, I must also admit to a recurring sense of guilt that however good a friend my ex-client friends may have gained, it may not be equal to what they have lost.

Exercise Exploring Post-therapeutic Relations with Former Clients

1. Together with a partner, discuss what post-therapeutic social relationship or friendship with your past therapist/s you might have wished to have or would never wish to have. What provokes each of these responses?

2. Discuss your experience, if any, of working with a client with whom you could imagine a social relationship or friendship at an appropriate time following the ending of the therapeutic relationship. What was it about this client that provoked this desire for you? How did you deal with it?

3. Discuss your experience, if any, of working with a client who expressed his or her desire to establish a social relationship or friendship at an appropriate

time following the ending of the therapeutic relationship. How did you deal with this request? What other ways, if any, can you consider might be appropriate for you to have dealt with this request?

Summary

As well as being concerned with issues surrounding the ending of therapy, Phase Three plays a pivotal role in the exploration of the potential bridging of the therapy-world with that of the client's (and, indeed, the therapist's) wider-world relations. In this, Phase Three, as I have proposed it, brings to the fore the foundational Principles of existential phenomenology – relatedness, uncertainty and existential anxiety – in that the concerns it addresses can be seen to be direct expressions of these Principles' possibilities and consequences. In doing so, Phase Three emphasises that the practice of existential therapy is not only a matter of professional expertise but also a *moral* enterprise grounded in these three critical Principles. Perhaps most obviously, this aspect of existential therapy is expressed during Phase Three when direct attempts are made to address the necessary relational negotiation with the wider-world that clients must undertake in order for their novel, post-therapeutic worldview to remain at least partially tenable.

The ending of existential therapy can, and often does, provide clients with a sense of elation – for what has been achieved, for the novel possibilities of living that have been initiated, and the genuine sense of choice, freedom and responsibility which accompanies them. At the same time, the ending of existential therapy can also be a period of sober reflection and some regret for both the client and therapist. For the client, the uncertainty of a new beginning which does not include the security of a therapy-world and the reliability of the therapist's care must now be faced and lived with. For the therapist, the sense of loss and sacrifice may be felt in a much more diffuse fashion. For both, I suspect, the death of their therapeutic relationship enfolds them in an embodied awareness of what is, what could have been and what will be.

10

Addenda:

Existential Therapy with Couples
Existential Therapy with Groups
Time-limited Existential Therapy
Existential Supervision

The primary focus of this book has been on practising existential therapy from an open–ended, one–to–one perspective. While this form of existential therapy remains by far the most common, this should not lead readers to suppose that it is the only means by which to practise this approach. Existential therapists also work under settings and circumstances that involve both therapeutic work with *couples* and with *groups* and under *short-term or time-limited conditions*. While these alternative forms of practice deserve their own extended explication, nonetheless it is appropriate for this text to address and summarise briefly some of the more pertinent features of each. Equally, the increasing professional significance placed upon therapeutic *supervision* raises numerous relevant questions and concerns regarding how existential therapy might best interpret and make use of supervision without compromising its foundational Principles. While this text can only touch on and address the most immediate issues raised by these important variations in focus and practice, nonetheless it is hoped that the points it makes will encourage readers to pursue these topics in greater detail.

Existential Therapy with Couples

A great deal of existential therapy with couples parallels one-to-one work with individuals in terms of its focus and overall aims of descriptive clarification and challenge. A substantial amount of that which has been described throughout this text, for example, would be equally applicable in work with couples. Nonetheless, it remains my view that significant emphases specific to therapy with couples can be noted and articulated. Among these, I believe the most significant to be the following:

1. A couple is seen inadequately if it is perceived only as made up of two people who interact with, and relate to, one another in various ways. As well as acknowledging the worldview of each partner in the couple, what must also be recognised is the existence of the couple itself as a structure made up of, but not equivalent to, the separate and combined aspects of the worldviews of each person in the couple. In other words, the couple-construct as a distinct structure containing its own worldview requires clarification and challenge.

2. Viewed in this way, the investigatory focus of existential couple therapy is only tangentially upon each individual partner in the couple, A and B. Far more prominently, it is attuned to the *couple-construct,* which expresses a particular way of inter-relating that has been co-constructed by the couple (that is to say, which exists between A and B). If the existential therapist fails to adequately explore the couple-construct, he or she will likely focus greater attention upon the worldview of one partner to the detriment of the other's.

3. The couple-construct is likely to be initially presented and considered by each partner in the couple predominantly from the focus of conflict, with its dysfunctional elements being highlighted as its primary defining structural components. It is also likely, however, that many of the worldview structures and their existential uncertainties, which both underpin and identify the couple-construct, have never been made sufficiently explicit by either partner. The attempt to do so is likely to reveal that (a) each partner has made little if any distinction between his or her own particular worldview and that of the couple-construct, other than with regard to the conflictual aspects between them, and (b) when considered more adequately, the couple-construct is likely to reveal numerous structures which both partners value and wish to continue to maintain. This latter point may well serve to provide the couple-in-conflict with the insight that they are also, in part, a couple-in-agreement and, thereby, permit the awareness and experience of connectedness as well as that of dividedness.

4. The couple-construct's presenting conflict is initially perceived by each partner from his or her own worldview. This viewpoint is typically maintained with either insufficient or only bellicose direct communication between the partners. The conflicts threatening the couple-construct reveal existential insecurities focused on questions of continuity, dispositional stances and identity. They are commonly expressed by one or both of the partners in the following ways:

   i. One partner expresses the view that the other threatens the continuity, dispositional stances (such as values, beliefs and aspirations) and/or established identity of the couple-construct in some way, be it focused upon his or her behaviour, statements or overall attitude towards it. For example, one partner holds the view that the other no longer wants to be in the relationship, or is expressing the desire to alter the couple-construct's structure, or who is no longer identifiable as he or she used to be in the relationship.

   ii. One partner expresses the view that he or she has changed, or is changing, in ways that are acknowledged to threaten the continuity, dispositional stances and identity of the couple-construct. The structures of the couple-construct that are being highlighted are deemed to be 'out of touch', no longer relevant or in conflict with either or both partners' current worldview stance. For example, one partner no longer sees the value in remaining in the couple, or argues that to do so will hinder his or her own interests and aspirations, or that he or she has changed in ways to which the couple-construct cannot accommodate.

iii. Both partners express dissatisfaction with some aspect or aspects of the current couple-construct and either may wish to change it but don't know how, or are concerned that any such changes, if accomplished, may be unsustainable and/or may threaten each partner's own worldview. For example, both partners express the view that they are trying to be the sort of couple that neither one of them wishes to be any longer but are worried that any new couple-construct won't work out. Often, couples express such concerns through the metaphor of the couple-construct's 'illness', the possibility of its 'death', and the fears and concerns surrounding what 'life after the death of the couple-construct' may be like for either or both partners in the couple. It is not unusual for both partners, who might otherwise claim to disagree with one another on practically every other issue, to agree on the 'illness' of the couple-construct. Often, by simply pointing out this shared assumption to them, the existential therapist may increase the possibility of the couple's willingness to address its concerns from a less combative stance.

5. In individual therapy, the primary structures and embodied existential insecurities of the client's worldview are clarified and challenged so that the presenting problems can be considered in relation to them. Working with couples re-focuses this enterprise so that the investigation is predominantly concerned with the clarification and challenge of the structures and existential insecurities which maintain and define the couple-construct so that the couple's presenting problems can be considered in relation to it. From a practical standpoint, the existential therapist remains attuned to the statements made by either or both partners regarding any aspect of the couple-construct rather than concentrate on each partner's own personal worldview statements. The exploration of these concerns with both partners may well facilitate clarification of the couple-construct's limitations, ambiguities and contradictions with respect to each partner's aspirations, needs and desires for him or her self, the other partner, and for them as a couple.

6. From an existential standpoint, an important, if rarely acknowledged, complexity in couple work emerges: individual therapy can only focus indirectly upon the client's other-construct. In individual therapy relational encounters with others are limited to the client's direct engagement with the therapist-as-other. In the case of couple therapy, however, each partner engages not only with the therapist-as-other, but also experiences the direct presence of the other partner within the therapy-world. This presence brings a relational complexity to the therapy-world that, in turn, attunes each partner not only to his or her own worldview, but also to the other partner's and, in doing so,

allows the exploration of the couple's co-created couple-construct to become more accessible to investigation and clarification.

7.   Throughout couple therapy, the existential therapist stays within a predomi-nantly Phase One focus that concentrates on the descriptive clarification of the consonant, competing and contradictory views held by each partner with regard to the couple-construct, treating each perspective as being initially equally experientially valid. This stance requires the therapist's willingness to attend not only to the partner who is currently speaking but also to the other who remains silent. By so doing, the therapist accesses with increasing adequacy the couple-construct that has emerged through the holding of both partners' maintained stances, whose ambiguities, conflicts and contradic-tions are the basis to the couple's presenting problems.

8.   In the service of this investigative enterprise, I have developed a particular sequence for working with couples. This sequence follows a repeated five-session pattern made up of the following:

   i.   The existential therapist meets with both partners together for sessions one and two.
   ii. The existential therapist meets with each partner individually for sessions three and four.
   iii. The existential therapist meets with both partners together for session five. This sequence is then repeated until such time as couple therapy ends.

The rationale for this sequence is to enable each partner to expose, clarify and consider his or her experience of co-habiting the couple-construct both in the direct presence of the other partner and under circumstances more akin to those of individual therapy. While the majority of these investigations are conducted with both partners present, the individual sessions allow each partner to engage in explorations that, although significant, are likely to be assessed as being too threatening or difficult to be engaged with while the other partner is present. Nonetheless, at some point during these individual sessions, whatever has been presented is considered from an imagined pos-sibility of the other partner's having been present. Often, this permits the communication of at least some of that which was explored to the other part-ner either in-between sessions or during their next session together.

   In particular, this enterprise can be greatly assisted by the existential therapist's focus on the inter-relational realms of encounter (as discussed in Chapter 8) to enable the couple's mutual validation of the accuracy of what each has attempted to express. For instance:

Therapist: Jill, you've talked about how it hurts for you when Jack questions his love for you. Can you repeat to Jack as directly and clearly as possible what it's like to hear that?

Jill: I feel like I'm being squeezed into a tiny box [**I-focus**]. I can't believe that after all we've worked for over the years, you'd be so easily prepared to give up on us! [**We-focus**]. I can't make any sense of you! [**You-focus**]. And I don't know what you think I've done to you that you would want to hurt me in this way! [**You-focus**].

Jack: But I don't ...

Therapist: Jack, before you give us your response to Jill's statements, could you repeat what you heard Jill just say?

Jack: Yeah. She basically said she hates me [**You-focus**].

Therapist: You heard Jill say: 'I hate you.'

Jack: Yes.

Therapist: Jill, is what Jack heard what you intended to say to him?

Jill: No! I—

Therapist: [To Jill] Wait. Can you repeat to Jack what you intended to say?

Jill: I don't hate you [**You-focus**]. If I did, I wouldn't be here. I still love you [**I-focus**]. But you've hurt me really badly when you said that you were wondering whether you still loved me [**You-focus**].

Therapist: Jack, what did you hear Jill say now?

Jack: That she doesn't hate me but that I've hurt her a lot [**You-focus**].

Therapist: Jill, is what Jack heard what you intended to say to him?

Jill: Yes. But not all of it. He missed out that I still love him [**I-focus**].

Therapist: Jack, did you hear that part of Jill's message, too?

Jack: Yeah ...

Therapist: Okay. So is there anything you want to say to Jill?

Jack: I'm sorry. I didn't want any of this to happen. I don't know what to do [**I-focus**].

Therapist: Jill, what did you just hear Jack say?

Jill: That he's sorry and he didn't want this to happen and he doesn't know what to do [**You-focus**].

Therapist: Jack? Has Jill heard you accurately?

Jack: Yeah ...

Therapist: Okay. So, Jill, in the light of what Jack said, is there anything you want to say to him?

Jill: That I believe him [**You-focus**]. But I don't think that's good enough [**I-focus**]. I think I deserve better than that [**I-focus**]. I think we both deserve better than that [**We-focus**].

Jack:	I do, too [**We-focus**].
Therapist:	Okay. So although neither of you entirely agrees with what the other has expressed, would it be correct to say that you both do agree that you both deserve better?
Jack:	Yes.
Jill:	Absolutely.
Therapist:	Okay. So that's something that, in spite of your numerous disagreements, you both agree on. So ... let's stay with that a bit. What is the 'better' that you each agree you deserve?

9. Viewed from the perspective of existential therapy's focus on the descriptive exploration of the couple-construct, the most likely consequences of this investigation are that:

   i. One partner's worldview is altered in such a way that what had intensified tensions between it and the couple-construct is either diminished or alleviated.
   ii. Both partners' worldviews are altered in such a way that what intensified tensions between them and the couple-construct is either diminished or alleviated.
   iii. Significant and shared aspects of the couple-construct are altered so that it more adequately reflects relevant aspects of either or both partners' worldviews.
   iv. The couple-construct remains in too much conflict with either or both partners' worldviews such that it cannot be maintained or altered and ceases to exist.

Although this brief exploration of existential therapy with couples reveals numerous similarities with individual therapy, readers will, I hope, have gained an initial sense of the added complexity of clarification and challenge that it imposes. Typically, there is a more intrusive quality to the therapist's interventions in that they must often restrain more spontaneous discourse between the couple in the interest of clarifying whether each has heard the other accurately and how this accuracy might further expose that which exists in the couple–construct that may be provoking the greatest worldview tensions for either or both partners. Although working in this way with couples can be highly stimulating for the existential therapist, I would recommend that existential therapy with couples might be best left to those therapists who have already gained a substantial amount of experience in working on a one–to–one basis with clients.

Existential Group Therapy

Existential group therapy is well–represented in that one of the acknowledged modern classics on the general topic of group therapy has been written by a world-renowned author who also happens to be the leading representative of contemporary North American existential therapy. The fifth edition of Irvin Yalom's *Theory and Practice of Group Psychotherapy* (Yalom and Leszcz, 2005) incorporates numerous viewpoints and ideas that are directly influenced by his understanding of, and approach to, existential therapy. Similarly, Yalom's well-received novel, *The Schopenhauer Cure* (2006) contains an accessible exploration of group therapy from a broadly existential perspective. Although I would recommend both books to all readers interested in this topic, I remain in agreement with Hans Cohn's judgement that Yalom's explorations of group therapy provide an excellent focus on the thematic existence concerns (such as meaning/meaninglessness, isolation and death anxiety) likely to arise in the course of group therapy, but do not truly discuss a way of working with a group in an explicitly existential manner (Cohn, 1997). Unfortunately, this same critique holds for the great majority of other attempts to discuss this topic (Tantam, 2005).

Literature on practising existential group therapy – as opposed to exploring existential themes in group therapy – is scarce. It is, in fact, Cohn's own brief account of it that I believe says more on the topic than anything else I have read (Cohn, 1997).

Cohn begins his discussion by reminding readers of the foundational Principle of relatedness. From a group therapy standpoint, therefore, each member of the group cannot be considered as a wholly separate entity, but rather as a co-existing focal point within a specified relational context and setting (the group). For Cohn, the focus of existential group therapy lies in the exploration of the discerned *relational disturbances* as expressed by, and within, the group, rather than in the internalised problems of distinct and separate individuals. It is the group itself, the way of its being and relating, that provides a particular set of circumstances within which disturbances appear, and through which these same disturbances can be observed, clarified and challenged. The group, as well, is its own narrational subject – what occurs within the group and what is brought into the group from outside by its members makes up its narrative content and context.

Although the existential therapist has a particular task to perform – which is that of assisting 'in the process of clarifying the relational and communicative disturbances and potentialities of the group' (Cohn, 1997: 55) – Cohn insists that it is a distinctive feature of existential group therapy to consider the therapist as a valid and active member of the group. From Cohn's perspective, the existential therapist is just one of any number of interpreters rather than its primary one. In addition, the therapist is neither discouraged nor prevented from contributing to group discussion via the communication of his or her own views, thoughts and concerns. In a broad sense, Cohn's account of the existential group therapist is one which acknowledges the therapist's special role in setting up and maintaining the structural conditions within which group therapy can occur. At the same time, Cohn is reluctant to bestow upon the existential group therapist anything that singles him or her out as possessing an authority that is a major determinant of the direction of group discourse. That the therapist presents material that seems worthy of disclosure to him or her should not suggest nonetheless that the therapist can have any idea as to who in the group might receive these disclosures, what reaction they might provoke and who, if any one at all, might benefit from them. Indeed, with regard to the typical role of the existential group therapist, Cohn is adamant that 'the group is the therapist of the group' (Cohn, 1997: 46).

It is my view that Cohn's account of existential group therapy, however brief, provides an initial overview as to its possibilities, as well as indicating how it diverges from other contemporary approaches. Although he does not use the term, I would suggest that Cohn is proposing a primary focus that rests upon what I would identify as the *group-construct*. In emphasising this focal point, the major tasks of existential group therapy become those of:

a. The descriptive investigation of the group-construct as revealed through the interactions between the various group members with each other within the group;
b. The descriptive investigation of the group-construct as revealed through the interactions between the various group members in response to what each brings to the group from outside the group;
c. The descriptive investigation of the relational tensions that arise between the group-construct and relevant aspects of each group member's worldview;
d. The descriptive investigation of the impact of those challenges presented by the group-construct upon any individual member's worldview;
e. The descriptive investigation of the impact of those challenges presented by each group member's worldview upon the group-construct.

As a final comment on existential group therapy, readers may recall that in an earlier section of this text the question of the artificiality or unreality of the therapy-world was considered. It was argued that in being made up of (usually) only two directly present participants, the therapy-world is inter-relationally less complex than the wider-world. Made up of a multitude of participants with differing views, expectations, demands and behaviours, the impact of the wider-world upon the client's worldview cannot ever be fully replicated in the therapy-world. Considering this conclusion from the standpoint of existential group therapy, it can be seen that what may be the most significant, as well as the most taxing, challenge for both the existential therapist and the clients who, together, make up the membership of the group, is precisely its *inter-relational complexity*. Undoubtedly, it is the multitude of participants whose differing insecurities concerning their own and/or the group's continuity, dispositional stances and identity impact upon one another that generates this complexity. At the same time, this group-generated complexity arises *within* a structured and distinct therapy-world with its explicit and mutually agreed setting, frame and contractual conditions. As such, the therapy-world of existential group therapy provides a structure that is both more closely akin to each group member's wider-world relations than any one-to-one form of therapy could ever hope to offer. At the same time, however, this same structure is also sufficiently different from each group member's wider-world relations to be able to provoke the disclosure of, and challenge to, each group member's currently maintained worldview. It is the enterprise of existential group therapy to 'hold the tension' between the therapy-world and the wider-world so that the group-construct generated within the therapy-world is neither too alien nor too indistinct from group members' various wider-world group interactions.

Time-limited Existential Therapy

Existential therapy is often perceived to be a long-term or open-ended enterprise. Of course, it can be so, but the assumption that this is a necessary condition is a false one that is probably based upon caricature interpretations of existential therapy as an intellectually dominated enterprise centred upon the examination of abstract 'higher-order' ideas and concerns. Hopefully, readers will have by now been dissuaded from associating such views with the practising of existential therapy. Because, increasingly, both state- and insurance-funded therapy providers insist upon short-term, focused therapy for patients and clients, it is of critical importance that existential therapy is neither dismissed nor side-lined as a valid approach within time-limited conditions.

This challenge was taken up as far back as 1997 by Freddie and Alison Strasser in their text *Existential Time-Limited Therapy: The Wheel of Existence* (1997). Rather than see short-term approaches as imposing limitations upon existential therapy, Strasser and Strasser argued that this way of working contained various advantages. First, time-limited therapy 'mirrors, in many respects, the time-limited nature of human existence ... [such that] clients are brought face-to-face with issues of finitude and temporality in a very direct and immediate way' (Cooper, 2003: 130). Second, Strasser and Strasser suggest that the explicit reminder to clients that the therapeutic encounter is time-limited is likely to 'intensify the client's commitment to the therapeutic process, encouraging the client to bring to the fore anxieties or concerns that, in a less time-pressurised environment, she might tend to withhold' (ibid.: 131).

Existential time-limited therapy as described by Strasser and Strasser retains a close proximity to many of the key focus points and practices that have been detailed in the structural model discussed in this text. The descriptive clarification and challenging of the client's presenting issues in relation to his or her overall worldview remains the key feature of the approach. What varies is the extent to which the therapist is more focused, active and directively challenging in the questions and reflections offered to the client. These more dynamic interventions focus explicitly upon how the client's presenting issues are expressed and impact upon the foundational Principles of relatedness, uncertainty and identity as well as various existence themes such as temporality and choice, and upon existential insecurities focused on questions relevant to the client's experiences of continuity, dispositional stances and identity.

The structural model advocated by Strasser and Strasser is visualised by them as a dynamic 'wheel of existence'. At its hub is what they refer to as the client's 'moving self' (an idea in this current text which has been extended and expressed as the client's worldview) while each particular area of existential focus forms one of the wheel's various spokes. In this way, the inter-connectedness between the moving self and any presenting existential issues is made explicit (Strasser & Strasser, 1997). Further, Strasser and Strasser argue that through this diagrammatic visualisation of the wheel of existence, the descriptive clarification of the client's presenting concerns can be accelerated insofar as that an immediate and distinctive inter-relational focus is established and maintained from the very start of the therapeutic encounter. In this sense, their model provides a structural context that can often be experienced as being akin to an intensive 'hothouse' environment that identifies and challenges rigid and limiting worldview sedimentations.

If anything, this focused approach may be experienced by the client as being overly challenging in that it can very rapidly expose and make explicit fixed, often contradictory meanings, values and beliefs that have been maintained by the client in an insufficiently reflective or covert way. As a counter-balance to this, Strasser and Strasser also emphasise the value and importance of the therapist's caring, respectful and accepting stance toward the client so that the relational context under which the investigations are carried out is experienced by the client as being sufficiently secure to hold the often intense emotion-laden insights that are likely to occur.

Strasser and Strasser's pioneering work in time-limited, or short-term, existential therapy is being increasingly taken up by other practitioners, especially in Australia, where Alison Strasser now lives and works. At the same time, variations on short-term, intensive existential therapy are currently being developed by several other practitioners and detailed descriptions of their models are likely to be published over the next few years (Rayner & Vitali, 2014; Stephenson, in preparation). Although many similarities exist, one important distinction that has arisen between approaches centres on the issue of goal-focus and goal-setting. Strasser and Strasser remain cautious about pre-setting any desired goal-outcomes. They argue that once the client's presenting problems have been made explicit, it is appropriate for therapeutic enquiry to find its own direction and focus so that whatever goals may be identified will emerge out of the encounter rather than be pre-set as conditions of encounter. In this, they remain very much in line with the more open-ended approaches to existential therapy such as that of the structural model being presented in this text. In contrast, other practitioners, mainly working under conditions approved by the UK National Health Service (NHS), have developed approaches that focus on identifiable pre-set goals that then become the focus of descriptive investigations closely aligned to those discussed in the present text (Rayner & Vitali, 2014; Stephenson, in preparation).

Whatever the approach taken, what has begun to emerge with regard to short-term existential therapy is that not only is it a feasible enterprise for therapists and clients to undertake; it is neither too diffuse nor too 'intellectual' in comparison to other approaches. Indeed, if anything, its rapid and explicit exploratory impact requires some caution in being applied and should always be tempered by the therapist's attentive presence and engagement with the client.

Existential Supervision

The supervision of therapists by their colleagues has become one of the primary requirements for continuing professional practice. Just about every Professional Body concerned with therapy emphasises the importance of supervision and, typically, specifies that its members must engage in it under regular and ongoing approved conditions. Although existential therapy is no different in that its members adhere to these governances, the very concept of supervision, and in particular what its meaning and purpose might be understood to be, has remained an ongoing source of debate.

What has been written about existential supervision remains somewhat limited. Nonetheless, the paucity in material is counter-balanced by the quality of discussions presented by contributors. In many ways, the issues surrounding supervision have provided existential therapists with a focus through which to address the wider debate as to what constitutes existential therapy and what may be distinctive about its practice. As such, it is not entirely surprising to discover that the majority of papers on existential supervision are concerned with basic questions such as: '[W]hat makes an "existential supervisor"? More importantly, is there such a thing as "existential supervision" and what are its characteristics?' (Pett, 1995: 117). Equally, a recurring question centres upon whether existential supervision should focus upon an existentially informed process of enquiry or should provide the basis for discussing therapeutic issues from the perspective of differing insights derived from theorists and practitioners linked to existential phenomenology (Pett, 1995; Wright, 1996).

Currently, disagreements between authors who have approached this topic remain at least as common as their agreements. For example, Regina Wright writes that what most distinguishes an existential approach to supervision is its 'lack of doctrine' (Wright, 1996: 154) and its openness to what may emerge as opposed to preconceived assumptions about what to expect, look for, or identify. Whereas, for Diana Mitchell, the very possibility of existential supervision is questionable since its demands for 'a certain kind of exploration concerned with the themes and issues that emerge in the therapeutic relationship' (Mitchell, 2002: 91) are in stark contrast to jointly agreed explorations carried out in existential therapy wherein the topics under discussion are chosen by the client. That both Wright and Mitchell are existential therapists, yet their views on supervision reveal significant divergence, should clarify the depth and extent of differing opinion within the approach. In general, I am in agreement with Mitchell's conclusion that the undertaking of any sort of existential supervision must 'accept that there are already aspects of supervision ... that are at odds with existential thinking and the practice of therapy' (Mitchell, 2002: 96). Nonetheless, I am also in agreement with both Wright and Mitchell in their recognition that what might be called existential supervision promotes 'a questioning attitude towards the theories and beliefs' (ibid.: 93) that are held with regard to the aims of supervision.

In my view, the most significant contributions to the debates surrounding existential supervision have appeared in two papers published by Simon du Plock

(2007, 2009). In the first of these, du Plock proposes 'an experiential approach utilising some aspects of existential therapy to facilitate the concept of "supervision"
per se' (du Plock, 2007: 31). Rather than provide yet another model for supervision, du Plock attempts to elucidate an attitudinal stance that takes the therapeutic
relationship itself as its primary focus. He challenges existential therapists to make
clear 'what we, the practitioners, want existential-phenomenological supervision
to signify' (ibid.: 34). Focusing upon a relationally attuned approach to supervision
(which he clarifies through the use of several experiential exercises as practical
examples), du Plock conceptualises 'supervision as a piece of practical research into
our openness to and limitations on being in relationship with clients. In such an
approach the supervisor and supervisees become co-researchers of the phenomenon "relationship"' (ibid.: 38).

In his second paper (2009), which centres upon the analysis of a phenomenological study focused upon the meaning of supervision carried out by du Plock
and 18 existential therapist co-researchers, he highlights the significance of relatedness as the focus point for a triad of inter-connected narratives:

1. The client's narratives of experience of being, <u>as they are reported by
   the supervisee</u>.
2. The narratives of the experience of being in relation with the client, <u>as
   they are reported by the supervisee</u>.
3. The supervisor's and supervisee's currently lived experience of
   relatedness as it unfolds, and enfolds them both, <u>in the space of the
   supervisory encounter</u>. (Du Plock, 2009: 302)

Among the significant concerns pointed out by du Plock is an obvious one that,
nonetheless, is often missed: the client who is the focus of the supervisory encounter is not present in the room. Rather, it is 'the-therapist-who-meets-the-client'
(ibid.: 302) who is in the supervisory encounter and whose recounted experience
of therapeutic encounters remains the primary focus of the supervisory encounter.

As space conditions permit only a brief summary of du Plock's research conclusions, I urge readers to seek out and engage with the paper. The points that follow
provide a précis to its concluding arguments:

1. Existential supervision centres upon the co-creation of a discursive opening
   through which the 'non-judgemental and non-directive clarification of aspects
   of being human ... as they emerge in therapeutic practice' (ibid.: 313) are
   able to be descriptively clarified.
2. Existential supervision encourages supervisees 'to dwell often in a place of
   "un-knowing", and to tolerate and even cultivate accompanying anxiety' (ibid.).
3. Existential supervision attempts to establish a 'democratic and non-hierarchi-
   cal relationship' (ibid.).
4. Existential supervision addresses the ambiguities and paradoxes of existence, 'rather than make interpretations or use categories of pathology which
   limit the appreciation of the client's way of being' (ibid.).

5. Rather than be concerned with the investigation of the non-present client's problematic issues, existential supervision principally focuses upon the degree to which the supervisee is able and willing to establish and maintain increasingly adequate encounters with the client.
6. Existential supervision explores how supervisor and supervisee are, themselves, in relation with one another and how the investigation of their relationship might serve to enhance the quality of the supervisee's encounters with clients.

Considered together, the arguments presented by the great majority of existential therapists who have written about existential supervision suggest a challenge to the dominant perspectives adopted with regard to the meaning and function of supervision. In part, the concerns expressed are contained within the term itself. *Super-vision suggests an act of over-seeing.* From this standpoint, supervision suggests notions of viewing, judging and/or interpreting *from above* and, therefore, contains the implicit assumption of the supervisor's superiority in expertise, status and power. None of these features sits easily with existential phenomenological theory.

From this over-seeing standpoint, supervision concerns itself primarily with *formative, normative and restorative functions* in that it focuses upon the building up and development of the supervisee's understanding of theory and applications of skills and techniques (the formative function); the protection of clients through the supervisor's policing of the supervisee's professional behaviour (the normative function); and the amelioration of the client's presenting issues as understood and clarified through the 'lens' of the supervisor's and/or supervisee's preferred model (the restorative function).

However, there exists another means with which to consider the meaning of supervision. From this alternate perspective, *super-vision suggests an act of seeing-over.* From this interpretative focus, supervision provides the supervisee with the opportunity to view and consider again both that which occurred in an encounter with the client as well as that which may have been missed or insufficiently considered regarding that encounter *as re-viewed from the perspective of the supervisee* and as clarified through the investigative challenges of the supervisor under a set of relational conditions encouraging of a truthful dialogue. Specifically, this view invites the supervisee to consider and explicate that which has emerged for him or her in the course of the therapeutic encounter being recounted that continues to impact in some noticeable way upon either his or her sense of being a therapist, or of being a person, or both. This seeing–over approach to supervision is principally focused upon the supervisee's actual experience of being a therapist and practising therapy either in relation to a particular client, or with clients in general so that it can be compared to the supervisee's assumptions, beliefs and values as to what it is to be a therapist and to practise therapy.

While all forms of supervision that acknowledge professional regulation must in some way pay heed to the formative, normative and restorative functions of supervision, it remains the case that it is the second interpretation of supervision with which existential supervision most resonates. Nonetheless, this dual focus should not be seen as yet another case of 'either/or' options. Issues surrounding the formative, normative and restorative functions of supervision cannot always be dismissed. Nor should they be. For instance, at times, focusing the supervision on different ways of understanding a client's concerns or behaviour, including ways that focus upon a particular philosopher or practitioner, are invaluable. At the same time, it seems to me to be contrary to any existential enterprise if the supervisory process were to engage exclusively or principally only with questions centred upon 'what would philosopher/practitioner X think or do?' In the same fashion, it makes little sense to me to argue that existential supervision's primary concerns are those of interpreting various facets of therapeutic encounters in order to illuminate some existential principle or to address existential phenomenology's way of understanding thematic existence concerns. These sorts of theory-highlighting entertainments would soon become a rather empty and power-imbalanced enterprise that I can't imagine any supervisee would find to be of much value or that any existential supervisor would be interested in promoting. Obviously, ways of considering the client's concerns from theoretical and/or practical perspectives are always likely to emerge within the supervisory discussion, but even when they do the focus of existential supervision can still remain upon the re-viewing of the supervisee's experience of being a therapist in a specific encounter and the related concerns it raises. The challenge remains for existential supervision to find the means to hold the tension between these two interpretations of supervision and to navigate between them through some shared agreement.

Nonetheless, while still adopting a both/and perspective, it is evident that existential supervision's primary concerns lie with the shared attempt to open up the supervision-world space for an exploration of that which the supervisee considers to be problematic or a block to his or her ability to stay with and accept the client's way of being so that it can continue to be descriptively explicated and challenged. As such, the focus is primarily on the relational and contextual conditions in the encounter between the supervisee and his/her client and what issues or obstacles exist, have been created or have arisen for the supervisee in maintaining as open, challenging and non-defensive a relationship as possible with the client.

In accordance with this primary focus, I would suggest that existential supervision, in common with existential therapy, concerns itself with a descriptively focused exploratory process centred upon the supervisee's worldview stance regarding what are the necessary conditions for him or her to be a therapist, what is required in order to permit the practising of therapy as envisaged and desired by the supervisee and how these are being enhanced or challenged by or within a specified encounter with a client. In turn, this focused exploration of the supervisee's worldview as considered from his or her professional identity as a therapist is likely to bring to awareness those relational tensions and concerns or general ways of being that define and maintain the supervisee's worldview in general. This understanding reveals a link between existential supervision and the process of existential therapy. Although it is not therapy *per se,* existential supervision can often be experienced as therapeutic. Nonetheless, it remains the case that whatever may be touched upon in the course of existential supervision that is experienced by the supervisee as having wider ramifications extending beyond the professional to the personal should always be brought back to its relationship with, or impact upon, the therapeutic work being undertaken with the particular client under discussion.

For example, my supervisee, Jonas, had been grappling with a recurring sense of distraction that arose whenever he engaged in a therapeutic encounter with his client, Melanie. Jonas had noticed that the minute Melanie began to speak, he seemed to drift away such that he was barely able to recall what she had been saying. As we explored Jonas' reaction, utilising various descriptive challenges as detailed in the structural model discussed in this text, Jonas began to focus on how he experienced Melanie's way of being, particularly as expressed through a habit she had of waving her hand dismissively whenever he challenged a specific area of concern that Melanie brought to therapy. He realised that this dismissive hand-waving had far more general interpretative connotations for him that were relevant to several past failed romantic relationships in his life. Had this been a therapeutic session, the focus would have remained upon the further descriptive clarification of Jonas' wider experience of failed relationships. As a supervisory encounter, however, what took precedence was the exploration of the relation between this personal life insight and Jonas' drifting away during therapeutic encounters with Melanie and, in turn, how his connecting insight could be of value not only in keeping Jonas more focused on Melanie's statements, but, as well, how his connecting Melanie with his failed relationships might open up novel therapeutic means of descriptive exploration of Melanie's issues.

In turn, Jonas' clarification of the effect that Melanie's repeated gesture had on him allowed him to address concerns regarding how he imagined I viewed him both as a therapist and as a person and whether at some level his therapeutic failures with Melanie were leading me towards a dismissive attitude towards him. Again, the concerns being raised by Jonas within the immediacy of the supervisory encounter opened exploratory possibilities that were relevant both to Jonas' professional and personal identities. As his supervisor, I could point to the relevance of exploring the impact on both, but encouraged the explicit exploration of the professional implications of his concerns. As well, however, it led me to question whether the stance I adopted towards Jonas as his supervisor had a dismissive quality about it that I might recognise and, if so, what was my response to this in terms of how I saw my self, and hoped I was being seen, as an existential supervisor and, more generally, as a person. Once again, as with existential therapy, the principal method employed in existential supervision is the supervisory encounter itself. That which is presented and explored within the immediacy of this encounter is likely to have direct relevance and impact upon the supervisee but, once again in common with existential therapy, it may, at times, also – or even primarily – have its impact on the supervisor.

Finally, from the perspective being presented, existential supervision need not be limited to supervisory encounters between existentially attuned supervisors

and supervisees. Insofar as its primary concerns rest upon the descriptive exploration of the supervisee's way of being a therapist and practising therapy and the
challenges and obstacles being experienced through the attempts undertaken to
express this stance, existential supervision can be an exciting and valued experiential alternative to more 'over-seeing' modes of supervision. Existential supervision is less concerned with training supervisees to be better existential therapists
than it is about encouraging supervisees to 'own' the model they espouse in ways
which are attuned to their own embodied experience of being a therapist and
practising therapy.

Conclusion

It has been the aim of this text to provide readers with a detailed exposition of existential therapy.

Part One presented an overview of existential phenomenology as relevant to therapeutic practice. It began by emphasising three key foundational Principles – relatedness, uncertainty and existential anxiety – through which the various thematic concerns of existence are considered. In this way, I have attempted to offer an account of existential phenomenology that is less concerned with highlighting its varied ways of interpreting particular themes of existence than it is with the exploration of experiencing *being* and being-with-others in ways that are attuned to the impact and implications of existential phenomenology's foundational Principles.

Part Two detailed a three-phase structural model for practising existential therapy. It identified various descriptively focused, relationally attuned qualities and skills intended to provide interested readers and practitioners with a way of experiencing being and being-with-others, as identified in Part One, that can be applied within the professional context of therapy.

The structural model under consideration follows a general sequence centred upon the co-creation, co-habitation and closing down of what I have termed the therapy-world. In doing so, each phase under discussion raises various associated focal points to be addressed within the boundaries of that therapy-world, so that its inter-relational possibilities can be discerned and experienced as fully and openly as its co-habitants will permit.

Although the structural model can be seen to be rigorous in its overriding investigative aim of disclosing the lived world of the client, it is hoped that readers will also have gained some genuine sense of the situated freedom permitted to client and therapist alike within the therapy-world that is the setting for such explorations. It was, in part, with this in mind, that I decided to append various exercises following discussion of each of the major points raised. Although they served an instructional purpose that offered a means for readers to experiment with these points and to gauge their own responses to them, it is the possibility of their acting as experiential stimuli and catalysts to critical insight that, I believe, makes the engagement with them most worthwhile.

All forms of therapy entrust their practitioners with an 'awe-full' responsibility. This responsibility is not merely professional, containing ethical Codes of Conduct and the ability to apply learned skills in an appropriate and respectful manner. More than this, such responsibility lies in a set of moral Principles which each therapist seeks to convey in an embodied fashion – that is to say, through his or her very way of being-with and being-for the client who is present. Although structural models can only convey a modicum of this moral stance, it remains my hope that something of it has also been communicated throughout Part Two. Beyond skills, beyond rules and regulations, it seems to me that it is the *way* that the therapist responds to the presence of the other who is the client that makes all the difference.

Of necessity, the structural model being presented reflects my own personal interpretations of what existential therapy may mean and how it can be practised. Having been a student and adherent of this approach for around 30 years now, I hold no illusion that what I have gleaned, and attempted to communicate in this text, approaches anything resembling a 'final statement', be it personal or in general. Even so, the attempt, as maddeningly frustrating as I often continue to experience it to be, nevertheless manages to retain something akin to that spark of excitement and surprise that I experienced as an initiate of this approach. I hope that something of that disturbing thrill has been passed on to the reader.

In undertaking to write this text, it was my intent to delineate a structural model that could demonstrate a way of practising therapy from an existential perspective that remains:

- sufficiently open to description;
- structurally coherent;
- consistent with the key foundational Principles of existential phenomenology;
- distinguishable from other contemporary models and systems of therapy such that its aims, primary concerns and practices can be compared to and contrasted with them.

Whether or not I have succeeded in this is for the reader to decide.

Whatever the verdict, however, I am well aware that, like *all* structural models, it is limited, if only because it *is* a structure, in its ability to 'capture' and convey the ever-elusive *experience* of practising existential therapy. In this, it reveals the very same possibilities and limitations as those encountered when the process-like experience of worlding is structurally contextualised as the worldview. While the latter can express a truthful attempt to communicate and express that experience, that attempt can only be assessed and evaluated in terms of its relative adequacy rather than hope to achieve, or worse claim, its exact replication. Existential therapy, perhaps more than any other current approach, takes this understanding to the very heart of its enterprise. Whatever its limitations, the structure just described has sought to honour that aim.

Within such necessary and inevitable restrictions, it nevertheless remains my hope that readers and practitioners – and not least those who also identify themselves as existential therapists – will have been stimulated and challenged by what has been presented and that, more to the point, they will utilise such stimuli and challenges to identify their own working models and be willing to risk the communication of their conclusions.

I would be not only interested, but grateful, for any comments and critiques and alternative perspectives that readers might wish to offer. I can be contacted at the following email address: esa@plexworld.com

Many years ago now, I chanced upon a poem by e. e. cummings that has remained with me and served as a guiding light (even if I have, nonetheless, all too often blundered into the darkness). Ever since I began to write, I have known that I would someday include it as a means of stating that which I have yet to find my own words to express. As I was finishing the writing of the first draft of this book, I recalled the poem and knew for certain that it would provide the best summary of what I sought to express and, as well, its most appropriate ending.

seeker of truth

follow no path
all paths lead where

truth is here
– e.e. cummings –

References

Ablon, J.S. & Jones, E.E. (2002). Validity of controlled clinical trials of psychotherapy: findings from the NIMH Treatment of Depression Collaborative Research Program. *American Journal of Psychiatry, 159*, 775–783.

Adams, M. (2013). *A Concise Introduction to Existential Counselling.* London: Sage.

Al-Khalili, J. (2009). *The Secret Life of Chaos.* Documentary film directed by N. Stacey and produced by Furnace Ltd for BBC Television.

Al-Khalili, J. (2012). *Paradox: The Nine Greatest Enigmas in Physics.* London: Transworld.

Alexander, R. (1995). *Folie à Deux: An Experience of One-to-one Therapy.* London: Free Association Books.

Alvarez, A. (2006). The man who rowed away. *The New York Review of Books, 53*(13), 39–42.

Amiel, H. F. (189?). Journal Intimé of Henri-Frédéric Amiel. University of California Libraries. Available from: https://archive.org/details/amielsjournaljou00amieiala.

Anderson, H. & Goolishian, H. (1992). The client is the expert: A not-knowing approach to therapy. In S. McNamee & K.J. Gergen (Eds), *Therapy as Social Construction* (pp. 25–39). London: Sage.

Arendt, H. (1999). *The Human Condition, 2nd Edition.* Chicago: University of Chicago Press.

Barker, M. (2011). De Beauvoir, Bridget Jones' pants and vaginismus. *Existential Analysis, 22*(2), 203–216.

Barnett, L. & Madison, G. (Eds) (2012). *Existential Therapy: Legacy, Vibrancy and Dialogue.* London: Routledge.

Bates, Y. (Ed.) (2004). *Shouldn't I Be Feeling Better Now? Client Views of Therapy.* London: Palgrave Macmillan.

Berlin, I. (2006). *Political Ideas in the Romantic Age: Their Rise and Influence on Modern Thought.* Princeton, NJ: Princeton University Press.

Binswanger, L. (1963). *Being-in-the-World: Selected Papers of Ludwig Binswanger.* New York: Harper Torchbooks.

Bohm, D. & Hiley, B. (1995). *The Undivided Universe: An Ontological Interpretation of Quantum Theory.* London: Routledge.

Boss, M. (1957). *The Analysis of Dreams* (A.J. Pomerans, Trans.). London: Rider.

Boss, M. (1963). *Psychoanalysis and Daseinsanalysis.* New York: Basic Books.

Boss, M. (1977). *I Dreamt Last Night …* (S. Conway, Trans.). New York: Wiley.

Boss, M. (1979). *Existential Foundations of Medicine and Psychology*. Northvale, NJ: Jason Aronson.

Buber, M. (1970). *I and Thou*, 2nd ed. (R.G. Smith, Trans.). Edinburgh: T. & T. Clark.

Buber, M. (2002). *Between Man and Man* (R.G. Smith, Trans.). London: Routledge.

Bugenthal, J.F.T. (1981). *The Search for Authenticity: An Existential-Analytic Approach to Psychotherapy*. New York: Irvington.

Bugenthal, J.F.T. (1987). *The Art of the Psychotherapist*. New York: W.W. Norton.

Burman, E. (2008). *Deconstructing Developmental Psychology*, 2nd ed. London: Routledge.

Burston, D. (2000). *The Crucible of Experience: R.D. Laing and the Crisis of Psychotherapy*. Cambridge, MA: Harvard University Press.

Butler, J. (2006). *Gender Trouble: Feminism and the Subversion of Identity*. London: Routledge.

Cannon, B. (1991). *Sartre and Psychoanalysis: An Existentialist Challenge to Clinical Metatheory*. Lawrence, KS: University Press of Kansas.

Cherniss, J. (2006). Introduction. In I. Berlin, *Political Ideas in the Romantic Age: Their Rise and Influence on Modern Thought* (H. Hardy, Ed.) (pp. xxi–xxx). Princeton, NJ: Princeton University Press.

Claessens, M. (2010). Mindfulness based-third wave CBT therapies and existential-phenomenology. Friends or foes? *Existential Analysis*, *21*(2), 295–308.

Cohn, H.W. (1997). *Existential Thought and Therapeutic Practice: An Introduction to Existential Psychotherapy*. London: Sage.

Cohn, H.W. (2002). *Heidegger and the Roots of Existential Therapy*. London: Continuum.

Colaizzi, P.F. (2002). Psychotherapy and existential therapy. *Journal of Phenomenological Psychology*, *33*(1), 73–112.

Condrau, G. (1998). *Martin Heidegger's Impact on Psychotherapy*. Vienna: Mosaic.

Cooper, M. (2003). *Existential Therapies*. London: Sage.

Cooper, M. (2008). *Essential Research Findings in Counselling & Psychotherapy: The Facts are Friendly*. London: Sage.

Cooper, M. & McLeod, J. (2011). *Pluralistic Counselling and Psychotherapy*. London: Sage.

Correia, E.A., Cooper, M. & Berdondini, L. (2014). Existential psychotherapy: An international survey of the key authors and texts influencing practice. *Journal of Contemporary Psychotherapy (Special Issue)*.

Crotty, M. (1996). *Phenomenology and Nursing Research*. Melbourne: Churchill Livingstone.

cummings, e.e. (1965). *A Selection of Poems*. New York: Harvest.

De Beauvoir, S. (1986). *Ethics of Ambiguity* (B. Fechtman, Trans.). New York: Citadel Press.

Disney, W. (1941). *Dumbo*. Animated motion picture produced by the Walt Disney Studio and directed by B. Sharpsteen.

Du Plock, S. (2007). A relational approach to supervision: Some reflections on supervision from an existential–phenomenological perspective. *Existential Analysis, 18*(1), 31–38.

Du Plock, S. (2009). An existential–phenomenological inquiry into the meaning of clinical supervision: What do we mean when we talk about existential-phenomenological supervision? *Existential Analysis, 20*(2), 299–318.

Duncan, B.L., Miller, D.S., Wampold, B.E. & Hubble, M.A. (Eds) (2010). *The Heart and Soul of Change: What Works in Therapy.* Washington DC: APA Books.

Dyson, F. J. (1958). Innovation in Physics. *Scientific American, 199(3):* 74–82.

Einstein, A. (2001). *Relativity: The Special and General Theory.* London: Routledge.

Einstein, A., Lorentz, H.A., Weyl, H. & Minkowsli, H. (2000). *The Principle of Relativity.* New York: Dover.

Ellenberger, H.F. (1970). *The Discovery of the Unconscious: The History and Evolution of Dynamic Psychiatry.* New York: Basic Books.

Ellis, A. & Ellis, D.J. (2011). *Rational Emotive Behavior Therapy.* Washington, DC: American Psychological Association.

Evans, D. (2003). *Placebo: Mind over Matter in Modern Medicine.* London: Harper Collins.

Evans, R.I. (1981). *Dialogue with R.D. Laing.* New York: Praeger.

Eze, M.O. (2010). *Intellectual History in Contemporary South Africa.* London: Palgrave Macmillan.

Farber, L. (1967). Martin Buber and psychotherapy. In P.A. Schilpp & M. Friedman (Eds), *The Philosophy of Martin Buber* (pp. 577–602). LaSalle, IL: Open Court.

Farber, L. (2000). *The Ways of the Will: Selected Essays.* New York: Basic Books.

Feldman, D.P. (2012). *Chaos and Fractals: An Elementary Introduction.* Oxford: Oxford University Press.

Fine, C. (2010). *Delusions of Gender.* London: Icon Books.

Foucault, M. (1979). *A History of Sexuality Vol. 1: An Introduction.* London: Allen Lane.

Foucault, M. (1989). *The Order of Things.* London: Routledge.

Frankl, V. (1988). *The Will to Meaning: Foundations and Applications to Logotherapy.* London: Meridian.

Freedman, J. & Combs, G. (1996). *Narrative Therapy: The Social Construction of Preferred Realities.* London: W.W. Norton.

Friedman, M. (Ed.) (1964). *Worlds of Existentialism: A Critical Reader.* Chicago: University of Chicago Press.

Fromm, E. (2003). *Man for Himself: An Inquiry into the Psychology of Ethics.* London: Routledge.

Frosh, S. (2012). *A Brief Introduction to Psychoanalytic Theory.* London: Palgrave Macmillan.

Gadamer, H.G. (2004). *Truth and Method.* London: Continuum.

Gade, C.B.N. (2012). What is ubuntu? Different interpretations among South Africans of African descent. *South African Journal of Philosophy 31*(3), 484–503.

Gay, P. (1988). *Freud: A Life for Our Time*. London: J.M. Dent & Sons.

Gendlin, E.T. (2003). *Focusing: How to Gain Direct Access to your Body's Knowledge*. London: Rider.

Gergen, K.J. (2009). *Relational Being: Beyond Self and Community*. Oxford: Oxford University Press.

Gillett, G. (1995). The philosophical foundations of qualitative psychology. *The Psychologist, 8*(3), 111–114.

Gilliot (2009). *True dialogue for transformation and peace*. Available from: http://aidscompetence.ning.com/profiles/blogs/true-dialogue-for.

Giovazolias, T. & Davis, P. (2001). How common is sexual attraction towards clients? The experiences of sexual attraction of counselling psychologists toward their clients and its impact on the therapeutic process. *Counselling Psychology Quarterly, 14*(4), 281–286.

Gordon, E.F. (2000). *Mockingbird Years: A Life in and out of Therapy*. New York: Basic Books.

Gray, J. (2006). The case for decency. *The New York Review of Books, 53*(12), 20–22.

Havel, V. (2000). The first laugh. *The New York Review of Books, 46*(2), 20.

Hayes, S.C., Stroshal, K.D. & Wilson, K.G. (2011). *Acceptance and Commitment Therapy: The Process and Practice of Mindful Change,* 2nd ed. London: Guilford Press.

Heidegger, M. (1962). *Being and Time* (J. Maquarrie & E.H. Freund, Trans.). New York: Harper & Row.

Heidegger, M. (1976). *What Is Called Thinking?* (F.D. Wieck & J.G. Gray, Trans.). New York: Harper Perennial.

Heidegger, M. (1977). *The Question Concerning Technology and Other Essays* (W. Lovitt, Trans.). New York: Harper & Row.

Heidegger, M. (2001). *Zollikon Seminars: Protocols–Conversations–Letters* (F. Mayr & R. Askay, Trans.). Evanston, IL: Northwestern University Press.

Hills, J. (2012). *Introduction to Systemic and Family Therapy*. London: Palgrave Macmillan.

Hodges, H.A. (1952). *The Philosophy of Wilhelm Dilthey*. London: Routledge & Kegan Paul.

Hoeller, K. (1996). The tragedy of psychology: Rollo May's Daimonic and Friedrich Nietzsche's Dionysian. *Journal of the Society for Existential Analysis, 7*(1), 39–55.

Horney, K. (1991). *Neurosis and Human Growth*. New York: Norton.

Howard, K.I., Moras, K., Brill, P.L., Martinovich, Z. & Lutz, W. (1996). Evaluation of psychotherapy: Efficacy, effectiveness, and patient progress. *American Psychologist, 51*(10), 1059–1064.

Howard, K.I., Orlinsky, D.E. & Lueger, R.J. (1994). Clinically relevant outcome research in individual psychotherapy: New models guide the researcher and clinician. *British Journal of Psychiatry, 165*(1), 4–8.

Howe, D. (1993). *On Being a Client: Understanding the Process of Counselling and Psychotherapy*. London: Sage.

Howe, D. (2013). *Empathy: What it is and Why it Matters*. London: Palgrave Macmillan.

Hughes, R. (1991). *The Shock of the New: Art and the Century of Change.* London: Thames and Hudson.

Humphrey, N. (2002). Great expectations: The evolutionary psychology of faith-healing and the placebo response. In N. Humphrey (Ed.), *Mind Made Flesh: Essays from the Frontier of Evolution and Psychology* (pp. 255–285). Oxford: Oxford University Press.

Husserl, E. (1965). *Phenomenology and the Crisis of Philosophy* (Q. Lauer, Trans. & Introduction). New York: Harper Torchbooks.

Husserl, E. (1977). *Cartesian Meditations: An Introduction to Phenomenology* (D. Cairns, Trans.). The Hague: Nijhoff.

Husserl, E. (2012). *Ideas: General Introduction to Pure Phenomenology*, vol. 1 (D. Moran, Trans.). London: Routledge.

Iacovou, S. (2013). The existential review – a presentation by Mick Cooper. *Hermeneutic Circular: The Newsletter of the Society for Existential Analysis, July,* 15–16.

Ihde, D. (1986a). *Experimental Phenomenology: An Introduction.* Albany: State University of New York.

Ihde, D. (1986b). *Consequences of Phenomenology.* Albany: State University of New York.

Irigaray, L. (1985). *This Sex Which is Not One* (C. Porter, Trans.). New York: Cornell University Press.

Irigaray, L., Hirsch, E. & Olson, G.A. (1995). Je—Luce Irigaray: a meeting with Luce Irigaray. *Hypatia, 10*(2): 93–114.

Jacobsen, B. (2007). *Invitation to Existential Psychology.* London: Wiley.

Jaspers, K. (1963). *General Psychopathology*, vol. 1 (J. Hoening & M.W. Hamilton, Trans.). London: Johns Hopkins University Press.

Jaspers, K. (2009). *Man in the Modern Age.* London: Routledge.

Johnstone, L. (2013). *UK Clinical Psychologists Call for the Abandonment of Psychiatric Diagnosis and the 'Disease' Model.* Available from: www.madinamerica.com/2013/05.

Jordan-Young, R. (2011). *Brain Storm: The Flaws in the Science of Brain Differences.* London: Harvard University Press.

Joseph, A. (2009). An Inquiry into sexual difference in Ernesto Spinelli's Psychology: An Irigarayan critique and response to Ernesto Spinelli's psycholgy. VDM Verlag: Saarbrücken, Germany.

Kagan, J. (2000). *Three Seductive Ideas.* Cambridge, MA: Harvard University Press.

Kahneman, D. (2012). *Thinking, Fast and Slow.* London: Penguin.

Karlsson, G. (1993). *Psychological Qualitative Research from a Phenomenological Perspective.* Stockholm: Almqvist and Wiksell International.

Kaye, J. (1995). Postfoundationalism and the language of psychotherapy research. In J. Siegfried (Ed.), *Therapeutic and Everyday Discourse as Behavior Change* (pp. 29–60). Norwood, NJ: Ablex.

Kennedy, J. F. (1962). Commencement Address at Yale University, June 11, 1962. The American Presidency Project. Available from: www.presidency.ucsb.edu/ws/?pid=29661.

Kirschenbaum, H. & Henderson, V.L. (1990). *Carl Rogers Dialogues*. London: Constable.

Korzybski, A. (1995). *Science and Sanity: An Introduction to Non-Aristotelian Systems and General Semantics*, 5th ed. Englewood, NJ: Institute of General Semantics.

Kvale, S. (1994). Ten standard objections to qualitative research interviews. *Journal of Phenomenological Psychology, 25*(2), 147–173.

Laing, R.D. (1960). *The Divided Self*. Harmondsworth: Penguin.

Laing, R.D. (1967). *The Politics of Experience and the Bird of Paradise*. Harmondsworth: Penguin.

Laing, R.D. (1982). *The Voice of Experience*. Harmondsworth: Penguin.

Laing, R.D. & Cooper, D.G. (1964). *Reason and Violence: A Decade of Sartre's Philosophy*. Harmondsworth: Penguin.

Laing, R.D. & Esterson, A. (1964). *Sanity, Madness and the Family*. Harmondsworth: Penguin.

Langdridge, D. (2013). *Existential Counselling & Psychotherapy*. London: Sage.

Längle, A. (2005). The search for meaning in life and the existential fundamental motivations. *Existential Analysis, 16*(1), 2–14.

Levinas, I. (1987). *Time and the Other* (R.A. Cohen, Trans.). Pittsburgh, PA: Duquesne University Press.

Levinas, I. (1999). *Totality and Infinity* (A. Lingis, Trans.). Pittsburgh, PA: Duquesne University Press.

Longmore, R.J. & Worrell, M. (2007). Do we need to challenge thoughts in cognitive behaviour therapy? *Clinical Psychology Review, 27*, 173–187.

Luborsky, L., Diguer, L., Seligman, D.A., Rosenthal, R., Krause, E.D., Johnson, S., Halperin, G., Bishop, M., Berman, J.S. & Schweizer, E. (1999). The researcher's own therapy allegiance: A 'wild card' in comparisons of treatment efficacy. *Clinical Psychology: Science and Practice, 6*, 95–106.

Luborsky, L., Rosenthal, R., Diguer, L., Andrusyna, T.P., Berman, J.S. & Levitt, J.T. (2002). The dodo bird verdict is alive and well – mostly. *Clinical Psychology: Science and Practice, 9*, 2–12.

Luca, M. (2004). *The Therapeutic Frame in the Clinical Context: Integrative Perspectives*. London: Brunner-Routledge.

Lundin, R.W. & Bohart, A. (1996). *The Theories and Systems of Psychology*, 5th ed. New York: Houghton Mifflin.

Macfarlane, A. (2006). Some reflections on John Ziman's 'No man is an island'. *Journal of Consciousness Studies, 13*(5), 43–52.

McGartland, M. & Polgar, S. (1994). Paradigm collapse in psychology: The necessity for a 'two methods' approach. *Australian Psychologist, 29*(1), 21–28.

Madison, G. (2002). 'Illness'... and its human values. *Existential Analysis, 13*(1), 10–30.

Madison, G. (2014). Palpable existentialism: A focusing-oriented therapy. *Psychotherapy in Australia, 20*(2), 36–42.

Mahrer, A.R. (2000). Philosophy of science and the foundations of psychotherapy. *American Psychologist, 55*(10), 117–125.

Mahrer, A.R. (2004). *Theories of Truth, Models of Usefulness*. London: Whurr.

Mahrer, A.R. (2006). *The Creation of New Ideas: A Guide Book*. Hay-on-Wye: PCCS Books.

Mankell, H. (2002). *The Fifth Woman*. London: Vintage.

May, R. (1969). *Love and Will*. New York: W.W. Norton.

May, R. (1981). *Freedom and Destiny*. New York: Dell Books.

May, R. (1983). *The Discovery of Being*. London: W.W. Norton.

May, R. (1990). An open letter to Carl Rogers. In H. Kirschenbaum & V.L. Henderson (Eds), *Carl Rogers Dialogues* (pp. 229–255). London: Constable.

Mearns, D. & Cooper, M. (2005). *Working at Relational Depth in Counselling and Psychotherapy*. London: Sage.

Mencken, H. L. (1917). The Divine Afflatus. *New York Evening Mail* (16 November).

Merleau-Ponty, M. (1962). *The Phenomenology of Perception* (C. Smith, Trans.). London: Routledge & Kegan Paul.

Merleau-Ponty, M. (1964a). *The Primacy of Perception* (C.W. Cobb, Trans.). Evanston, IL: Northwestern University Press.

Merleau-Ponty, M. (1964b). *Sense and Non-sense* (H. Dreyfus & P. Dreyfus, Trans.). Evanston, IL: Northwestern University Press.

Messer, S.B. & Wampold, B.E. (2002). Common factors are more potent than specific therapy ingredients. *Clinical Psychology: Science and Practice, 6*, 21–25.

Midgley, D. (2006). Intersubjectivity and collective consciousness. *Journal of Consciousness Studies, 13*(5), 99–109.

Milgram, S. (1974). *Obedience to Authority: An Experimental View*. New York: Harper and Row.

Miller, F.G. & Kaptchuk, T.J. (2008). The power of context: Reconceptualizing the placebo effect. *Journal of the Royal Society of Medicine, 101*(5), 222–225.

Misiak, H. & Sexton, V.S. (1973). *Phenomenological, Existential, and Humanistic Psychologies: An Historical Survey*. New York: Grune and Stratton.

Mitchell, D. (2002). Is the concept of supervision at odds with existential thinking and therapeutic practice? *Existential Analysis, 13*(1), 91–97.

Moerman, D E. & Jonas, W.B. (2002). Deconstructing the placebo effect and finding the meaning response. *Annals of Internal Medicine, 136*(6), 471–476.

Moss, D. (Ed.) (1999). *Humanistic and Transpersonal Psychology: A Historical and Biographical Sourcebook*. London: Greenwood Press.

Nishida, K. (1990). *An Enquiry into the Good*. (Masao Abe & Christopher Ives, Trans.) New Haven, Connecticut: Yale University Press.

Norcross, J.C. (Ed.) (2002). *Psychotherapy Relationships That Work: Therapist Contributions and Responsiveness to Patients*. Oxford: Oxford University Press.

Norcross, J.C. & Wampold, B.E. (2011). Evidence-based therapy relationships: Research conclusions and clinical practices. *Psychotherapy, 48*(1), 98–102.

Parks, T. (2006). *Rapids*. London: Vintage.

Peavey, F. (1997). *Strategic Questioning Manual*. Available from: www.thechangeagency. org/_dbase_upl/strat_questioning_man.pdf.

Pett, J. (1995). A personal approach to existential supervision. *Journal of the Society for Existential Analysis, 6*(2), 117–126.

Pilgrim, D. (2000). Psychiatric diagnosis: More questions than answers. *The Psychologist, 13*(6), 302–305.

Piper, W.E. (2004). Implications of psychotherapy research for psychotherapy training. *Canadian Journal of Psychiatry, 49,* 221–229.

Pope, K.S. (1990). Therapist–client sexual involvement: A review of the research. *Clinical Psychology Review, 10*: 477–490.

Pope, K.S., Sonne, J. & Holroyd, J. (1993). *Sexual Feelings in Psychotherapy: Explorations for Therapists and Therapists-in-Training.* Washington, DC: American Psychological Association.

Rasmussen, S. (2004). The imperfection of perfection. *The Psychologist, 17*(7), 398–400.

Rayner, M. & Vitali, D. (2014). CORE Blimey! Existential therapy scores GOALS! *Existential Analysis 25*(2): 296–312.

Rennie, S. (2006). The end … or is it? *Existential Analysis, 17*(2), 330–342.

Rogers, C. (1990). This is me. In H. Kirschenbaum & V. L. Henderson (Eds), *The Carl Rogers Reader* (pp. 6–28). London: Constable.

Røine, E. (1997). *Group Psychotherapy as Experimental Theatre.* London: Jessica Kingsley.

Rothko, M. (2006). *The Artist's Reality: Philosophies of art.* New Haven, Connecticut: Yale University Press.

Rowan, J. (2001). Existential analysis and humanistic psychotherapy. In K.J. Schneider, J.F.T. Bugenthal & J. Fraser Pierson (Eds) *The Handbook of Humanistic Psychology* (pp. 447–464). London: Sage.

Rowan, J. & Jacobs, M. (2002). *The Therapist's Use of Self.* Maidenhead: Open University Press.

Russell, B. (1913). On the Notion of Cause. *Proceedings of the Aristotelian Society 13*: 1–26.

Russell, B. (1946). Philosophy for Laymen. Universities Quarterly 1, Bertrand Russell Society. Available from: www.users.drew.edu/~jlenz/br-lay-philosophy.html.

Salkovskis, P. M. (2002). Empirically grounded clinical interventions: Cognitive-behavioural therapy progresses through a multi-dimensional approach to clinical science. *Behavioural and Cognitive Psychotherapy, 30*(1), 3–11.

Sands, A. (2000). *Falling for Therapy: Psychotherapy from a Client's Point of View.* London: Macmillan.

Sartre, J.P. (1973). *Existentialism and Humanism* (P. Mairet, Trans.). London: Methuen.

Sartre, J.P. (1985). *Existentialism and Human Emotions* (B. Frechtman, Trans.). London: Citadel Press.

Sartre, J.P. (1991). *Being and Nothingness: An Essay on Phenomenological Ontology* (H. Barnes, Trans.). London: Routledge.

Sears, T. (2010). *A Phenomenological Critique of How Sexuality is Understood in Existential Thought.* Unpublished MA Dissertation, London School of Psychotherapy and Counselling Psychology, Regent's College.

Shanon, B. (2003). Hallucinations. *Journal of Consciousness Studies 10*(2): 3–31.

Sherwood, P. (2001). The client experience of psychotherapy: What heals and what harms? *Indo-Pacific Journal of Phenomenology, 1*(2), 24. Available from: www.ipjp.org.

Selleri, F. (Ed.) (2013). *Wave–Particle Duality.* New York: Plenum.

Siderits, M. (2003). *Empty Persons: Personal Identity and Buddhist Philosophy.* Burlington, VT: Ashgate Publishing.

Siegelman, E. Y. (1993). *Metaphor and Meaning in Psychotherapy.* London: Guilford Press.

Smith, D. L. (1991). *Hidden Conversations: An Introduction to Communicative Psychoanalysis.* London: Routledge.

Smythies, J. (2014). The nature of consciousness and its relation to the brain. *Journal of Consciousness Studies, 21*(1–2), 183–202.

Spiegel, D. (Ed.) (1999). *Efficacy and Cost-Effectiveness of Psychotherapy.* Washington, DC: American Psychiatric Publishing.

Spinelli, E. (1994). *Demystifying Therapy.* London: Constable.

Spinelli, E. (1995). Afterword. In R. Alexander, *Folie à Deux: an Experience of One-to-one Therapy.* London: Free Association Books.

Spinelli, E. (1997). *Tales of Un-knowing: Therapeutic Encounters from an Existential Perspective.* London: Duckworth.

Spinelli, E. (2001). *The Mirror and the Hammer: Challenges to Therapeutic Orthodoxy.* London: Continuum.

Spinelli, E. (2005). *The Interpreted World: An Introduction to Phenomenological Psychology*, 2nd ed. London: Sage.

Spinelli, E. (2006). The value of relatedness in existential psychotherapy and phenomenological enquiry. *Indo-Pacific Journal of Phenomenology,* Special Edition on Methodology, *6*, 15. Available from: www.ipjp.org.

Spinelli, E. (2007). Existential psychotherapy, *The Yalom–Spinelli Seminars* (DVD 1). Danish Psychotherapeutic Society for Psychologists (DPSP). Distribution: www.yseps.com.

Spinelli, E. (2008). The existential approach. In S. Haugh & S. Paul (Eds), *The Therapeutic Relationship: Perspectives and Themes* (pp. 51–64). Hay-on-Wye: PCCS Books.

Spinelli, E. (2013). Being sexual: Human sexuality revisited, Part 1. *Existential Analysis, 24*(2), 297–317.

Spinelli, E. (2014a). Being sexual: Human sexuality revisited, Part 2. *Existential Analysis, 25*(1), 17–42.

Spinelli, E. (2014b). Existential coaching. In E. Cox, T. Bachkirova & D. Clutterbuck (Eds), *The Complete Handbook of Coaching*, 2nd ed. (pp. 91–103). London: Sage.

Spinelli, E. (2014c). Being sexual: reconfiguring human sexuality. In M. Miten (Ed.), *Sexuality: existential perspectives* (21–60). Ross–onWye: PCCS.

Spinelli, E. & Horner, C. (2007). The existential–phenomenological paradigm. In S. Palmer & A. Whybrow (Eds), *The Handbook of Coaching Psychology: A Guide for Practitioners* (pp. 118–132). London: Routledge.

Spinelli, E., Coleman, C., Coleman, S. & Strasser, F. (2000). Caught in the middle: Training MPs in dispute resolution. In *Hansard Society Reports: Under Pressure – Are we Getting the Most from our MPs?* (pp. 37–44). London: House of Commons Publishing.

Stadlen, N. & Stadlen, A. (2005). Families. In E. van Deurzen & C. Arnold-Baker (Eds), *Existential Perspectives on Human Issues: A Handbook for Therapeutic Practice* (pp. 133–142). Basingstoke: Palgrave Macmillan.

Stern, D.N. (2004). *The Present Moment in Psychotherapy and Everyday Life.* New York: W.W. Norton.

Stephenson, L. (in preparation).

Strasser, F. & Randolph, P. (2004). *Mediation: A Psychological Insight into Conflict Resolution.* London: Continuum.

Strasser, F. & Strasser, A. (1997). *Existential Time-limited Therapy: The Wheel of Existence.* Chichester: Wiley.

Tantam, D. (2005). Groups. In E. van Deurzen & C. Arnold-Baker (Eds), *Existential Perspectives on Human Issues: A Handbook for Therapeutic Practice* (pp. 143–154). Basingstoke: Palgrave Macmillan.

Tetsurô, W. (2009) *Stanford Encyclopedia of Philosophy.* Available at: http://plato.stanford.edu/entries/watsuji-tetsuro.

The Age (2005) Life is about compromise. Available from: www.theage.com.au/news/hugh-mackay/life-is-about-compromise/2005/06/26/1119724522651.html.

Thelen, E. (2005). Dynamic systems theory and the complexity of change. *Psychoanalytic Dialogues, 15,* 255–283.

Thorne, B.M. & Henley, T.B. (2004). *Connections in the History and Systems of Psychology,* 3rd ed. New York: Houghton Mifflin.

Tillich, P. (1980). *The Courage to Be,* 2nd ed. New Haven, CT: Yale University Press.

Trüb, H. (1947). Vom selbst zur welt. *Psyche I,* 41–45.

United States Institute for Peace. Youth and Violent Conflict: Study guide for teachers and students. Available at www.usip.org/sites/default/files/Youth-and-Conflict-Study-Guide.pdf.

Valle, R.S. & King, M. (1978). *Existential–Phenomenological Alternatives for Psychology.* Oxford: Oxford University Press.

Van Deurzen, E. & Adams, M. (2011). *Skills in Existential Counselling & Psychotherapy.* London: Sage.

Van Deurzen, E. & Arnold-Baker, C. (Eds) (2005). *Existential Perspectives on Human Issues: A Handbook for Therapeutic Practice.* Basingstoke: Palgrave Macmillan.

Van Deurzen-Smith, E. (1988). *Existential Counselling in Practice.* London: Sage.

Van Deurzen-Smith, E. (1994). Courting death: Mortal ambitions of existential analysis. *Journal of the Society for Existential Analysis, 5,* 2–22.

Van Deurzen-Smith, E. (1997). *Everyday Mysteries.* London: Routledge.

Wade, J. (1996). *Changes of Mind.* Albany, NY: SUNY Press.

Wahl, B. (2003). Working with 'existence tension' as a basis for therapeutic practice. *Existential Analysis, 4*(2): 265–278.

What is critical reflection? A resource for teachers seeking to constantly improve their skills. Posted by Sacha. Available at: http://ehlt.flinders.edu.au/education/DLiT/2008/CriticalReflection/index.html.

Whitehead, A. N. (1999). Quotes by Alfred North Whitehead. *Oxford Dictionary of Quotations.* (p. 814). Oxford: Oxford University Press.

Wilson, G.D. & Rahman, Q. (2005). *Born Gay: The Biology of Sex Orientation.* London: Peter Owen.

Wittgenstein, L. (2001). *Tractatus Logico-Philosophicus*. London: Routledge.

Wong, P.T.P. (Ed.) (2012). *The Human Quest for Meaning: Theories, Research and Applications*, 2nd ed. London: Routledge.

Wright, R. (1996). Another personal approach to existential supervision. *Journal of the Society for Existential Analysis,* 7(1), 149–158.

Yalom, I. (1980). *Existential Psychotherapy*. New York: Basic Books.

Yalom, I. (1989). *Love's Executioner and Other Tales of Psychotherapy*. Harmondsworth: Penguin.

Yalom, I. (2001). *The Gift of Therapy*. New York: HarperCollins.

Yalom, I. (2006). *The Schopenhauer Cure*. London: Harper Perennial.

Yalom, I. (2007). Existential psychotherapy: Facing death anxiety. *The Yalom–Spinelli Seminars* (DVD 2). Danish Psychotherapeutic Society for Psychologists (DPSP). Distribution: www.yseps.com.

Yalom, I. & Leszcz, M. (2005). *Theory and Practice of Group Psychotherapy*, 5th ed. New York: Basic Books.

Yalom, I. & Spinelli, E. (2007). *The Yalom–Spinelli Seminars*. 2 DVDs by the Danish Psychotherapeutic Society for Psychologists (DPSP). Distribution: www.yseps.com.

Ziman, J. (2006). No man is an island. *Journal of Consciousness Studies, 13*(5), 17–42.

Zimbardo, P. (1969). The human choice: Individuation, reason, and order versus deindividuation, impulse and chaos. In W.J. Arnold & D. Levine (Eds), *Nebraska Symposium on Motivation, 17* (pp. 237–307). Lincoln, NB: University of Nebraska Press.

Index

Cohn, H.W.
  on authenticity, 47
  on *befindlichkeit*, 143
  British School of existential therapy and, 104
  on choice, 42
  on death anxiety, 51
  on dreams, 205
  on *erlebnis*, 52
  on group therapy, 242–243
  on the past, 55
  on spatiality, 56
Colaizzi, P.F., 1–2, 10–11
conflict, 91–93, 110–111, 237–238
consciousness, 100–101
consonant conflict, 92–93
contextual healing, 134–135
continuity, 69–70, 72–73, *73*, 86, *179*
contracts, 127–131, 211–213, 229
Cooper, D.G., 95
Cooper, M., 26, 47–48, 103, 116, 244
counter-transference, 12, 198–199
couples, 236–241
covert disclosures, 192–193, 194–195

daimonic, 202–205
dasein, 15
daseinsanalysis, 12, 103
death anxiety, 10, 51–52, 85–86, 107
Descartes, R., 17, 31, 101
description, 150–151
descriptively focused attunement, 142–147
descriptively focused enquiry
  body focus and, 157–158
  immediacy and, 163
  metaphorical attunement and, 158–160
  narrational scene-setting and, 160–162
  noematic and noetic elements and, 153–155
  phenomenological method of investigation and, 149–153
  strategic questioning and, 155–156
Diagnostic and Statistical Manual of Mental Disorders (DSM-V), 93, 94
dialogical attitude, 113–115
dispositional stances, 69–70, 72–73, *73*, *179*
dissociation, 74–80, 182–186
dissonant conflict, 92, 93
dreams, 205–211
Du Plock, S., 246–247
dualism, 13–15, 30–31
Dumbo Effect, 131–132, 229
dynamical systems theory, 24–25, 89–90

eigenwelt (own world), 176
Einstein, A., 23–24

embodied existential insecurities, 68–71, 72–74, 179–180, *179–180*, 238
embodiment, 66–67
empathy, 145
epoché (bracketing), 149–150
erlebnis, 52
erotic attraction, 198–200
Esterson, A., 95
existence precedes essence, 33–36, 62, 98
existence tensions, 172
existential analysis, 103
existential anxiety
  overview, 29–30, 31
  practice and, 106–107
  sedimentation and, 79
  worlding and, 61–62
  worldview and, 61–62
existential group therapy, 241–244
existential phenomenology, 2–3, 13–15
existential polarities, 172–176
existential relatedness. *See* relatedness
Existential Therapies (Cooper), 103
existential therapists
  acceptance and, 111–112
  dialogical attitude and, 113–115
  empathy and, 145
  as executioners, 217
  experiential immediacy and, 112–113
  as Fools, 166
  post-therapeutic relations with former clients and, 232–235
  as present others, 110–111
  unexpected encounters with clients, 213–214
  use of 'self-as-other' and, 170–171
  See also intimacy
existential therapy
  Colaizzi on, 1–2
  dualism and, 13–15, 30–31
  existential phenomenology and, 2–3
  foundational Principles of, 3–4, 11–13, 30–31, 117. *See also specific Principles*
  historical background, 103–104
  im/possibility of, 9–11
  inter-relational implications of, 126
  as investigative enterprise, 108–109
  philosophical assumptions of, 3–4
  as placebo, 134–135
  structural model for, 5, 12–13, 123–126. *See also specific phases*
  as theatre, 133, 144
  thematic existence concerns and, 2–3, 9–10, 33, 57, 117. *See also specific themes*
Existential Therapy (Yalom), 107
Existential Time-Limited Therapy (Strasser and Strasser), 229, 244–245